THE LONG ROAD

TO TEHACHAPI

by Judy Barras

With illustrations by Bud Barras

TITLE PAGE - An overview of the Tehachapi Valley as seen from Black Mountain in 1963 (U. S. Department of Agriculture Soil Conservation Service)

Second Edition
Published by The Downtown Improvement Committee of
The Greater Tehachapi Chamber of Commerce

This book was designed and set up by Judy and Bud Barras in the press room of The Tehachapi News and printed by Sierra Printers, Inc. of Bakersfield, California U.S.A.

Contents

Acknowledgments

For invaluable contributions, through correspondence, interviews, association and friendship, I am indebted to the following people, who do not represent the whole of my contacts, but who unfailingly contributed to my knowledge and understanding of the Tehachapi regional history. It is their story; I have only recorded it.

Among them are several long-time residents, some of whom are descendants of pioneers, who spent many hours sharing their knowledge of the past: Sherman Chitwood, Hazel Dickerson, Harvey Hicks, Duncan Monroe, Victor Phillips, and Elizabeth and Charles Powell.

Others who have graciously answered questions and offered their observations include: Clyde Brite, Perry Brite, Dr. W. Harland Boyd, Joe Leiva, Walter Hicks, Mrs. Elizabeth Pedigo, Walter Marx, Doctors Harold and Madge Schlotthauer, Dr. Lon Denison, J. C. Jacobsen, Don I. Carroll, Brad Krauter, Elliott J. Wyman, Bruce Eisenman, E. J. and Laura Jones, Judge William and Sarah Woods, Chester Gilbertson, Herb and Ola Mae

Force, and many others who, by just a comment or word, added to the information.

From the following organizations and companies valuable resource material was obtained: Mrs. Inez Pettijohn and Miss Mary Lou Wertz of the Reference Extension, and Mrs. Nina Caspari of the Historical Collection of the Beale Memorial Library of Kern County in Bakersfield, as well as Mrs. Edythe Eisenman, Tehachapi Branch librarian; Mrs. Lillian Wiggins, Director-Curator of the El Monte Historical Museum; Karl Backes of Monolith-Portland Cement Company; William A. Meyers, Company Historian of Southern California Edison Company; Lt. Fred Johnson of the California Correctional Institution at Tehachapi; Mrs. Kay Koski, Tehachapi City Clerk; Mrs. Joann Siglin, Administrative Secretary for the Tehachapi Unified School District; Andrew Anderson, Assistant General Public Relations Manager, Southern Pacific Company; Ed Duffy, Public Relations Representative, and Arnold Magnuson of the Bakersfield office, Southern California Gas Company; Frank E. Wagers, Deputy Surveyor and Frank Souza of the Map Room, Kern County Surveyor's Office; John Donofrio, Assistant Archivist, Bank of America Archives in San Francisco; Helen Goring, Librarian of the Los Angeles Department of Water and Power Library in Los Angeles; Librarians of the Huntington Library in San Marino, California; Librarians of the Special Collections Department of the Library of the University of California at Los Angeles; Peter E. Hanff, Coordinator, Technical Services, The Bancroft Library of the University of California at Berkeley; Miss Merrilee Gwerder, Director of History Room, Wells Fargo Museum in San Francisco; Librarians of the California State Library in Sacramento; officials of the National Archives in Washington, D.C.; Mrs. Hilda C. Farlee, Librarian, Los Angeles Public Library in Newhall.

I am particularly grateful to Wilbur Foley of La Crescenta and Kathleen S. Riley of Torrance, who allowed me to recount their family's wagon train adventures across the United States and along the Southern Trail to California.

In the actual composition of this book, my thanks go to Sherman Chitwood, Harvey Hicks, J. C. Jacobsen, Warren Johnson, and Brad Krauter, who read portions of the manuscript and offered their criticism; to Ben Capanas for his technical reading and suggestions of comfortable English usage; and particularly to Warren and Richard Johnson, co-publishers of The Tehachapi News, who allowed me the use of their press equipment, press room, and expertise in composition, as well as Ron Johnson for his assistance in composition, and Joan Johnson for proofreading the galleys.

Finally, without the companionship in exploration, encouragement in research and writing, and collaboration in composition, of my husband Bud Barras, this contribution to the history of Tehachapi would not have been made.

Judy Barras
Tehachapi, California
September 1975

The Road

The winds of time
 have dimmed the ancient trace
Of mountain men who coursed a western plain
To brave the Yuma streams; no tracks remain.
And by old river beds the storms erase
A toilsome path that won a lonely place
Where padres paused to pray; like driven rain,
The sand has filled their footprints. All in vain
Such trails were sought as ages could efface.

But, O, My Sweet,
 no winds of chance or change
Can turn the will or kill the heart's desire
When there are hills to roam or heights to scale!
Though we may leave our traces on the range
For time to dim, it cannot quench the fire
Of venturing that lights the distant trail.

Ardis M. Walker

—ONE—

Imagine yourself in the Mid-Nineteenth century. In Europe and Asia ancient civilizations have crested in the tide of monarchy, while in the young, new world of America, a whole vast Western part of the continent was practically devoid of the influence of white men.

Mile stretched into mile where no man had explored in the name of westward expansion or under the guise of Manifest Destiny. In the Southern Sierra Nevada Range of California, where that great mountain chain drops down into a peaceful valley, to rise again in the south as the Tehachapi Range, the land was uncharted as the fifth decade of the Nineteenth Century dawned, except for a single line marking a trail through the pass which John Charles Fremont traveled in 1844. Known today as Tehachapi Canyon, Fremont called it Pass Creek. It alone appeared on maps of the time to hint that life existed in the canyons, by the streams, and in the four basins which, today, comprise the Tehachapi Valley system.

Only occasionally had the land known the footfall of the white race. Trapper-explorers Jedediah Strong Smith and Ewing Young, guide and frontiersman Kit Carson, had been through the Tehachapis earlier in the century.

As the middle years of the century appeared, however, change was imminent. The land was about to assume a new character and a character of men who have been part of the American scene since the first Europeans touched the Eastern seashore when, in the Seventeenth Century the Mayflower, as well as other vessels of its character, came in search of new lands.

The men and women who first settled the Tehachapis, as well as those who followed, didn't just suddenly appear on the scene. They came from many walks of life, with divergent and sundry backgrounds, in different ways. For all of them, it was a long journey. Some crossed oceans; others crossed only a continent. All had one common bond: it was a long road, in some instances requiring many years of travel.

Throughout time immemorial there has been an intuitive idea to guide kindred spirits; it whispers, "on the other side of the sea, over that mountain, across the desert, what is there for me?"

Yankees had been visiting California since the late 1700's, as vessels sailed from Boston, around Cape Horn, searching the Pacific coastline for otter, docking at the coastal port of Monterey. Until the mid-1820's the only way to visit the Western shore was by sea. Then, the first overland expedition reached California, led by Jedediah Smith in 1826, arriving at Mission San Gabriel on November 27, after a long journey over the Old Spanish Trail. It wasn't until November 1841, however, that the first overland emigrant train was organized and journeyed to California. The Bartleson-Bidwell party headed for Northern California. Within a week of its arrival a second train reached Southern California. The American overland migration had begun in earnest.

The financial depression of 1837 influenced many settlers in the Eastern and North-Central states to seek new lands to the West. Their journey was often towards Texas or Oregon. In the Forties and Fifties (even before the discovery of gold in California), the Federal Government's Doctrine of Manifest Destiny justified their sometimes aggressive plunge westward, preaching its right to inhabit and govern the Continental Empire from coast-to-coast.

The pressures of a growing population, the lure of a new land, mineral wealth, and the fur trade, influenced the citizens, thousands of them, to uproot from their homes and be replanted onto the virgin soil of the West. In this great tide that swept over the nation, men, unknown to themselves at that time, were indeed destined to set their course West to the valleys isolated in the mountain fastness of California's Southern Sierras, where, to the east, lay a desolate desert and to the west a fermenting, swampy plain inhabited by aboriginal Indians.

The first settlers in the Tehachapis were called Southern Democrats, a result of their fiercely loyal allegience to that gist of political thinking active in the Southern United States in pre-Civil War days. On the long journey, many of these settlers stopped for a while in Texas and then, impelled — some by boldness and others by the urge to seek new territory — continued to the American settlement of El Monte, California, which was established in 1851.

The history of this region would be incomplete without some knowledge of this colorful era. Much of the flavor and character of the first few decades of an evolving Tehachapi Community, was carved by the frontier attitudes which served the immigrants well along the long road.

The first rut in the road to Tehachapi was indelibly marked on the map of history as long ago as when the first ship reached America's shores. The history of Tehachapi was born and nurtured in the minds of men who sought new lands and traveled the road to get there. It began in no one place nor at any one point in time; but it did cross the vast oceans, passed over the Eastern Coastline of the Americas, and sailed around Cape Horn. It crossed the uncharted wastes of an unknown land and, while only a few stories are here told of a few families, their joys and sorrows, trials and tribulations, were repeated over and over again by scores of others who traveled the same road.

By sea clipper and land clipper the first settlers came to Tehachapi, some to stay for a short time, others for a lifetime.

This is their story.

—TWO—

When the first pioneer wagon arrived at El Monte, the terminus of the Southern Emigrant Route, it was little more than a settlement of a few American families. Spanish settlers had named the site because of the many willow trees and high meadows then flourishing (1). El Monte was situated along the banks of the San Gabriel River, where American

6

families had lived since 1850, but it wasn't until the arrival of the Texan Ira Thompson, with his party of several wagons in 1851, that a community was actually established.

It was to this point hundreds of pioneers journeyed along the trail from Texas to California, a trail also called the Gila or Southern Trail. But all followed more or less a similar rutted wagon road, a road later to become the route of the Butterfield Stage Line, and later still a railroad line which to this day carries passengers westward along an artery of travel first emblazoned so many years ago.

That road was first blazed by Captain Philip St. George Cooke, commander of the Mormon Battalion, an expedition which left Santa Fe, New Mexico, in October 1846, to join forces with the beleaguered Stephen Kearny in San Diego, during the aggressive days of the Mexican-American War. The Mormons were eager to make the hazardous trip. Forced to leave Missouri and Illinois, refused admission into Arkansas, the Mormon Church sought any avenue to enable its adherents to reach the Far West, where they hoped for refuge and respite. With the formation of Cooke's Battalion, 339 strong intrepid Mormon men, accompanied by a few women, wives of some of the volunteers, undertook the journey with fifteen wagons and a herd of animals as well as provisions for sixty days.

They walked. Marching southwest from Ojo de Vaca the battalion began to blaze the trail that others would follow. They made their way over Guadalupe Pass to the San Pedro River, turned north and proceeded down the valley of that stream about fifty-five miles, and then headed west to Tucson. Continuing northwest to the Pima Indian villages on the Gila River, they picked up the trail of General Kearny, who had made the journey from that point a short time before but without wagons. They moved west along the south side of the Gila, and crossed the Colorado River.

After traveling over the desert wastes of Southern California, the battalion veered north, passed Vallecito, the first place after the long desert trek where there was grass, and then through a pass hardly wide enough for a wagon to squeeze through, with perpendicular walls of rock about fifteen feet high. Cooke and his men with only hammers and axes, widened the gap (known today as Box Canyon in Anza-Borrego National Park), so that future travelers could pass through.

On to San Diego the Mormon Battalion marched to join in battles which led to the winning of California for the United States — and statehood.

Cooke recorded his experience in accurate terms: "History may be searched in vain for an equal march of infantry . . . . With almost helpless labor, we have dug deep wells, which the future traveler will enjoy. Without a guide who had traversed them, we have ventured into trackless prairies where water was not found for several marches. With crowbar and pick and ax in hand we have worked our way over mountains which seemed to defy aught save the wild goat, and hewed a passage through a chasm of living rock more narrow than our wagons . . . Thus, marching half naked and half fed, . . . we have discovered and made a road of great value to our country."

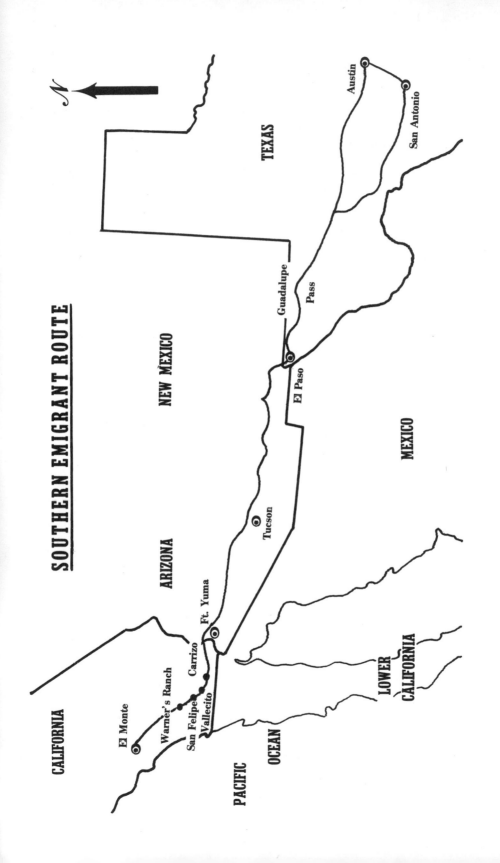

Other roads from Arkansas and Santa Fe merged with Cooke's new track, which became the trail of the future simply because a few wagons left ruts in the earth. In later years improvements occurred; some areas were avoided in favor of better conditions but, more or less, the line of march of the Mormon Battalion became the line of march of the Southern Trail (2).

Except for an occasional scarcity of water, there were few problems until the Guadalupe Pass. There men labored long and hard to drag the wagons over the mountain trail. Another difficult area was the eighty miles of desert between Tucson and the Pima Indian villages, where men and animals suffered from the heat and total absence of water.

After crossing the Colorado River a short distance below the mouth of the Gila, the last ninety miles of desert from the river to the creek, especially in late spring and summer, were perhaps the most difficult of all with intense heat, hot winds, and a continuing lack of water. West from the river, just below today's Plaster City, the trail crossed what is now Highway 80, heading towards the Carrizo Gap — through which flows Carrizo Creek, then into the Carrizo Corridor, a twenty-mile stretch of washes, to Vallecito.

The wagon trains rejoiced to stop for a while at the ranch of Jonathan Warner's, granted to him by the Mexican government and a landmark even for Twentieth-Century travelers. Warner came to California in Young's 1830 Overland Expedition which, after its arrival at San Gabriel Mission, continued fur trapping into Northern California.

Rest and respite, replenishment of provisions at Warner's Ranch near the end of the long road, and then onward to trail's end, north through Temecula and El Monte at last.

In later years wagon trains from the Southwest entered Southern California through the Cajon and San Gorgonio Passes, but it was by way of the Southern Emigrant Route that the first settlers destined for the Tehachapis came.

—THREE—

When the wagon train captained by Nathaniel Vise pulled into "the Monte" in December 1852, the passel of covered wagons with their tired and trailworn families were glad to know the end of the journey was at hand. Many of their friends had arrived before them by several months. They had all left Texas together in the spring of 1851. Joining a group from Arkansas, the train strung out 100 wagons long.

Occupying a few of the wagons was the family of the widow Ann Clifton Wiggins and her five children — four boys and one girl, Ann's husband Archibald Wiggins, having died before they left for California. Two of the boys, Francis Marion and William Clifton, became early residents of the Tehachapis. Francis didn't arrive to take up ranching in Brite Valley until 1870, remaining in El Monte; while William Clifton left soon after their arrival in the Southland for San Francisco, and came into the Tehachapis toward the latter part of the 1850's. For many years he was a Justice of the Peace and schoolteacher in Old Town.

9

The Wiggins family began their long journey across the Continent at Massachusetts, living for a time in the states of Pennsylvania, Virginia, Kentucky, and Missouri. It may have been while they were in Kentucky, when Oliver Wiggins was a "right-hand man" of explorer-trapper-guide Kit Carson who had been in California in the 1820's, that they were influenced by Carson's stories of the West and decided to pick up again and head west. Vise, another neighbor, left with them and they headed for Texas. Here, in the spring of 1851, they joined a train from Arkansas for California, but not before Francis and William Wiggins married, Francis to Elizabeth Dircks and William to Mary Dircks (3).

Proceeding along the Southern Trail, they encountered few problems. They didn't lack for food and had little trouble with Indians, although in a few places there was a shortage of water and forage for the animals — they drove quite a few cattle, losing some stragglers along the way to Indians.

According to T. J. Cross, a pioneer settler of Springville, California, who was also in the Vise train, they didn't shoot any game on their trip, but had lots of fish whenever they came to a stream. And they stopped along the way at a couple of settlements to buy supplies.

Somewhere in Arizona the wagon train split up. While meeting with Indians about the slaughter of their cattle, Vise discovered a captive white woman; although her skin had been dyed, a white spot behind one ear revealed her race. After negotiating for her "purchase" she joined the group, which was joined by, among others, the Wiggins families. They all went to San Diego rather than El Monte, where the woman was reunited with her family.

Several months passed by. Finally they proceeded north to El Monte where many of their friends were already settled. Enroute through Warner's Ranch they had some difficulties with Indians and stayed there about a month, arriving at the Monte in December 1852.

In 1861 the Vise and Wiggins families were united by the marriage of Ellen Vise to Thomas Jefferson Wiggins, one of the four brothers. Ellen's father had earlier left his name to history when in the early 1850's, while taking up land in the Kaweah River country, he developed plans for a town which he called Visalia; when he was there it was only a stockade on Mill Creek where a few white families lived within its walls.

—FOUR—

It was a long journey. For the patron of the family, Johannes Petersen Nordbo, it began with his birth in Norway and ended at his death in Texas. A vast ocean was sailed; interminable miles of uninhabited country were crossed, as the Nordbo family joined the great migration westward.

John Nordbo was a child of ten years when the great adventure began. His role in Tehachapi's history was in the far distant future. Anglicizing the family name to Narboe, he played a prominent role in the region's early development. Particularly in the 1860's, he exploited the mining of salt off the shallow but wide lake in the eastern end of the valley — called

10

by him Narboe Lake but known today as Proctor, and also discovered silver and gold nearby. He burned the first lime in the region in 1877 at Antelope Canyon.

But that was in the future. It is the family's adventure, told partly in the words of Johannes Nordbo, that excites us now. Not all Tehachapi's settlers were native-born Americans; some journeyed from foreign shores.

At the age of sixty-four years Nordbo left Norway with his wife and four children. Although an advanced age for a man to decide to uproot himself for a new life, he had experienced suppression of his talents and abilities in his native land, declaring the restrictive Norwegian laws and conventions a "straight jacket."

In 1837 Nordbo wrote his friend Hans Larsen Rudi a revealing letter of the immigrant's journey. It said in part:

"Your honored letter was received with joy and heartfelt pleasure it having been delayed almost two years. A man who returned to Norway from here brought it back with him . . . . he delayed until he had assembled about one hundred eighty persons, both young and old, most of them being from the Stavanger region, the group coming in two brigs. The cost of the passage for each person amounted to thirty two dollars. They were packed together so closely and had such slight realization of the importance of good ventilation that almost all became ill of diarrhea, seasickness and so forth.

"A few took passage from Gothenburg on American ships. These arrived in good health after a six weeks voyage. For people of eastern Norway it is best to go to Frederickshald and thence to Svefesund. A short way south of there one meets many large open boats which are constantly going southward along the coast to Gothenburg with cargoes of lumber. One can go along for nothing by helping the two men on one of these boats in hoisting sail or rowing a little when necessary . . .

". . . At the far end of the pier is a small house where there are several customs officers who can speak English who usually have a small boat. For a few shillings one of the officers will let you accompany him out to the American ships that lie close by. There they will ask twenty specie dollars for passage. If you can get your board included in the passage well and good although it costs more. If not you will have to supply yourself. If a ship to New York cannot be had, it is possible to go to a port further north in America such as Boston . . . When one arrives in America, one takes a southwesterly route. People who live in the interior of the country usually travel by land. The emigrants from western Norway do not care to go by land and prefer to travel by boat as they are accustomed. The people of eastern Norway are afraid of the water; those of western Norway fear the land.

". . . A person from eastern Norway who is not altogether too tenderfooted will be well advised to go by road inland. He should obtain an axe to indicate that he wants work, and a couple of shirts for change, two combs to keep himself clean, and a cloth to wrap up some food if he so wishes. This is all that should be taken along if one does not have enough money for passage by water. In the evening when he asks for lodging, he should offer to cut some wood; this is always well received.

11

He will then also get supper and breakfast before he leaves, and for dinner he should do the same. In this manner he can travel through the entire country — and he will make us happy by coming here.

"We intend to move from here in a few weeks. We must first sell eight acres of land which we have here [he was writing from Ottawa, LaSalle County, Illinois], and we will auction off a ten acre field of wheat, together with our live stock which includes seven oxen, four cows, a hog and one mare together with the eighty acres, all of which must be converted into money, should net us two hundred dollars, and the wheat field one hundred dollars.

"This western country is far different from the eastern states. Perhaps you will recall what I said the last time I had a talk with you — that I would not stop in my travels until I had reached the westernmost part of the state of Missouri. That we have been unable to reach our destination before this must be laid to our poverty, as well as to the unfortunate sea voyage. Had we arrived without any mishaps, we would have come far enough the first year. It is very easy to raise cattle here and likewise to cultivate the soil. This year as well as last year we have had nothing with which to feed the cattle except what my two sons have cut on the prairie, amounting to about thirty tons. We have had no stable for the cattle this winter, since such are not used here, and that is very unfortunate. The winter here is very cold, and this second winter has again been very long.

"The land in the state of Illinois consists largely of prairie with little of woods except along the rivers and creeks. The summer may be compared to an earthly paradise but the winter on the contrary may be likened to 'Brieflaaen.'

"If I am fortunate enough to find satisfactory and good land where we are now going, I shall take four claims, each of 160 acres, which is a farm large enough for one family."

Nordbo thought he would live in Missouri, but continued instead to Texas, where he finally secured a measure of success. He settled a large ranch of 1,920 acres near modern Dallas after their arrival in 1841, and also practiced medicine, living without undue hardship until his death at the age of eighty-five in 1855.

His journey to Texas joined him to a migration of other Americans into the new frontier. It was an easy journey to the territory; there were a variety of roads to travel. By 1836 up to 30,000 Americans were in Texas, most of them settling there because of the availability of land. When, in 1837, the United States Government recognized Texas as a republic, after its independence was won from Mexico the previous year, it was inevitable that more settlers would converge on the new lands.

In 1856 John Narboe, now married to Johanna Elizabeth Knight, travelled in a wagon train to El Monte, California. Other Texans were there before them, and farther north, still others were settled already at Tehachapi. Soon, he was, too.

—FIVE—

Not all the wagon trains had an easy time of it — fear and tragedy stalked the John Brite family, traveling from Texas to California in 1853-54. While camped at the head of the Gila River, they learned of an Indian fight farther up the trail. One evening while John's wife Amanda was cooking, Indians came into camp. As she removed the lid from a pot an Indian woman took a biscuit and Amanda swiped at her. This so upset the Indians that to avoid a problem John whipped his wife on the spot. According to their grandson Vance Brite, who heard the story often, "We asked her if she cried, and she said she did because it hurt!" But the Indians were satisfied.

After crossing the Colorado River one of their two infant children died. Forced to bury her along the trail, they burned a fire over her grave to disguise it and to prevent looting by Indians in search of clothing.

The Brites' journey took seven months and three weeks, according to Mrs. Sarah Glenn who settled in Glennville and was also in the train. She, too, remembered the visit by the Apache Indians, and that Jim Houston, another member of their party, was shot by them while attempting to recover twenty-three head of stolen horses.

No doubt one of the biggest cargoes moved by the emigrants along the trail was cattle. Long before the romanticized Texas drives into the Midwest, major cattle drives to California occurred contiguous with the families' movement. The herds, which crossed the desert as early as 1848, were still going strong in the mid-1850's. Most of the stock was destined for San Francisco and Stockton, where it was sold for as low as $5.00 a head. A glut of beef flooded the market and drove the price down from the $16.00 to $20.00 a head paid in the spring of 1852.

A Los Angeles newspaper reported at the end of 1854: "A man recently in from the Colorado informs us that there are large parties of immigrants on the road — most of them will go up the country by way of the Monte and San Gabriel. They have a large amount of stock and they are generally better fitted-out than the immigration of any previous year. There is a large amount of stock being driven over this year — mostly from Texas — amounting during the past eight weeks to something like 6,000 head of cattle across the Colorado. Among the others, Mr. Dunlap has crossed 500 head; Erskine, 800, and a Mr. Ryne, who lost so many cattle last year by the Apaches, has over a 1000.''

Dunlap is probably the same man who was in the Glenn-Brite train as that name appears in the records along with mention of his cattle; and there is every reason to believe the Brites and Glenns drove cattle as they entered the cattle business soon after settling in their respective California communities.

The California cattle drives continued on a regular basis even though there was a general decrease in the demand for beef until the outbreak of the Civil War. After the war ended there was a brief revival, but the uncertainty of the market and greater promise offered on the northern trails, resulted in an end to the historic California drives.

Soon after their arrival at El Monte in the latter days of 1854, John Brite moved his small family into the Tehachapi Valley, where they have enjoyed the reputation of being the first permanent family to settle.

Although Dick Shackelford didn't arrive in the Tehachapis until the spring of 1864, he was one of the region's earliest settlers to use the Southern Trail. In 1849 his father Montgomery Bell Shackelford, a Kentuckian by birth, who had been a scout of the frontier as well as a member of the Texas Rangers, brought his family to California, stopping at Mission San Gabriel during the winter of 1849-50. The "dangers of the desert, the fear of savage Indians and of wild beasts and the perils, seen and unseen, connected with that large expedition traveling with wagons and ox-teams" were memories of Dick Shackelford, although only a seven-year-old when the trip was made.

As he grew to young manhood, he engaged in teaming, plying his trade between San Bernardino and Los Angeles. He worked at the Frasier River in 1862, in charge of a pack train to and from the mines. Although Shackelford had been in the Tehachapis as early as 1856, it was another eight years before he became a resident, pioneering in the region's cattle industry and an owner of considerable acreage in the southeast section of Brite Valley.

—SIX—

By 1868 a well-defined busy track existed between Texas and California, when still another Tehachapi pioneer traversed the Southern Trail.

Alcie Rogers was twelve years old when she made the journey in a train captained by her father William Rogers. Migration was not a new event in the Roger's family history; it began in England several centuries before. An Adamic-bridge moves swiftly through time as William was the son of Ralph, who was born in 1760 in South Carolina. He was in the American Revolution, fighting in that great extended battle which hastened the migration westward. Several generations past, John Rogers the Martyr, was burned at the stake in Smithfield, England during the reign of "Bloody Mary," Mary, Queen of England.

Nine years after their journey to California, in 1877 Alcie Rogers married Francis Foley; during that decade he ranched near where the Tehachapi Mountain Park dresses the landscape today. Foley also traveled the Southern Trail in 1856.

A granddaughter of William Rogers, Lula Allen Coe, often heard the stories of that adventurous trip in 1868; in her later years she recorded the tale.

* * *

Grandfather William Rogers started out for California . . . with ox teams from a place near McKinney, Collin Co., Texas, in May, 1868. Traveling with him were his four daughters, Sarah, Margery, Clarissa, Alcie, also his two sons, Thomas G. and Dennis. Tom's family, his wife Fannie and two children, Lizzie and Nelson were with him. George Foley who afterward married Sarah Rogers was also in the train (4).

As they journeyed along other wagons joined them from time to time, helping to form quite a large train. They used ox teams because they

14

furnished the most practical means of transporting the heavy covered wagons and they could endure more hardships and go longer without water than the horse or mule . . . They had to take great care of them, sometimes going without water themselves in order that the oxen might drink. When rocks and bumpy ground made the hoofs of the animals sore the pioneers made shoes of leather for the beasts. While the animals were very slow, making from two to five miles an hour, they were safe and sure.

When the travellers camped at night, the wagons were drawn together to form a circular corral, the tongue of each wagon being placed in the back end of the wagon in front of it, as a protection against Indians and wild animals. They camped in this enclosure.

It was the custom for the men to stand guard two at a time in watches of three or four hours during the night. One man in the train refused to stand guard. He was notified by the corporal he would either take his turn as guard or they would put him out of the corral. But this man got into his wagon with a shotgun and said he would shoot the first man who touched his wagon. So Ben Rogers, the corporal, who had been serving in the Civil War and was not afraid of man or beast said, "Come on boys, let's put him out." They took hold of his wagon, rolled it out and left him and his family exposed to the danger of the Indians. The next night he was ready to stand guard.

Everything went well with the train on the first party of the journey, while the oxen were fat and fresh and travelling was still a welcome change from settled life. When they came to the Concho River, they had a great time bathing and fishing. One of the men caught a cat fish that weighed sixty pounds. They put a hole through its gills and two men carried it on their shoulders, its tail dragging the ground.

After leaving the Concho River they came to the dry "staked plains," ninety miles across. As there was not water for the oxen in any of that region, they travelled day and night without camping, taking three days and nights in which to cross it. They would stop awhile at night to let the oxen lie down and rest, then drive on as long as they could endure it.

One afternoon, about three o'clock, Mr. Gutherie's team gave out and lay down. Some of the men said, "We can't stop here," so they pulled out of the train and went on. Mr. Gutherie came around to Grandfather Rogers and said, "Uncle Billie, are you going on and leave me, too?" Grandfather Rogers answered him, "No, indeed! If we can't do any better, I will take you in my own wagons."

Then he went out into the sage brush and prayed. In a short time there arose a cloud out of almost a clear sky and poured out a refreshing shower of rain, which cooled the atmosphere to such an extent that the oxen, rested and refreshed, arose and walked off across the desert. They reached the Pecos River in due time, arriving there before the people who had gone on and left them.

They found the river almost overflowing its banks. The oxen were so thirsty, they could hardly be restrained from jumping into the river before they could be loosed from the wagons.

The river was so high they could not ford it, and there was no bridge

15

nor ferry on which to cross. They had to provide some means of getting across. They took a wagon bed and turned it bottom side up, putting empty water barrels under it, thus making an improvised ferry boat. Then some of the men took a rope and swam across the river, making a cable by which they drew the ferry boat back and forth, by this means carrying all their supplies across the river. They made the oxen swim across, pulling the wagons. It was a long tedious task, taking them several days.

By this time the novelty of the trip had worn off, and travel more and more had become a burden. From here they took their way across the sand and desert and mountains to El Paso on the Rio Grande River. Their train had increased to about thirty wagons by this time.

They traveled up the Rio Grande River about 100 miles. In the meantime they stopped and made camp for several weeks to rest and recuperate, also giving their teams a chance to graze and rest, thus regaining their strength to continue their journey to the end.

One night while they were camped at this place, some Mexicans stole some of their oxen and drove them into the mountains, thinking the men of the train would be afraid to follow them on account of Indians. But they did not know with whom they were dealing for most of the young men had just come out of the war and were not in the least afraid to go after the oxen. Which they proceeded to do, recovering them without the loss of one.

They did not have any real battles with the hostile Indians. Tom Rogers, one of whose duties it was to go on ahead and look out for camping places as to water, grass and protection, had some skirmishes with them. Some of the other trains saw signs of Indians as they came upon the charred wrecks of other caravans that had been annihilated by the savages.

There was one account of a train mistaking the first sight of giant cacti for distant bands of Indians. The scouts rushed back and got the wagons rounded in battle array, but found out their mistake as they ventured out again.

So they took up again their long, hot, tiresome journey across New Mexico and Arizona. For days and days nothing to be seen but desert sand, rocks, and cactus. The fear of the Indians was exceeded only by the dread of an exhausted supply of water.

Their arrival at Maricopa Wells was very well remembered for they felt they were out of danger of the Indians, and were nearing their journey's end. Here the train broke up more or less and each one went their own way.

When they came to Ft. Yuma, the U. S. Government gave them supplies, flour, bacon and coffee. There was one account that it took them three weeks to build rafts to get across the Colorado River.

They yet had 250 miles of almost the worst part of the whole trip, the sandy desert waste this side of Yuma. No water! No feed! Just sand and rocks! But, finally, after six months of a long tiresome trip, they reached El Monte, California. Here they were met by some of the family who had preceded them a year or two . . .

They could hardly realize that they had at last reached California and were through traveling. A trip like this is an experience long to be remembered.

—SEVEN—

Peak years in the migration pattern of the United States were 1855, 1875, 1887, and 1923 to 1946. The completion of the intercontinental railroad in 1869 as well as the connecting rail link within California in 1876, brought new waves of settlers to the West. Through the years other distinct acts within the framework of California's history have affected the historical pattern of the Tehachapis, an indication that pioneers ever appear in the unfoldment of history.

Coincident with the arrival of John Brite's family at El Monte in the winter of 1854-55, were events to the north which, in only a few short months, opened up a wild and virgin territory to new settlers. The Brites are historically known as the first permanent white settlers in the Tehachapi Valley. If they were, they were preceded by a number of miners, followed quickly by a few other families. This is what happened.

El Camino Viejo was the first major trail to inland California. It had been used prior to 1800 as a refugee road, enabling Spanish fugitives to travel between the Pueblo de Los Angeles and the San Francisco Bay area unobserved by coastal settlers.

In 1851 the Los Angeles Court of Sessions granted certain rights-of-way across the San Francisco Rancho, a Mexican land grant, which had been withheld in the original grant. They detailed the "Tulare Road to the Mines" by way of ex-Mission San Fernando, Rancho San Francisco, the Canada of Alamos (San Francisquito Canyon), Rabbit Lake (Elizabeth Lake) and northward. This is probably the earliest governmental acknowledgment of the road that was so important to Tehachapi's early growth. In later years there were more appropriations, subscriptions, and expenditures to make a passable road across the Rancho San Francisco than all other Los Angeles County roads combined.

In October 1853 a railroad survey party of Lieutenant Stoneman opened a "most excellent wagon road from Lake Elizabeth (near the crest of the pass of San Francisco) direct into the Tulare Valley by way of the canon de Las Uvas." "The pass of San Francisco can," according to an observer, "by a little work in digging down a few points where the stream impinges upon the steep mountain sides, be made a very good wagon road, so that the only obstacle which now presents itself to a very good means of land transit from Los Angeles to the mining region is the pass of San Fernando; and a few hundred dollars and barrels of powder would do much towards removing the obstacle."

In June 1854 the editor of the Los Angeles Star, William A. Wallace, accompanied Lieutenant Edward F. Beale and his party to Fort Tejon, located in the Canada de las Uvas.

"We started early and rode through the San Francisco Rancho to the mouth of Turner's Pass," Wallace wrote in his diary, "where we halted near a little arroyo . . . This rancho is inaccessible except by a trail over the mountains. . . . there are numerous vallies (sic) making up into mountains.

17

"About noon we left camp and traveled through to near the top of the pass, seventeen miles," he continued. "Through the whole length of it runs a little stream of clear water . . . . The road through the pass is very bad, winding through the sandy bed of the arroyo, with many steep pitches and the wagons were much retarded."

The next day the party reached the top of the pass where "we came into a beautiful valley some three miles wide and ten long . . . . This is the lovely valley of Elizabeth Lake just at the entrance of the Great Desert — one of the most delightful spots in nature." Thousands of other travelers would pass the same way.

During the summer of 1854 a gold discovery on the Kern River as well as the establishment of Fort Tejon, brought graphically to the attention of Los Angeles businessmen the need for a suitable wagon road northward. By August, perhaps as a result of commentary in his own newspaper and pressure brought to bear upon the citizenry, the editor of the Daily Alta Californian reported that "a road has been cut through the solid rock affording a fine wagon track where heretofore a pack mule could barely scramble." Within two months the county formed a road district to improve the wagon road from the Mission to the Rancho San Francisco at a cost of $1,000.

Ever at the forefront of providing modern transportation to the Pueblo's citizens, Los Angeles businessman Phineas Banning offered stagecoach travel as well as freighting to Fort Tejon by the end of the year. Because of the hardships of the road the citizenry said it was "impossible." Banning was prepared, however, to prove the ability of an able driver to mount the pass safely. In December he was at the reins of a stage to which, according to Major Horace Bell, ". . . were harnessed a half dozen well fed, panting and foaming mustangs." Upon reaching the summit of San Fernando Pass, Banning's nine passengers, who had mounted the pass on foot, wondered how the stage could ever descend the other side. He insisted it could be done: ". . .that a man who couldn't drive a stage safely down that hill was no driver at all . . . ."

Bell described the descent: "Now he cracks his whip, tightens his lines, whistles to his trembling mustangs, and urges them to the brink of the precipice, and in a moment they are going down! down! down! racketty clatter bang! Sometimes the horses ahead of the stage, and sometimes the stage ahead of the horses, all, however, going down! . . . Finally, the conglomeration of chains, harness, coach, mustangs and Banning were found by the pursuing passengers in an inextricable mass of confusion — contusions, scratches, bruises, batters, cracks and breaks, forming a general smash and pile up in a thicket of chaparral at the foot of the mountain.

" 'Didn't I tell you so,' said Banning, 'a beautiful ascent far less difficult than I anticipated. I intended that staging to Fort Tejon and Kern river should be a success. Gentlemen, you see my judgment is good.' "

The road was open. Within two months Bell and David Alexander, Banning's partner, drove over the road, which had been additionally improved, with heavy ten-mule teams, the first commercial train to head north. "We had a terrible time of it, however," Bell recalled, "and in the San Francisquito Canon were caught in a snow storm, and were three days in going one mile, building our road as we advanced."

Banning's demonstration stimulated popular subscriptions to further construct the road; appropriations from merchants and business houses in Los Angeles and El Monte were forthcoming. This enabled a "small army of men armed with shovels and picks, . . . to repair parts of the road which the stagecoach in its descent had knocked out of joint."

During the next four years wishful newsmen described the road as in "excellent condition". But it was still the original rutted track; the worst spots graded with picks and shovels, sloping chutes dug into overly steep creek banks, and bogs corrugated with brush or saplings.

An event of national significance undoubtedly renewed interest in the pass and road. In 1858 the Butterfield Stage Line inaugurated transcontinental service. That summer a number of Los Angeles citizens contributed a total of $3,000 and an additional $5,000 was appropriated by the County Board of Supervisors. New improvements were made on San Fernando Hill and through Rancho San Francisco. Under the supervision of contractor G. Allen, the work was completed in August, in time for the arrival of the first Butterfield stage.

—EIGHT—

In the Age of Space it is still possible to repeat, in some measure, the several-weeks' journey of early travelers on the northern route from El Monte and Los Angeles. In 1973 on a summer day of searing heat and blazing light we began our journey at the San Fernando Pass. There was no point beginning in Los Angeles, as change over the years has obliterated the trace men once took to the outland — to the farthest edge of civilization at San Fernando Mission, or into the wild country beyond.

In Spanish days the gateway to the San Fernando Valley was today's Burbank; it appears on old maps as "Puerto Suelo." During the Spanish and Mexican eras, ox-drawn carretas moved over this route between Pueblo de Los Angeles and the Mission. With American occupation of the Pueblo, Cahuenga Pass was often used as the thoroughfare, a more practical route for wagons than Puerto Suelo.

As traffic passed swiftly by at the north on Highway 14, and bulldozers marked a modern freeway to our south, we hiked up the almost forgotten slope to the "cut" where, over a hundred years before us, Tehachapi's pioneers had struggled with their wagons and carriages.

Today it is known as Beale's Cut, but even before the Lieutenant Colonel appeared on the scene in the mid-1850's, as part of the initial road development a shallow cut was first made in the solid rock at the top of the mountain. When Beale was awarded his franchise in 1862, he hired men to cut fifty feet deep into the sandstone with pick and shovel, and widened it to about fifteen feet. (Some authorities, however, suggest the second cut was actually made a short distance from the first.)

Rates were established for the toll road by the Los Angeles County Board of Supervisors and, depending on the type of vehicle and produce, travelers were charged: "Team of 12 animals 2.75; 10 animals 2.75; team of 8 $2.50; of six $2; four $1.75; two $1.37½; one 75 cents. Loose animals, cattle, et cetera 10 cents each; 1 man and horse 25 cents; sheep 4 cents each; pack animals 25 cents each."

Winfield McNamee walks his team through Beale Cut in 1907 (Goldcamp Museum, Rosamond, California)

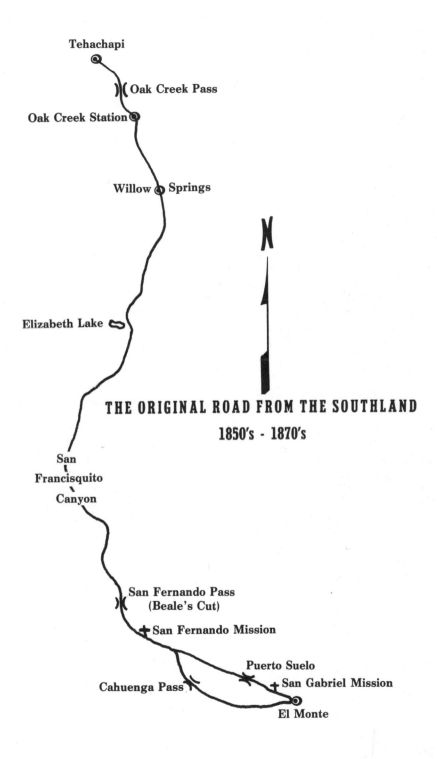

Tehachapi

Oak Creek Pass

Oak Creek Station

Willow Springs

Elizabeth Lake

N

THE ORIGINAL ROAD FROM THE SOUTHLAND

1850's - 1870's

San Francisquito Canyon

San Fernando Pass (Beale's Cut)

San Fernando Mission

Puerto Suelo

San Gabriel Mission

Cahuenga Pass

El Monte

For twenty-two years Beale's toll road was the mainstream of traffic and continued to be the major outlet from Los Angeles northward until the early 1900's. It was even used for a short while by automobiles.

In 1910 San Fernando Pass, then called the Newhall Grade, was replaced by a tunnel; the tunnel was replaced by a new road in 1939; and Highway 14 was replaced by a modern freeway system in the 1970's.

We left Beale's Cut with regret, but our journey northward had to be completed in the latter hours of daylight, as compared to the longer trip of yesteryear, when it took travelers to and from the Tehachapi Valley from eight to twelve days to make the trip, depending upon their transportation.

Continuing northward on Highway 14 our next stop was at an historic marker designating the stage stop and waystation of Lyon's Station, operated for many years by Sanford Lyon and including a depot, a store, post office, telegraph office, and a tavern. Before Lyon, however, the pioneer Hart family of the Tehachapis, first operated the station.

Hart's Station was an important stop as early as the Kern River gold rush of the 1850's, operated by Josiah Hart from 1854 until 1858, when he moved to Cummings Valley. Hart, born at Hardin County, Kentucky in 1794, was a frontiersman in the truest sense of the word. His early years were influenced by the spirit of men like Daniel Boone. In the 1820's he hunted buffalo and antelope in the Red River Valley, shipping game down-river to various markets. Migrating westward from Texas he, too, crossed to El Monte by way of the Southern Trail. Until his establishment of a public "stopping place" he leased a portion of the Azusa Ranch (5).

Hart's or Lyon's Station, as it was later known, was important until the 1870's when the Southern Pacific Railroad reduced the need for a stage line.

A correspondent for the New York Herald, Waterman L. Ormsby, having ridden the Butterfield Stage across the continent wrote this impression of part of his journey, after leaving San Fernando Mission: "The road leading through the new pass is rugged and difficult. About the center of the pass is, I believe, the steepest hill on the entire route. I should judge it to be 500 feet from the level of the road, which has to be ascended and descended in the space of a quarter of a mile; . . . certainly it is a very steep hill and our six horses found great difficulty in drawing our empty wagon up.

"The road takes some pretty sharp turns in the canyon and a slight accident might precipitate a wagon load into a very uncomfortable abyss.

"Eight miles from San Fernando (Mission) we changed horses again at Hart's rancho, having made nearly ten miles per hour in spite of the bad condition of the roads . . . from this point the road leads through San Francisco Canyon, 12 miles long."

With the searing sun on our western flank, we drove through the bustling communities of Newhall and Saugus. The early road followed what is approximately Ash Street, then Newhall Avenue. Approaching the Santa Clara River, we looked in vain for signs of the pioneer road. At the mouth of San Francisquito Canyon a waystation known as Moore's had been located; in 1860 it was also called Holdansville, but no sign of it remains. We did see "The small jagged peaks of the mountains on either side," described by Ormsby as "looking much like rows of upturned human profiles."

Slowly we ascended the canyon, quietly searching the landscape, creeping along the almost deserted paved road which in Ormsby's time "was very rocky." For about two miles the pavement did give way to dirt, as hugging the hillside we felt for a few moments like stage passengers of old must have, only with tighter control over our own horses, and certainly in greater comfort.

Finally achieving the top of the pass, we continued to Elizabeth Lake where another station had served the travelers. At this point the road split: traffic headed for the San Joaquin Valley struck off to the northwest toward the Tejon country; and traffic destined to the desert, Owens Valley, or the Tehachapis, veered to the northeast — our route. Virtually no road construction was necessary from the lake into the Tehachapis as the flat plains and natural contours of the hills were easily traversed.

Willow Springs in 1886 (Jake Dearborn and Goldcamp Museum, Rosamond, California)

After crossing a low range of hills, we headed across the western Antelope Valley, described by some early travelers as a "desolate hell," by others as "paradise." We arrived at another important stop on our jaunt, the waystation of Willow Springs. Folklore to the contrary, this was never a stop on the Butterfield line, which used the Tejon Pass, but other companies as necessary to the growth and survival of the desert and Eastern Sierra communities made it an important locale. Buildings constructed in the early Twentieth Century by erstwhile gold miner and developer Ezra Hamilton dominate the community today. Two mementoes of the past, however, exist: the crumbling adobe walls of the station and the watering trough which quenched the thirst of man and beast alike.

After establishing a boarding house at Willow Springs about 1862, Adelia and Nelson G. Ward operated the stage station there for about ten years. They also kept a number of teams for travelers (6).

Willow Springs is the most important historic spot in Kern County, according to Richard C. Bailey, Director of the Kern County Museum. It was a rest stop and watering hole for Indians of the distant past. Some authorities suggest Father Francisco Garces stopped there in 1776 on his way back from his expedition into the San Joaquin Valley. After Jedediah Smith left San Gabriel Mission in January 1827, he headed for Northern California by way of Oak Creek Pass and the Tehachapis, as did Ewing Young, who was accompanied by Kit Carson, in 1830. John Fremont, who wrote an eloquent account of his journey through the Tehachapis and over Oak Creek Pass in 1844, stopped at Willow Springs. And the pioneers who opened up the Tehachapis, as well as teamsters and travelers to Eastern California, stopped at this famous watering hole.

As the heat of day gave way to a desert evening of tranquil air and a western sky of shimmering red light, we returned to the Tehachapi Valley. For days afterward we spoke of our journey, which had repeated in a small measure the trek of Nineteenth Century travelers who paved the way for this century, and beyond.

Ruins of the Willow Springs Stage Station in July 1973

As the flood of miners poured into the Kern River country in the 1850's, some passed through the Tehachapi Valley. The earliest survey of the region, conducted in 1854 by H. S. Washburn for the Surveyor General of California, delineates the "Los Angeles and Kern River Road" entering the Tehachapi Valley by way of Oak Creek Pass and crossing to the west. While the majority of travelers to Kern River went by way of Fort Tejon, heavy teams also went through the desert, Jawbone Canyon and Kelso Valley, and lighter wagons went through the Tehachapi Valley.

Survey notes made in preparation of the first official maps of the Tehachapis are descriptive as well as prophetic. In 1855 a general description of the "township is, about 5/6 of it, adapted to agricultural purposes, nearly one half of which is good, first rate tillable land, and the other half well adapted to the raising of stock. Timber, there is a plenty of oak, situated at the foot of the hills, skirting the valley, and pines in large quantity to the southward about 3 miles.

"There are an abundance of springs, but no running streams nor are there any beds of branches or creeks to indicate that there is ever an excess of water for drainage. The chief cause of this no doubt is, that the heavy rains of winter fall here in snow, and the soil being very porous, absorbs that as it melts. Nowhere in California have I seen greater inducements for the enterprising and hardy settler."

Specifically referring to the township which embraces the City of Tehachapi and its immediate farmland, Washburn wrote in the fall of 1854:

"More than half of this township is susceptible of cultivation, and none of it but was in some way adapted to farming purposes. Fully 1/4 is very rich and would produce any and all the cereals abundantly. Timber is scarce, except on Tehachapi Creek, where there are oaks 8 feet in diameter, and, some 50 feet to the first limbs." He added, "Good springs are numerous. A good road can be easily made south to Los Angeles and Northwest into Tulare Valley or to Kern River."

During the same month, while surveying the township directly west of the Tehachapi Valley which includes Brite Valley and Water Canyon, Washburn observed: "Gold is found in all the gulches south of this section." He generally described the land as "of first quality for farming purposes, fine springs and groves of oaks abound. Considerable mining is carried on in the rainy season in the hills and gulches on the South."

The 1855 survey map shows the claim of John Brite to Section 18, Township 32 South, Range 33 East, but the field notes do not mention any improvements on the section. On the other hand, Washburn carefully noted two settlers he found in Township 32 South, Range 32 East — a man named Arnold and "Keller's claim" where he found a "Board House and field with ditch fence and Smith's Shop."

Los Angeles was aware of the activities of survey parties in the northern county which, until 1866, included the Tehachapis. Colonel Norris's survey of the Elizabeth Lake area was mentioned in the Los Angeles Star in May 1854. Later that year Norris also surveyed part of the Tehachapi region. It is not unreasonable to assume the men who saw the Tehachapis spoke of their impressions — not just wrote about them in field notes.

—TEN—

During the 1850's and 1860's settlement in the Tehachapis continued to be controlled by other events. A gold discovery in the camp of Dogtown, far north in the Owens Valley country, brought an influx of miners along the existing roads, including through the southern San Joaquin Valley and the Tehachapi Valley. More people saw the country.

In late summer of 1861 a "new road to Coso" was applauded. "From Elizabeth Lake, take the Tehachape (sic) road to Oak Creek; thence to Willow Springs at western end of Salt Lake; thence due north up a broad arroyo, through some low hills, seven miles to the Plains; making 18 miles in all, to mouth of Walker's Pass from Willow Springs." The writer of these directions mistook the Tehachapi Pass for Walker's, a not uncommon error then. In February 1862 a "good deal of travel through the valley toward Coso mines," was reported in a Los Angeles newspaper; the valley was Tehachapi. "A 60 horse steam engine taken through by way of the valley and Walker's Pass (sic Tehachapi) for Coso Mines." Rather than head out to the "plains" seven miles from Willow Springs, some travelers went to Oak Creek where there was water and rest and "thence striking out upon the desert along the foot of the Sierras . . . ."

Although there was a good deal of traffic through the Tehachapis during this period, permanent settlement was slow due mainly to the Civil War and continuing Indian problems.

—ELEVEN—

The War between the States was fought a few thousand miles from California; but in the Pacific States sympathizers were vocal and active in their support of both sides to the conflict. An immediate result in this area was the abandonment in 1861 of Fort Tejon as the soldiers manning the fort and protecting the countryside were needed in the fight "back home." Area residents, suddenly concerned about the lack of protection from the "incursion and inroads of the Indians," pleaded with Army Headquarters at San Francisco to maintain the fort, but to no avail. There is no evidence that serious Indian problems occurred in the immediate area of Tejon, as settlers came into the region and assumed the ancestral lands of the native inhabitants. To the north and east, however, increased attacks on settlers, fomented by misunderstandings and insensible attitudes by some whites, was experienced within a year, adding to the fears of Tehachapi's settlers.

Particularly in the Owens Valley there were frequent reports in 1862; by May it was claimed the Indians were in almost "undisputed possession of the whole Owens Valley." In September a meeting was held on an island in the South Fork of Kern River; an "outlaw element" from bands living there, as well as near Tehachapi and on the desert, agreed to attack settlers in the Owens Valley the following winter and spring.

One Tehachapi family felt the ramifications of the spring offensive. The Harts, from their initial arrival in the mid-1850's in the Tehachapis, engaged in freighting. While hauling merchandise from Los Angeles to Kern River on July 3, 1863, as they passed through Kelso Valley, Martin Hart, Oliver Burke, Moses Hart, William Dawson, and James Hazlum were ambushed by a band of about "40 Tehachapis." Martin Hart was killed with a shot in his head; his step-brother, Oliver Burke, although shot in an arm returned the fire, killing an Indian. Dawson, carrying the wounded Burke to safety, was fired upon; again Burke was hit, this time in the side. He asked Dawson to put him down and as he lay dying, fired once more, but died preparing to shoot again. Moses Hart, Dawson, and Hazlum decided to abandon their teams and wagons, and escaped.

The Indians captured the goods, "dressed themselves in the clothing that formed part of the load, and took two cases of pistols as a portion of their plunder." In their own folklore of the region, descendants of the Indians recall stories of an attack "near Piute Mountain." After killing some white men, they captured the wagons and "a lot of the clothes were spread over the bushes and could be seen from below." Perhaps this is the same episode.

A future Tehachapi settler, Fred Fickert, while residing in Owens Valley in 1865, participated in an Indian attack there. According to historian W. A. Chalfant, ". . . a general council of whites was held at Lone Pine determined to inflict a crushing blow on the Indians by destroying their settlement near the mouth of Owens River," this attack being their reaction to an Indian raid on a settlement at Haiwei.

Reaching the Indian camp at daylight on January 6, the party, including Fickert, attacked. While less than a dozen of the guilty were in camp, the invaders killed all of the village's inhabitants, of whom at least three-quarters were innocent of any possible participation in the Haiwei act.

In 1856 John Brite led the few families in the area in defense of an expected Indian attack, as explained by him in a letter to his friend in El Monte, Dr. Barton:

"I take this opportunity to inform you that we are all well at present, but not doing as well as we might. Times are squally here. — The Indians have broke out on the Four Creeks, and have driven off a great many cattle. They have stolen 3 or 4 hundred head of horses from Santa Barbara, and carried them up into the mountains on Tule River. The mines on Kern River have quit work and forted up. There have been two fights on Four Creeks, and the Americans were whipped both times. An Express came in from Kern River this morning. They expect to be attacked in a day or two.

"The settlers have all gathered into my house. — We hardly know what to do. I think you had better come up and get your cattle and take them to a more safe place. I am sure that all the stock in this valley will be stolen in a few days. Uncle Davy Smith is going to start for Los Angeles in the morning with a letter from the miners at Kern River to the Sheriff of Los Angeles, to raise a company to come to their assistance. If you come up, I want you to bring me five or six pounds of lead.''

The anticipated attack at Kern River was a result of the plunder of settlers' stock on the Tule River which caused a counterattack on a nearby rancheria by some of the white setlers. Although on May 1, 500 Indians were reported ready to assault Keysville, within a month the uproar died down, and no action was ever taken against the white settlers either at Kern River or Tehachapi.

"Uncle Davy Smith" was a welcome transient in the Tehachapi Valley during 1856, as one of the first mail riders between Los Angeles and the Kern River Valley. The following year he operated a semi-monthly stage which left Los Angeles immediately after the arrival of the steamer at San Pedro Harbor. He journeyed north by way of Fort Tejon to the Kern River and Visalia, carrying the United States Mail on Route 12544.

There is a delightful story involving Amanda Brite in the region's folklore. One day while she was alone at home and John was in Los Angeles on a lengthy buying trip she observed some "savages" around the house. As she feared the results of their finding John's store of whiskey, she overturned the barrels. Just what John's comment was when he returned to find his liquor gone, is not known!

During the same period the settlers were concerned about Indian attacks. They were also bothered by raids of Southern sympathizers. In April 1863 M. M. Welher of Kernville wrote in alarm: "Since the news of the surrender of Lee's army, the assination (sic) of Lincoln and Seward and the surrender of Johnson's army, has reached here, the Rebs have been perfectly wild with excitement and rage, and have organized a guerilla (sic) band at Clear Creek, 15 miles from here, and threaten to annihilate us all, and I don't know but they will do it, but we intend to fight them to the bitter end.''

In September 1864 Colonel R. C. Drum at the Headquarters Department of the Pacific was informed by Captain John C. Smith, Second Infantry, commander of a temporary unit stationed at Fort Tejon, "The cessionists are arming at Tehachapi, sixty miles from this post, led by Harpending, one of the champions of the pirate crew, lately of Keysville.''

In April 1865 twenty-five armed men, many of them "rebels from Price's army,'' drove off a herd of 200 horses from George Cummings' ranch in Cummings Valley. The Los Angeles News, of decidedly Northern inclination, reported the event: "Mr. Cummings is a strong Union man and the blow was especially aimed at him. Thus do our military authorities allow Union men to be plundered and take no measure to pursue the rebel guerrilas (sic). General Mason refused to allow Capt. Ledyard's company of calvary at Drum Barracks to go in pursuit. Adjutant Drum says a force of infantry can be sent. The idea of sending infantry after a gang of well-mounted guerrilas (sic), who were a hundred and fifty miles away in the first place, and had 3 or 4 days start besides is worthy of the source from whence it came. The military authorities are not very anxious to protect the property of Union men.''

In a few weeks the News again reported, "The party who stole Mr. Cummings' stock, at Tehachepe (sic), are said to be in the vicinity of San Bernardino,'' which was sometimes a gathering place for guerrillas in hiding.

A meeting took place in the early summer of 1865 which also caused much concern. The Visalia Delta reported on June 6: "A large number of desparate (sic) characters, disaffected Southern men and worthless reprobates from civilization" had moved to the Clear Creek area. In a pretense of immigrating to Arizona or Mexico, the leaders of the meeting, which numbered 200 people by the time it congregated in the northern Tehachapi Valley, hoped to inflame them to "such madness as to attack such towns as Kernville, Visalia, etc. after supplying their wants, getting hold of all money, arms, and horses, they could gather to force their way out of the country." Fortunately for the settlers, most of the men, while willing to leave the country but unwilling to partake in wanton robbery and its side effects, disbanded. However, Lovic P. Hall, editor in 1862 of the Visalia Equal Rights Expositor, who was one of the leaders and a strong advocate of the secessionist cause, didn't give up. The "Notorious Hall and several returned Confederate soldiers aware that California would probably be too warm for them, carried out so much of the plan as they thought safe, gathered all the horses they could belonging to Union men, and started on their travels." They, too, disappeared into the fastness of the isolated San Bernardino Mountains.

Horace Bell, whose observations of the early American occupation of Southern California are a joy to read, placed the notorious Mason and Henry gang in the Tehachapis. While John Monroe, alias John Mason, and James Henry, alias Spotty McCauley, pretended to be sympathizers of the Southern cause, they used the war as an opportunity to mask their true employment: leaders of an outlaw band. Wrote Major Bell in his "Reminiscenses of a Ranger":

"During the dark days of the Civil War the locality [he was referring to Tehachapi] gained an evil repute on account of one patriotic citizen named Mason, who collected a gang of cutthroats, unfurled to the balmy breeze the three barred banner of the lost cause, declared for the Southern confederacy, and robbed and murdered all who failed to pay tribute. The gang became the terror of the country, ruined the reputation of the wintery pass, and where the mad career of the gurillas (sic) would have ended had not a woman stepped in and caused the death of the chief, is left to conjecture. That is to say, the chief became enamoured of the charms of the wife of one of his band, was smiled on by the fair and fickle one, which caused the reverse of a smile from the outraged husband who ended the amorous dalliance of the two guilty lovers by putting an end to the redoubtable Robin Hood of the windy pass. On the death of the leader the band disbanded and has passed into the history of Tehachapi."

Bell's account of Mason's death is more theatrical than the Los Angeles News tersely reported comment in April 1866: "Mason, one of the late distinguished firm of Mason & Henry was killed a few days since in Tejon Canon by some citizens . . . It seems there were several of his clan together and they all got off except the chief, . . ." James Henry was caught and shot near San Bernardino. He had stopped to rest in a canyon and while he was asleep a posse sighted him. A fight followed and he was shot.

TWELVE

Near Clear Creek in 1864 another gold discovery the following year brought about the founding of the town of Havilah by Asbury Harpending (late of Civil War infamy). Visalia immediately initiated a concerted effort to obtain the trade of the new mining settlement. At the same time, Los Angeles recognized the new source of revenue, and began its own campaign.

In May 1865 a petition was presented to the Los Angeles County Board of Supervisors "praying . . . to aid in the construction of a free pass through the mountains beyond Oak Creek, for a wagon road to the mines." Recognizing the benefit the Board appropriated $1,000 for a road fund, to be augmented by contributions of $3,000 to $4,000 from merchants and businessmen in Los Angeles and along the route-of-way.

Within a month E. K. Dunlap, the superintendent, left for the mountain country beyond Oak Creek "with a party of laborers, to open the work." Accompanying him was Doctor James B. Winston, a Los Angeles businessman who intended to visit the mines, stopping along the way at Oak Creek and Tehachapi to solicit subscriptions. The crew found a "good natural road for the whole distance with the exception of about six miles, . . . the section now under contract." In December the road over the mountain was completed and in fine condition, "heavy teams experiencing no difficulty in passing with freight."

Most of the natural road from Los Angeles to Havilah has disappeared under the wheels of progress — new roads, plowing, the winds of time. But in one short stretch of about a mile-and-a-half, from the Bill Cuddeback Cabin on White Rock Creek northwest through Section 35, time stood still. In May 1975, packs on our backs and only cows watching our progress, we walked that virgin stretch and wondered at the skill of Jehus whipping their steeds through the canyon to crest the first range of hills. The rut of the coach and wagon have washed away, but two stretches of about a hundred feet clearly exemplify the labor in building and compacting the road.

The road from Los Angeles to Havilah and beyond brought public transportation to the region for the first time. Stage coaches were a weekly occurrence, when the firm of John J. Tomlinson began service to Havilah on May 9, 1865. There is no evidence that at this early date the stage went into the Western Tehachapi Valley where most of the population was gathering in settlement. Rather, it went from Oak Creek Station up the road towards Cameron Station, but about half-way on the Cameron Road veered to the north through a cut in the northern slope. Then it crossed over to the Salt Lake or Sinks of the Tehachapi, and entered the White Rock Creek region over the newly constructed mountain road by way of Tollgate Canyon. A mail route was established between Los Angeles and Havilah and Tomlinson was awarded the contract. This was a welcome addition to one observer who was ". . . glad the department has at last performed an act of justice to the people of that section through which the route passes, they will now be enabled to communicate with the outside world." Another stageline through the

Tehachapis during this time was operated by George Andrews, using the same route.

The developing mines of the Owens Valley, Coso Range, and the Panamints, as well as construction of the railroad through the San Joaquin Valley in the early 1870's, instigated other stage routes through the Tehachapi Valley in an east-west direction. And more people came through the Tehachapis.

—THIRTEEN—

As a result of the Havilah gold rush, citizens in the northern extremity of Los Angeles County, long isolated from the mainstream of growth experienced in the southern city, began to think about politics and progress, not just gold and roads. On March 15, 1866, a meeting was held in Havilah because "a large portion of the citizens of the southern portion of Tulare county" saw a need for self-government. This idea was concurred with by residents of the Tehachapis. Action was swift; before the State legislature adjourned in the spring, a bill passed forming the county of Kern from portions of Tulare and Los Angeles Counties. One of the new county's townships was "Tehachpa (sic) . . . situated on an elevated plain, about one hundred and thirty miles from this city . . . has a salubrious climate and rich soil, producing larger and better crops of cereals than almost any part of the State and less liable to rust; the people are intelligent and industrious, and mostly engaged in agricultural pursuits, and their industrious agricultural community will be a great accession to the new county, and will add greatly to the wealth . . . ."

—FOURTEEN—

The end of the Civil War and of serious Indian outbreaks; the first real estate boom in Southern California; the opening of new roads and commencement of public transportation, all contributed to an influx of settlers to the Tehachapis in the late 1860's. By then the original many-thousand-acred Tehachapi Valley was known as the four valleys of Tehachapi, Bear, Brite, and Cummings.

Most of the land was in the Public Domain. Private land grants of Spanish and Mexican origin were non-existent — except for the nearest grant which embraced the Tejon ranchos. As the pioneers arrived they claimed the land — by homestead, timber, mining, and pre-emption rights. Some settlers pre-empted the land by right of settlement and improvement, and eventually purchased it at $1.25 an acre without competition from others. Others filed on homesteads of 160 acres free-of-charge in exchange for five years' residence and cultivation, after which a certificate of patent was filed.

In 1867 James Williams moved his family into the Western Tehachapi Valley. Two years later he built the first commercial establishment in the town he founded known as Williamsburg and Tehachipa. Williams was one of the region's original subdividers and may well have been influenced in his real estate ambitions by a map published in 1868 by R.

31

H. Strech of San Francisco which was for sale throughout the state. It delineated the route of the Southern Pacific Railroad from Northern California to Los Angeles, ''giving boundaries of the lands granted by the Government to the former . . . This is a valuable work,'' commented the Tulare Times in advertising it, ''and parties interested in dealing in land should avail themselves of its information.''

In the early 1870's Williams sold lots in the pleasant small flat surrounded by oaks and with a swift stream flowing nearby. A small village grew up, offering all the services necessary to a growing community. The village was sustained by the continuing growth in the region and contributed to it as well.

The Mines

Gold Mine Found. In the newly made raceway of the sawmill recently created by Captain Sutter on the American Fork, gold has been found in considerable quantities. One person brought thirty dollars' worth to New Helvetia, gathered there in a short time. California, no doubt, is rich in mineral wealth; great chances here for scientific capitalists. Gold has been found in almost every part of the country.

In the Alta Californian,
March 15, 1848

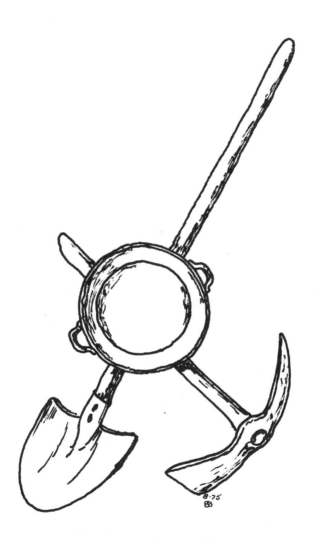

—ONE—

Gold brought many adventurers to California. Some found their way into the Tehachapis. The gold is still here: for some, the value is its weight of ore — for others its wealth is the stories. It tests the historian's metal to sift fact from fiction, especially in the light of determined story-tellers insisting that millions of dollars was mined in the Tehachapis (7). These are the facts which appear on the surface, leaving to you a search beneath the surface to find your own treasure.

Northwest of Tehachapi is Mormon Gulch, where history records men of that religious persuasion sought and found gold, sending it to Salt Lake City.

On a fresh spring day in 1975 I followed in their footsteps, walking up the gulch from the modern freeway which speeds by it so swiftly that few motorists look to the east to see its invitation. A slow-moving stream in that dry year meandered down to Tehachapi Creek as I walked upstream searching for any evidence of these first miners in the Tehachapis. I found nothing but seasonal flowers, cattle grazing on the hillsides, and a lost dog. But the history of the gulch was in mind as I walked along the streambank.

At the end of 1856 Peter D. Greene, later to excel as a leader of the region, on "Christmas night of that year struck camp in Mormon Gulch, near Tehachapi and here he prospected for a time . . . ." A company of Mormons preceded Greene to the gulch, leaving their name to history. In another dry year, during the winter of 1854-55, David Seeley, a settler of the Mormon community of San Bernardino, went to the Kern River mines with a fifty-man Mormon Colony. They intended to raise money for the community, but evidently did poorly as they stayed less than a month. It is not unlikely they passed through the Tehachapi Valley on their return to San Bernardino, or that another Mormon company stopped for a while to placer mine at the gulch.

The Mormons were active miners in California during the 1850's. In 1847, at the conclusion of the Mormon Battalion's march to San Diego with Lt. Cooke, some men went to guard from Indian raiders the Cajon Pass, located between the desert and San Bernardino. Issac Williams, owner of the Chino Ranch, offered to sell it and his cattle to Mormon settlers. The same year Brigham Young arrived in Salt Lake City with many of the faithful. Some of his followers were already working in the mines of Northern California, tithing to the church after arriving in an early wagon train over the Santa Fe Trail.

In March 1851, 150 wagons with 437 people left Utah for the Chino Ranch, arriving in June. Williams didn't sell to them after all, so they bought the Lugo San Berdino Ranch in September 1851 and began their settlement.

Young's plan was to connect a chain of stations from the Deseret State

Mormon Gulch where miners panned for gold as early as 1854

at Salt Lake City with a California harbor, for the reception of foreign converts, and with a larger visionary plan for a California State. By their brief mining venture in the Tehachapis, some of Young's followers unintentionally named a geographic landmark.

At the end of 1855 another company of miners sought placer gold in other gulches. One illustrative miner wrote of their adventures in a letter to the Los Angeles Star:

"Tay-ee-chay-pah Valley, California, February 23d, 1856.

"Since I have come to this place, some 3 months since, I have spent a considerable length of time in prospecting the various gulches and ravines by which we are surrounded, but as yet I have made no valuable discoveries, still I can by the least effort, and in almost any direction, find more or less gold, but not sufficient to justify me to work, yet from what I have got here from experienced miners, there are the strongest indications of deep and rich diggings imaginable.

"From every appearance there has at some time been a considerable stream of water run through this portion of the country, which, by some volcanic eruptions, has been either destroyed or removed to some other part of the land, and the general opinion is, could the old bed of this stream be found, that rich and extensive treasures would be the reward of any person whose energy might prompt him to test the matter.

"There has been but few claims discovered as yet that will pay more than eight or ten dollars per day to the hand as a general thing; however, some few are doing, I think, a little better, while others are not doing near as well.

"I candidly believe that all that keeps this from being a rich and extensive mining country is for the want of some few energetic industrious miners to prospect the country thoroughly, for as yet there has been no prospecting done by which we can tell anything. So much for mining."

In the spring of 1858 a new discovery was reported. Gold valued at $100 was washed out in one day by four men; and 300 buckets of auriferous earth produced the handsome sum of $60. It's no wonder men continued to come to the Tehachapis, especially from diggings such as the Kern River Valley which disillusioned them, when a Los Angeles paper reported: "Should such diggings as this be found in the Valley, it will soon become the scene of busy industry, and afford active and highly remunerative employment to those who are now engaged in the calm and peaceful life of husbandry."

That summer three parties worked the gulches. "Mr. Robinson made the first discovery of that gold was to be found there," commented the Star although not specifically saying just where in the area, "and is now at work, doing very well." The men earned from $10 to $18 a day, although they had formerly made as high as $25. Prophetically, Robinson complained "water was not as abundant on his claim as the wants of the company require." Throughout the gold mining era the lack of water precluded a big rush to the Tehachapi gold fields, such as occurred elsewhere and, perhaps, a genuine lack of extensive gold, as suggested by knowledgeable oldtimers today, did, too.

Robinson employed a party of six Chinamen who mined in a gulch about a mile distant from his claim. They also complained that all the intervening land along the foothills would pay well if "water could be obtained." Meanwhile the Chinese cut a ditch seven miles long and led what water there was along the top of the hill, which gave them the command of the gulches.

Chinese working in the Tehachapi "gold fields" was not unusual. Recruitment in their native country, particularly in Kwangtun province, by

37

agents for the railroad, timber, ranch, and mine interests, was a common occurrence when California became a state. After the Taiping Rebellion, ruin and resulting poverty and the horrors of war induced men to leave their homeland for foreign shores. Although American miners resisted their incursion, the Chinese were permitted to work if they were under contract to Americans. Conscript labor resulted. Foreign importers and Chinese middlemen were the principal contractors in a system which brought indentured emigrants to America. Until the debt of their travel ticket and expenses was paid, the laborer remained under the control of his "benefactor."

Robinson's claims may well have been in the area known today as the China Diggings. Although some tales say millions of dollars were recovered there, another oldtimer who had extensively searched the area commented, "That quartz just ain't that rich. Sure the Chinamen and others found gold. But millions? No, they never found that there."

A third party of men commanded by a Mr. Steward, also engaged in mining in the valley. They, too, were "doing well."

In March 1861 mining was pursued more extensively than ever and with better returns. Although a lack of water limited the activity to only three months, three men produced $4,500. The following year "Pioneer gulch" was opened, "a section of great extent and unparalled (sic) richness in that valley." The large numbers of men were quite satisfied with the yield.

The search for gold was not without problems. Violence shattered a camp on Christmas night in 1861. Aaron Hart, a son of Josiah and a chainman in the 1854 governmental survey (as was his brother Issac), lived in the valley and prospected for gold. At his home that night visitor P. Lewis accosted another guest, Joel H. Brooks, threatening to shoot Brooks. Hart and another man, David Hart, who was not related, temporarily settled the disagreement. Ill-feeling continued, however, until on January 8, they met again on a prospecting trip. This time Brooks was the aggressor and drew his gun. As he fired, Lewis used his pick, pan, and shovel for a shield, and avoided the shots, but Aaron Hart was wounded in the arm. Brooks told Aaron "to go home and when he got well he would shoot him again," which led to further arguing, this time between Lewis and a man called Ayres. Again, as he attempted to prevent a fight, Aaron was shot. Lewis then stole a horse, saddle, and bridle and "escaped to the upper country by way of San Pedro." Meanwhile Hart's wound mortified, and on January 21 "a respectable man and very popular in the community" died.

In the late 1870's J. J. Hendrickson gleaned a small fortune from the placer mines in the same hills where Chinese had mined, but he utilized hydraulic mining equipment also. This method required water pressure to beat the ground and, in fact, as a wholesale washing scheme materially changed the landscape. The hydraulic mining equipment was invented by an innovative miner who first employed it in Northern California. (In 1933 at the same location as Hendrickson's, E. R. Pierce and Associates reportedly invested $30,000 digging a two mile ditch. They built a million gallon reservoir on top of the mountain and installed a pipe line in a determined effort to reap their fortune in hydraulic mining.)

Once again, oral history records Hendrickson earned "millions." And yet other oldtimers insist he couldn't have, as "It just wasn't there!" Perhaps, in this case they're right because an 1873 newspaper item reports that two men "cleaned up $1438 in their hydraulic operation" next to Hendrickson. That requires a lot of multiples to reach millions.

In 1878 a rich strike above the China Diggings resulted in later claims which embraced a large area and the development over many years of the Pine Tree Mine. Rich ore was found in tunnels dug with the sweat of muscled men. Again, "millions," said some of the storytellers but the actual mine reports record a few hundred thousand dollars.

In 1869 a surveyor's report of an exploration through the Tehachapis two years earlier, surely added to the lore. General William J. Palmer wrote, "At Tehachapa Pass where we cross it, the mountains abound in gold, silver and copper. Gold placers are worked here."

Undoubtedly newspaper reports helped stimulate men to seek riches and then, when it was over, in the minds of other men, those reports became fact rather than the search itself. In the 1880's, when the Pine Tree Mine was extensively mined, a Bakersfield paper reported, "A slight mining excitement is growing up in the Tehachapi country." And, "In the Tehachapi section of the county gold mining is being profitably pursued and with increasing activity. Some large capitalists, it is stated, have recently become interested in the mines there." In the summer of 1891, a new owner of the Pine Tree Mine reopened the tunnel "and with the new apparatus now on hand great things are expected from the old claim, which has turned out barrels of money in its time." During the summer of 1897, with still another promoter guiding the miners, a report said, "They are employing about 24 men and the monthly dividends are in the neighborhood of $5,000."

This same mine, in the early 1940's, yielded another mineral: tungsten. Used principally in the manufacture of tool steel, some development took place in the gold tunnels as well as in new workings. Carl H. Claussenius produced several tons. Scheelite was also found east of the Pine Tree Mine on property owned by the Summit Lime Co., but neither claim was a major source of revenue.

It was not unusual for new discoveries in the Tehachapis to coincide with events elsewhere. But I don't believe it was only a coincidence; rather, the exploration for gold elsewhere reminded men that here, too, gold had been found and perhaps there was more.

In 1893 men from Tehachapi "were going to the mines in the desert." Two years later Eugene Garlock was one of them. Where a well of pure water filled the earth, allegedly discovered by Hamp Williams, Jr., who said, "In the year of 1893 I dug a water well 9 feet down. I found water and a lot of it. We called it Cow Wells," Garlock began his two-stamp mill, operated by a crude ten-horsepower oil engine. (Actually wells existed at that locale for many years providing stockmen with water long before Williams dug his.) In 1896 Garlock developed an eight-stamp mill at Cow Wells, which he renamed Eugeneville. Later it became known as Garlock. The Tehachapi paper reported, "The boom that is taking place in

Morjave (sic) desert mines is already showing its effect in our town and also in the town of Mojave. We will gladly welcome any development that will bring in money for the actual exploitation of the mines.''

As a result of the desert mining excitement during the rest of the decade many men searched the hills and gullies of the Tehachapis. Newspaper reports read:

(1894) ''Placer gold has been discovered in a mile and a half of Tehachapi and prospects well. From three pans of top dirt there was taken out 37½ of yellow metal one day this week. There are a number of men out prospecting and a rich find will not be a surprising event.''

(1894) ''Mining excitement in Tehachapi high and many people heading from the desert to dig for gold.''

(1896) ''A great many mining men have visited Tehachapi in the last ten days. Most of them coming from San Francisco. There is an air of secrecy and a no-nothing manner about them that betokens a great deal.''

(1896) ''Tehachapi mining matters picking up. Old mines are being opened up, new ones prospected for and some of the best ones being sold and others under contemplation of sale.''

(1897) ''Untold wealth is stored in the mountains of Tehachapi. This is destined shortly to become the richest mining district in California.''

And so it went, except from about that time the mining excitement died down, just as did the blatant reporting of the area's newspapers, quick invitations to gold-hungry men.

Years later still another event occasioned a new search for gold. In the depression years of the 1930's men scurried to the desert locating new prospects. And once again men looked in the Tehachapis, and looked, and looked. They found some gold; we could find it yet.

—TWO—

In the 1970's instead of the metal I sought the wealth of stories which abound. The common currency in the early days of Tehachapi's settlement was gold coin.

After his death in the 1870's, Jerry Glenn's brother Bob searched for a hidden treasure. Jerry lived in a tall house on a tall hill, somewhat east of Old Town. He was a cattleman. As was the custom of the day, men paid in gold coin. Bob knew Jerry had buried the coin under a tree near the house; there were no banks here then. The problem was what tree? He hunted for days, but never found the gold.

That story was passed around over the years, until one day a resident of Tehachapi bought a metal detector. He knew the area where Glenn lived and searched for the gold. He spent weeks at his avocation, but never found it.

Another story involves Indians; only in this case they were the victims, not the aggressors. In the days when the Spanish reigned over the countryside, and the Indian was little more than a slave, a gold train passed below the slopes of Sugarloaf Mountain, east of Tehachapi. It was coming from somewhere in the desert, so the story is told, headed for the coast and civilization. Driving burros laden with gold were Indians,

40

guarded by Spanish soldiers.

No one knows what prompted them to revolt, but they did. After overpowering and killing the Spaniards, the treasure was buried because gold was a curse, had brought them problems, and they wanted no part of it.

Sugarloaf is in Sand Canyon country. So is the locale of the next tale. In the old days a bandit was escaping with loot, saddle bags full of gold coins. Because the bags were so heavy, aware that a posse would eventually catch him, he decided to bury the money and return at a later time. The bandit sighted along three big rocks so he could find the place again and buried the loot at the foot of the third rock. The next event should be obvious in the telling of hidden treasure stories: the bandit was killed before he could recover the gold — which is still there, waiting. Or is it?

New story: some years ago a man homesteaded in Sand Canyon. He lived alone and remained aloof. Every morning it was his custom to take a walk. No one knew where, although he was observed heading out and coming back. On some occasions, down in Los Angeles, he was seen walking into a Federal bank, depositing gold nuggets, and receiving cash. The nuggets did not gleam with color, but looked old. Now, where did those nuggets come from — the Indians' horde or the bandit's?

If the next story is right, it wasn't the bandit's. As I told the tale to an oldtimer he said, "Nope, you've got it wrong," and proceeded to tell it right — or so he said. Rawley Duntley lived many years on his Oak Creek Canyon Ranch. He told the oldtimer this tale, which he said occurred about the turn of the century.

One day a bandit came riding over Oak Creek Pass, escaping from a posse. Aware they would eventually catch up with him and knowing he couldn't escape, he decided to bury heavy saddlebags full of gold, and return at a later time. The bandit sighted along three big rocks so he could find the place again, and also used an oak tree as a location point. He buried his loot.

Now the tale changes, for the bandit was on Duntley's ranch, some distance from Sand Canyon. Duntley had not yet seen the bandit, who hid by the corrals until the posse searched for him and rode off. The bandit went into the house. Right after he told his story about burying the gold, the bandit died. Duntley had a pretty good idea where the gold was buried, but he was a superstitious man, according to the storyteller. Figuring there was a "curse" on the treasure, he left it there; we can only presume it still remains untouched.

There was an old codger named "Slim" or "Swede." (After all these years the next storyteller couldn't remember which.) But he did remember Slim arrived in Arvin (in the San Joaquin Valley) each spring, dirty, ragged, and with money. For several months he'd board at a rooming house, buy some new clothes, and wait the passage of time, usually knitting.

The last time the storyteller saw him, he'd driven him to Tehachapi. After they stopped for supper, Slim asked to be driven south to the entrance of Antelope Canyon. "Now what do you do when you go away each winter?'' Slim was sked.

Slim replied, ''Well, up there somewhere (pointing to the Tehachapis), I've found a wet-weather spring. I keep hidden nearby, during the summer, some sluice boxes.'' He went on: ''About this time each year I return, set out the boxes, and let nature take its course. The water washes down the fine sand and my boxes capture the gold. Then, in the spring when the water starts to dry up, I come in, empty out the gold and hide my boxes. I'll tell you what,'' he promised the storyteller, ''next time I see you, I'll take you right to the spot.''

In the true spirit of all good tales, you know what happened. The storyteller never saw Slim again. He assured me he's covered those mountains up, down, and on both sides. He's never found the sluice-boxes — they, too, are still there — waiting.

—THREE—

As excitement elsewhere fomented the exploration and discovery of gold, other mineral discoveries accomplished the same thing. In 1900 major oil finds were made on the west side of the San Joaquin Valley which have produced millions of dollars through the years. That same year, the American Oil Company was incorporated at Tehachapi. Burt Denison was president, John Durnal was vice president, Albert Ancker served as Secretary with H. P. Bender as Assistant Secretary, and the directors were R. R. Taylor, L. F. Brite, and Frank Meehan. J. W. Murray was the Manager. The corporation drilled in several sections in the Sand Canyon area; one side canyon became known as Oil Canyon. Interest in the oil boom even resulted in the opening of a new saloon called the ''Oil Exchange'' in Tehachapi in February 1901. Perhaps the Exchange reaped a rich profit; the oilmen didn't.

In 1927 the Jameson Corporation also looked for oil prospects on the Pauly Tract north of Tehachapi. And in the 1940's some prospecting occurred in Cummings Valley.

The rush for uranium prospects following World War II produced a discovery in 1955 in the hills southwest of Oak Creek Road, on the north side of a small peak. The Atomic Energy Commission posted its result of a survey of uranium potentials in a map on March 15, 1955. Within six hours 143 new claims were filed with the Kern County Recorder, and in a week the total reached 477. The prospectors at Oak Creek dug a shallow surface trench and bulldozed a cut around the top of the hill, but no ore was produced.

The rush, continuing for several weeks, was likened by some observers to the gold rush of a century before. Now as then, the same thing happened: for some riches, for most only claims.

—FOUR—

Inasmuch as geologic action produced the minerals of the region, let us pause for a moment to take a good look at the land. What better way is there than to walk over it? A casual trek from Tehachapi into the surrounding foothills quickly reveals the contours and slopes of the valley floor; it's uphill or downhill any way you go. Moving into higher elevations, a brisk hike into narrow canyons, then up steep slopes take you to eagle-eye vantage points. The higher you go, the more rugged the backward, downward view until, if you could fly the currents of the winds, far below the awesome geologic history of the Tehachapi region would reveal itself.

In the beginning there was no dry land. Covering the area, as well as much of the Sierra Nevada Range, was a widespread sea. Today's explorer can find some evidence of this very early period known as the Paleozoic of over 185 million years ago. On the West Ranch properties (southeast of the Tehachapi Valley) and imbedded in a "shelf" on a ridge above the Mountain Park, seashells have been found, hinting at the depth of water that once filled the valley. Great thicknesses of silt, sand, clay, and limestone were collected and deeply buried during the Paleozoic period.

Next came the Jurassic and Cretaceous epochs of 75 million to 155 million years ago, when the crust of the earth was disturbed and great mountains created. Repeatedly as time passed, rock produced by fiery action intruded upon the earth and, accompanied by folding, changed the character of the once flat terrain. Great granitic rocks of different varieties intruded also and were firmly implanted by the end of the Cretaceous period.

Then began the Tertiary epoch of 75 million years ago. Uplifts, erosional intervals, subsequent burial, all accompanied by persistent folding, brought more change.

During the Miocene epoch, nine to twenty-eight million years ago, the land became more habitable, although, during this time volcanoes exploded and the land was again lifted and folded. Basaltic rock on a slope near the freeway west of Tehachapi as well as in certain locations of the Sand Canyon region is evidence of the early volcanic activity that moved the land. But peace reigned more often than not during this period.

Many more eons elapsed; the land continued to change, to lift up and come down. Then, in the late Pleistocene of six million years ago, the range known today as the Sierra Nevada was lifted up to rest at its present elevation.

Finally, possibly as late as the beginning of the Recent epoch of .011 million years ago, further faulting occurred and dislocated remnants of the Tehachapi erosion surface, forming a series of depressions and producing what is now called the Tehachapi Valley system.

All through time, as volcanic outbursts pierced the occasional serenity of the jumbled and tilted land, rains fell. The inland sea had long ago disappeared, but from high in the mountains falling rain loosened silts, sands, and gravels, which were carried downward.

Canyons were deepened. In areas where mountains spread out the land was filled and formed. Where streams emptied into the ever-forming large valley, alluvial fans were deposited.

Today, four major valleys compose the system: to the west is Cummings

Valley, about six miles long, two and one-half miles wide, and with a mean elevation of about 3,800 feet; Bear Valley lies northwest of Cummings and is about three miles long and two miles wide. (This valley is in two levels: at the Fickert Ranchhouse it is about 4,300 feet, while a terrace above it is from 300 to 500 feet higher.) Brite Valley is the highest in the system, at a mean elevation of 4,400 feet, and also the narrowest, less than a mile wide, and five miles long. The largest valley is Tehachapi — ten miles long, three and one-half miles wide, its mean elevation 4,000 feet.

Two major mountain ranges surround the valleys. To the north is the Sierra Nevada. In the immediate area of the Tehachapi Valley, its highest elevation is about 6,500 feet. To the south is the Tehachapi Mountain Range, with its highest points Cummings Mountain at 7,753 feet, and near Double Mountain at 7,988 feet. The Tehachapis swing westward into the San Emigdio Mountains, which in turn trend north-of-west into the Coast Range.

These mountain masses separate the Mojave Desert in the east from the San Joaquin Valley in the west. They are also responsible for the variant climate which is often a source of conversation for Tehachapi's residents.

Several major streams feed the land with water, although they are usually not seasonable. Chanac, Cummings, Brite, Tehachapi, China Hill, Antelope, Blackburn, White Rock, Sand, and Cache creeks, flow into the valley's system, in some instances draining into the San Joaquin or the desert.

The floor of the Tehachapi Valley is, for the most part, one vast alluvial plain. Through studies of wells dug in historic times, it is estimated the depth of the alluviation is not less than 344 feet. This fill appears deepest at the railroad siding of Summit, about one-half mile east of the City of Tehachapi, where the recorded elevation is 4,032 feet.

One of the most interesting features in the main valley is two rocky hills. The one closest to the city near the county airport rises to an altitude of about 100 feet above the surrounding plain and consists of mostly bare rock. It is rugged in character. The other hill is in the eastern Tehachapi Valley near Sand Canyon Road. It is about half-a-mile in length from north-to-south and about half as wide at its base. Probably not less than 200 feet high, its bare, rocky, precipitous slopes are in striking contrast to the surrounding landscape. The isolation of these two hills suggested to a geologist seventy years ago that the alluvial infilling of the valley reached a great depth and the rock surface upon which the alluvium rests was quite irregular.

The oldest rocks in the region are bands of gneiss, schist, recrystallized limestone, and quartzite. It is granitic rock, however, that constitutes the bulk of the mountains, and it was into this mass that limestone in large inclusions sank when the granite was in a syrupy state.

The landscape is ever changing. The earthquake of 1952 changed water courses, opened cracks in the earth, and caused other geologic phenomenon of importance to scientific studies. These changes are miniscule when compared to the evolving landscape of millions of years.

From great seas to continuous volcanic activity, from the creation of the mountain ranges and deep-filled alluvium valleys which dominate the scenery today — the landscape was formed.

—FIVE—

More than other areas of the Tehachapis the terrain of the Sand Canyon region demonstrates the geologic changes that have occurred. Evidence, especially of the Miocene epoch, is vivid there today. During that period, when the land became more habitable, palms and reeds grew in shallow marshes at the shores of lakes. The faunal assemblage found there today indicates a plains environment, although the presence of water is not an indication of lush growth. It was a semi-arid region with localized deposits of water above ground — the attraction for the unique animal life of that time and place.

While hiking the countryside, one finds it hard to imagine the horses and other herbivorous animals that once roamed the land. We would not recognize them now. The horse is a commonplace Western American animal of the Twentieth Century, introduced by the Spanish conquistadores. He has little resemblance to the grazing animal of millions of years ago. Then he was about the size of a Collie dog with the unusual physical characteristic of three toes. Some scientists theorize the horse, as well as a camel which lived in the same locale, originated in North America, migrated to the Old World across the Bering Strait landbridge, and at some distant time disappeared entirely from this continent.

Bruce Eisenman searchs for fossils in Sand Canyon in October 1974

45

As the result of a fossil find near Sand Canyon in the early 1900's, scientists from the University of California undertook a series of expeditions. Bone collections were made in 1914 and 1915, revealing the fossil remains of grazing animals. The distinct horse fossil was called Merychippus Tehachapiensis. The collections made at Sand Canyon as well as at nearby Cache Peak and at Ricardo in Red Rock Canyon, were the precursor of an extensive study of early mammals in Western North America. Again, in 1934 and 1935 further explorations and collecting occurred there. By this time, however, the Cache Creek area was renamed Horse Canyon for obvious reasons.

Sandstone quarry ruins at Sand Canyon in April 1975

Several years after the initial exploration for fossil remains, a new and different exploration of Horse Canyon began. A cowboy told several Bakersfield men about discovering some large petrified tree trunks. An exploratory party found the trees and recognized the beauty of moss agate. The tree trunks soon disappeared, but the bed of agate has yet to cease sharing its wealth. It would be safe to say that thousands of gemologists have since visited the Horse Canyon agate beds.

The agate, appearing as sagenite, banded, clouded, plume, and lace, is fashioned into jewelry specimens and book ends. It is the delicate moss-like growth, however, in various shades of green, as well as white, and sometimes appearing in brown, yellow, red, or black, that qualifies the material as a unique collectible. Specimens of petrified palm and palm root, cattails and reeds, have also been found and collected, as have petrified oak and sycamore logs, and chalcedony, chrysoprise, jasper,

46

opal, and quartz clusters, all of these having also attracted the rockhounds.

Bud Barras checks the green sandstone quarry at Sand Canyon in April 1975

Throughout the Sand Canyon region sandstone predominates in a variety of colors. At the entrance to a short canyon just west of Horse Canyon, several stone buildings and an extensive quarry of green sandstone is the location of an early industry in the region. Although the property was homesteaded by a man named McFarlane (8), at the beginning of 1887 the Tehachipa Building Stone Co., incorporated at Los Angeles, produced sandstone building blocks at its quarries for projects in Los Angeles and San Francisco. The blocks, which were later quarried by the Kern Development Syndicate in colors of green, blue, red, tan, and drab, were used in the construction of the Pasadena library building, and the Date and Fish Blocks in Los Angeles. Farther up "McFarlane's" canyon, a ridge above the floor is a jumble of dynamited blocks of buff-colored sandstone. In Horse Canyon deep red colors a hillside near the entrance, although the quarry may have been located in another canyon to the west.

As recently as 1950 the sandstone was utilized by several companies, including the Desert Rock Milling Company, Hidecker Rock Company, and the M & M Mining Company of Walter Eisenman and Tom Murray. The companies produced roofing granule material for a once popular exterior decor, mining in several locations throughout the general Sand Canyon area. The mining activity continued until about 1970, when that style of roof lost architectural favor at the same time as some inferior grades of roofing material gave to all rock gravel a bad reputation, which materially affected the market.

Although it was mined on only a small scale, worthy of mention is a product of the Fitrol Company of Los Angeles, which forty years ago mined a deposit of Fuller's earth in Sand Canyon. It is a clay used in fulling wool and deodorizing and clarifying oils, fats, greases, and other fluids. The Los Angeles company used it to treat petroleum oil, mining it in small tunnels and hauling the material by truck to a siding of the Southern Pacific Railroad Company.

Although it has no connection with mineral activity that occurred there, several juniper trees and pinon pines attract the eye for more than their beauty. Some early surveys of Sand Canyon were in the 1870's, and as the chainmen and surveyors marked their maps, they also marked bearing trees, which still grow along section lines near Sugarloaf Mountain.

—SIX—

In open spaces and hidden glades in the mountains south of the Tehachapi Valley, the sculptured ruins of Nineteenth Century stone artisans are mute reminders of an industry that continues to dominate the Tehachapi scene a century later.

The announcement in a March 1877 Bakersfield paper was brief and terse: "New lime kilns are being started at a distance of some six miles from town by Mr. John Narboe and I. B. Malin." The locale was Antelope Canyon. While they assuredly expected a return for their efforts, they could not foresee the results of their virgin venture.

The first kilns were quite primitive, built of large stones in a circular design to a height of several feet, with an opening at the top. The limestone was dumped into the "pot kiln" after being quarried and teamed from a nearby location. Wood, usually oak because of its high burning temperature, was piled on top and then fired (9).

When heated at high temperatures, the limestone lost its carbonic acid which passed off as a gas, while the oxide of lime for quicklime remained. This loss began at about 750 degrees F., but a temperature of over 1300 degrees F. was necessary before all the gas was driven off. When the stone was burned down, the arduous task of removing the lime from the depths of the pot kiln began. It came out in chunks as big as a jug, a bluish-white color when properly burned.

To make the lime "work," cold water was added and it immediately heated to a quick boil; the term "slake" is used to describe this chemical change. As more water was added the lime looked like a dough but only finer and usable as whitewash. To make mortar, less water was added.

Although the initial production of lime was intended for local consumption, by the 1890's it was shipped to Southern California.

Lime has a variety of applications. In the Tehachapi region it was used mainly in mortar for building, as a whitewash, and as a refractory in mining applications. As whitewash it lasted only a few years before peeling, so that salt was added to prevent this from occurring. Today it has several applications: it is used in mortar stucco and plaster by the building industry, and as a refractory for lining open-hearth furnaces. It is a soil additive for agricultural purposes or to stabilize roadbeds; a raw material for making glass and other chemical products; it is used in water purification, sewage treatment, pulp and paper manufacture; and in refining sugar and petroleum and in tanning.

The exact location of Narboe's kiln is unknown. In Antelope Canyon, however, at several different locations, the remains of a few "pot" kilns delight the eye. In June 1888 Godfrey Poirier built a large kiln adjacent to his quarry in Pine Grove Canyon, which is a branch of Antelope, running northwesterly out of the mountains. In Antelope Canyon, in addition to the Narboe-Malin operation, a Mr. Anderson built a large kiln in 1888. The Homestake Company, which operated a five-stamp mill at the mouth of Pine Grove Canyon prior to that year, also operated a lime kiln.

A major lime production operation in Antelope Canyon began in 1885 under management of the Union Lime Company, which is also known as the Summit Lime Company. For a while in the early Twentieth Century the company also had kilns in downtown Tehachapi. Four of them were located on the company's property near H and Hayes Streets adjacent to the railroad. The rock was hauled by eight-horse teams from the canyon quarries. Probably the main reason for the downtown kiln was a need to replace with fuel oil the common but dwindling wood supply. In 1906 Ferd Snyder opened kilns for the same reason and purpose, just east of the Union's.

In 1927 the Union Lime Company modernized, adding to its downtown facility a hydrating plant, installed by the McGann Manufacturing Company of Pennsylvania. This plant had a two-and-one-half ton capacity per hour, and operated twenty hours daily. Considerable pressure was required to hydrate lime, 250 gallons of water was used each hour. Hydrated lime was manufactured for only a couple of years; economic

The Union Lime Co. and Snyder Lime Co. kilns adjacent to the railroad and east of Tehachapi — Circa 1914 (Ed Wiggins Collection)

Hauling limestone from Antelope Canyon down G Street near Greene Street to kilns east of Tehachapi — Circa early 20th century (Ed Wiggins Collection)

factors, partly created by the nationwide depressions, closed the plant down and it never reopened. Hydrated lime has more than sixty applications, including various building methods, stucco work, soap manufacture, and fertilizer.

In Grizzly Canyon, two limekilns are in ruins: one was operated by Henry Seeger, the other by Thos. Lee. At Grizzly's mouth a dirt road exits from Water Canyon Road leading to the lime quarry and kiln of John J. Hendrickson's, an active valley resident in the late Nineteenth Century.

Hendrickson, born in 1841 in the village of Husum on the Western Coast of Schleswig-Holstein, followed his family's tradition by going to sea as a sailor. He first arrived in New York City in 1856; after three voyages as mate on the J. N. Hicks out of that eastern port, he shipped as a boatswain on the Minnehaha via Cape Horn to San Francisco. After arriving there in April 1862, Hendrickson left the sea to begin the occupation of thousands before him: miner.

He mined in the Inyos for a year, and then went to the Slate Range in San Bernardino County. Later, using a watercart filled by buckets dipped into the zanje or ditch that ran down Los Angeles Street, he supplied Los Angeles residents with water. Hendrickson also prospected for oil at Santa Paula and near the San Fernando Mission, but after he discovered large pools, learned the land was part of a large recorded grant, and not open to development.

About 1865 Hendrickson arrived in Havilah where he operated the Delphi Hotel with Andrew Denker. It was a profitable business with the stage lines running through town from Los Angeles to Visalia. When he moved to the Tehachapi Valley in 1867, he resumed his search for gold. He and Peter Greene opened new mining locations along Water Canyon Creek. He later sold them to John Brite, who wanted the water rights, not the minerals.

Hendrickson pre-empted a claim of 160 acres, took up a homestead of eighty acres, and bought an adjacent tract of 160 acres in the Eastern Tehachapi Valley. It was after he sold the farm that he entered the lime business near where he mined gold, shipping the lime to Los Angeles, Bakersfield, and Fresno, where a large trade had been established. During this period he also engaged in a mercantile business in Tehachapi for two years with A. Weill, who later established a large department store in Bakersfield. Lime from Hendrickson's kiln was used in the construction of their new building in 1887. He was appointed Tehachapi's postmaster in 1883, and served for many years as a school trustee, retiring to Bakersfield in 1905.

Mrs. Elizabeth Jane McVicar and John Hendrickson were married in 1880. She was born in Missouri in 1863, and brought across the plains by her parents Dr. Russell and Margaret Cooke Peery. Mrs. Peery claimed to be a direct descendant of Francis Cooke who, with his eight-year-old son John, sailed from England in 1620 on the Mayflower, to enter history as a member of the Plymouth Colony (10).

The history of lime began in the mountains south of the Tehachapi Valley; its continuity to the present is equally visible in the northeastern boundaries of the valley. A dry-looking terrain in the 1970's, the White

Rock Creek area was more fertile when men first settled there to farm. Water seldom courses through the bed now. Iron Springs no longer offers water, although Mud or Squaw Springs still quenches thirsty grazing cattle. Mostly dry farmers, the settlers reaped only a tolerable crop for their efforts. As the years passed they came and went, sold and resold the land. White Rock Creek and the Sand Canyon area are contiguous, and throughout both sections stockmen grazed their cattle. Isolated sheep camps as well as farm ruins can be found today.

Some of the early families are known. In the 1870's the Tungates lived in the flats just north of today's Highway 58 and west of White Rock Creek. Sometime in the 1880's a man named Freeman settled where a lone oak tree now grows in the shadow of Jameson Mountain. In the early 1870's the Harkins brothers and Bill Higgins cut wood for a living and tried to dry farm.

Dick Williamson came to the Tehachapi Valley in the 1870's, married a daughter of Mary Ann Haigh's in 1879 (11), and bought some sections at White Rock Creek about 1890. In 1905 he moved into Tehachapi where he was employed as the town watchman. Appointed a Deputy Marshall by the Board of Trustees in 1911 he served only a few months as he died later that year. Barns in various states of deterioration, the Tree of Heaven spreading its shade over a vacant house site, a gate into the yard hanging by its hinge on the sagging fence, a silent windmill marking the well — are all that remain of the Williamson Ranch in the mid-1970's.

Fred Boden moved to the Tehachapi Valley in the 1860's, operating a blacksmith shop in Old Town. In the 1870's he, too, bought farm property along White Rock Creek, selling it to his son Louis in 1894, when he moved to Garlock. Another lone oak tree marks that farm today.

Others also tried their hand at farming. John McConaha, Norcross and McLaughlin were there. Hendrickson ranched near the now dry lake bed, first called Salt or Narboe Lake, but known today as Proctor Lake. At the head of White Rock Canyon, a timbered cabin still stands. At this homestead William Cuddeback ran cattle and hogs for a while in the 1920's and 1930's. The hogs are supposed to have gone wild as has the land today. The names of many later-day visitors are carved on the cabin's walls, and it is home to a family of bats.

The early morning hours of a hot summer day are the most delightful time to visit the White Rock Creek region. Cottontail rabbits, coveys of quail, signs of deer, are seen in the occasional heavy stands of timber and thick underbrush of chapparal and sage. Often we have stopped to listen to the sounds of the morning and to feel the heat of the sun as it rose over the sheltered canyons and valleys. Our thoughts then were with the first settlers who broke the ground. The economic impact of the area, however, was yet to come.

While settlers in the White Rock Creek region struggled to make the land pay, another breed of men urged the land to share its bounty. An exploration of the canyons adjacent to White Rock Creek reveals a silent panorama of an early industry. Not far from Iron Spring, an unnamed canyon veers to the south; it can be entered by car for only a short distance. Then the faint wagon track becomes brush-crowded and so thick

Ruin of a primitive pot kiln near White Rock Creek in July 1972

that one is forced to take to his feet. Breaking our way through the underbrush on our first exploration of the beckoning track, we found a primitive pot kiln and, beyond it, the remains of a quarry. A short distance away another majestic kiln is hidden in the oaks. It must have been an artisan's labor of love as it is the finest example of stone masonry we've seen in the Tehachapis. Who built these kilns is not known; but in the latter days of the Nineteenth Century, two men from China made an earnest attempt to earn a living there. Artifact hunters in recent years have recovered considerable material near the kilns. Chinese opium tins as well as other distinctly ethnic material are all that remain of the Chinese endeavor. One of the men was named Ah Luk, although he was popularly called "Long Sam." He had an untimely death in 1907, when he was hit by a train at Keene.

John Narboe gave his name to a beautiful canyon that also leaves White Rock Creek to the west, near the head of which are the lime kilns of Andrew Vance. Snug against a hillside they have sat for years in quietude. Many men once fed the lime into the yawning ovens. They lived close by in a two-story bunkhouse, although it, too, has followed the way of the men, and disappeared.

Vance came to the Tehachapi Valley in the late 1870's. Although he did not purchase the land from Minor J. Bell until January 1898, he is supposed to have burned lime there several years before. He first built a pot kiln and, in the spring of 1901, constructed two patent kilns which modernized the technique of burning with furnaces lined in steel and brick. While the pot kiln took about two weeks to reduce the rock to lime, its fires burning day and night, the patent kiln reduced the time to only one day. Rock was still loaded into the top, with a furnace opening at the bottom, it was emptied from below and loaded into wheelbarrows.

Vance employed about twenty men: wood choppers, teamsters, furnacemen. By 1906, however, the kilns closed down, although in the spring, the Mountain Summit Lime Company, which had a large operation

Ruin of a ''majestic'' lime kiln used by Chinese miners near White Rock Creek in July 1972

in Tweedy Canyon near Keene, reopened them. According to Harvey Hicks, the only reason the Vance kilns were reopened by Jude Moore, Superintendent of Mountain Summit, was that when the Tweedy operation closed, 600 cords of oak remained. Mr. Hicks drove a wagonload of wood from Tweedy to Narboe Canyon and, after the wood was burned, the kilns shut down again. Mr. Hicks reminisced one day as we sat together looking at the ruins where he had once spent many days working, "It never did start up again."

Ruins of the Vance lime kiln in Narboe Canyon in July 1972

In the early 1890's J. W. Jameson came to the Tehachapi Valley and played a major role in its industry. He was born in Humboldt County and practiced law in San Francisco. He took an early interest in the lime industry that was mushrooming and lucrative north and south of the valley. Jameson bought acreage, including a mountain, for $1,800; some of the property was once owned by Fred Boden. In a cleft just west of the mountain which was about 400 feet high with limestone outcroppings all the way to the top, he opened his quarry in the mountain's side. The mountain also had a small clay deposit, and some chalcedonic chert was found near the middle of the slope.

Beginning in the mid-1890's Jameson burned lime in pot kilns. In the summer of 1903, however, he constructed two patent kilns which had a daily capacity of forty barrels each and burned oil at a cost of 50 cents per barrel, although some wood was used. The plant operated six months during the year, employing ten men. The lime was transported in barrels by wagon team to the railroad depot in Tehachapi. In 1904 the quarry opening was about 100 feet from the bottom of the canyon, with several smaller openings at other heights.

Jameson was a millionaire, but not because of the lime — it was oil. Investing heavily in the fields at Taft and McKittrick early in this century, when the boom occurred there he made his fortune. (It's no wonder he used fuel oil rather than wood!) Jameson continued to manufacture lime until 1920 when, after moving to Palos Verde in 1919, he formed and was president of the Blue Diamond Plaster Company of Los Angeles. Although he had big plans to improve his kilns to produce at higher yields, he never did. In 1921 much of the property was sold to the United States Potash Company (12).

—SEVEN—

In the throes of great growth during the early part of this century, Los Angeles lacked one necessary element: water. It went to the north for it, to the Owens Valley. In order to transport water from the valley to Los Angeles, the City built an aqueduct — and that required cement.

And so, after years of having had scattered attempts of farming and lime production, the White Rock Creek region proved its worth. It took a year for Los Angeles to complete negotiations; in June 1907 the final deeds were recorded by which the City acquired nearly 3,000 acres of land: from Mr. and Mrs. William N. Cuddeback, Mr. and Mrs. Andrew J. Blackley, and Mr. and Mrs. Harry Rose, including Sections 19 and 29 through 33.

Initially Los Angeles intended only to remove the lime and erect a giant cement works near a dry lake east of Mojave. The cement would be manufactured there; the rock to be quarried in the Tehachapi Valley and burned in kilns to be erected nearby, then hauled to the cement plant for mixing. However, the plant was finally built near White Rock Creek (13).

A year-and-a-half later, the City was finally ready to begin production. William Mulholland, the project's chief engineer, after returning from a trip "up the line" in January 1909, predicted they would be actively engaged in cement manufacture at the Tehachapi plant within two or three days. Mulholland blamed the long delay on the failure of the structural steel contractors to deliver the material for the building housing the machinery within the time specified. In an era when contractors didn't vie with inflationary and spiraling prices, Mulholland remarked: "The cost of the plant will come practically within the estimates of $350,000 made by Mr. Duryea, the city's cement expert . . . We now have work in hand that will call for 800 barrels of cement a day but inside of the next three months it is expected the place will be pushed to its full capacity of 1200 barrels. I am confident," remarked the optimistic Mulholland, "this cement can be turned out at a cost not to exceed $1.05 a barrel."

Just as the plant was ready to begin production, legal problems developed. The purchases of 1907 included the "Cuddeback Ledge" on a 160 acre tract three miles west of the mill, which was now claimed by J. W. Jameson. With title in contention the City leased the "South Quarry," located six miles southwest of the mill.

City of Los Angeles cement plant soon after its completion in 1909
(Los Angeles Department of Water and Power)

Great gashes in the mountains due south of Tehachapi and east of
Antelope Canyon mark this quarry. A 4,700-foot long aerial tramway was
constructed to bring the stone down to a bin at the base of the hill. With a
carrying capacity of thirty tons per hour, it was kept busy feeding the
hungry furnaces at the main plant. I remember well one spring day a few
years ago when Mrs. Rose Ford and I decided to visit the quarry. We
hiked up the wagon road that had been built almost seventy years ago
but, as happens when dirt tracks are neglected and unused, this one was
overgrown so that brush often impeded our progress. Up, up we went, the
view of the valley below spectacular, the promise of history above
beckoning.

We found the ruins of a once busy quarry. No buildings stood —
weather and vandalism had taken their toll, but fallen roofs at
brush-hidden sites indicated where they were. The diggings were bare
and stark; empty powder cans as well as the cable lay motionless on the
mountainside. From our lofty viewpoint we looked at the landscape below
and tried to trace the route of a narrow-gauge railroad, 5¼ miles long,
that transported the rock from the base of the mountain to the plant. A
careful exploration of the property known as Mountain Meadows does
reveal some of the contours of this long-ago railbed which at a maximum
grade of five percent closely followed the section lines. It wound its way to
the Southern Pacific's track, which was crossed by a subgrade crossing a
short distance north of Sullivan Spur. The rails terminated at the crusher
house.

The contractors were given sixty days to construct the tracks. Standard thirty-five pound rail and redwood ties were used, and a specially designed twenty-five ton steam engine and twelve side dump cars of ten-ton capacity were purchased. How prices have changed! The twelve quarry cars cost $4,282. The rails were $26 per ton; angle bars, $1.60 per cwt; bolts $2.75 per cwt. The 21,000 redwood ties cost 20 cents each. And the mine locomotive cost $3,275.

In the spring of 1912, when ownership of the "Cuddeback Ledge" was decided in Jameson's favor, Jameson in turn leased it to the City, thus the quarrying operations moved northward. Bolt, tie, spike, angle bar — all of it was transported and the narrow gauge placed in operation between the cement plant and the new quarry west of the mill.

Clay, a necessary ingredient in the manufacture of cement, was amply supplied by the lake near the plant. As early as the 1860's the Narboe brothers had mined salt from a saline stratum five to six feet deep. Then, the lake was seasonally covered with a shallow sheet of water that was a saturated solution of salt, muddy from the clay which was held in suspension. In the summer the salt crust was from three to four inches thick; 200 to 300 tons of a quality that was 92-98% pure were gathered each season. The crust was simply raked into heaps of 100 pounds or so and then shoveled into a scow which held 800 to 1,200 pounds each, which was hauled from the muddy bottom onto harder, drier ground. Salt production continued for a number of years. In fact when Los Angeles purchased the lime properties, the salt lake was also sold by the Cuddebacks and Blackleys. The Central Saline Mining Company, the Kern Development Mining Company, and the Tehachapi Saline Development Company each acquired one location.

There was optimism at the time that they would mine salt but, by August 1907, the City had plans to drain the lake and excavate a ditch two miles long and eighteen feet deep at one point. The lake had to be drained to obtain the clay which, as in the earlier salt mining, appeared during the summer. Another tramway was built there. With a carrying capacity of twenty-five tons per hour, the 5,800 foot long conveyance carried clay to a storage floor at the rear of the mill.

The Romans were first to discover that a mixture of volcanic ash and lime made by burning marble would bond together rocks and cut stone to build their roads, aqueducts, and other structures. The material was called "caementum," meaning literally pieces of rough, uncut rock. At the decline of the Empire, the formula was lost. In 1756 a similar cement which hardened under water was produced in England. It was not until 1824, however, that modern cement was discovered, when an English stonemason, Joseph Aspdin, found that mixing lime, silica, and alumina, then burning and grinding the mixture, made a strong cement. Since the concrete made with his cement looked very much like a rock formation on the Isle of Portland in England, Aspdin named his discovery "Portland cement."

Although the process has been refined, the basic production steps have changed little. The manufacture of cement begins at the quarry where huge crushers break the limestone into small pieces about the size of chicken eggs. The crushed rock is mixed with silica-alumina-bearing slag, shale, or clay, in rotating cylinders called ball mills where heavy steel or iron balls batter the mixture into powder. The powder goes to a tube mill that contains even smaller balls or pebbles of flint, which produce particles so fine that they can pass through a sieve that can hold water. This finely ground powder is then burned in kilns as large as eighteen feet in diameter and 500 feet long, which gives the material its binding quality, producing calcium silicates and calcium aluminates that react chemically with water to form a rock-like mass. The burning kilns are long, rotating steel cylinders, lined with firebrick to protect the steel from temperatures as high as 2,700 degrees F., maintained at the lowest end of the kilns. The cement powder, which is sometimes mixed with water to form a soupy slurry, takes about two hours to pass through the kilns. The tremendous heat, besides creating the chemical reaction, also produces the resulting material called clinker. The clinker, small pieces about the size of children's marbles, is cooked; a small amount of gypsum is added and finally more ball and tube mills regrind it. The final product is Portland cement, so finely pulverized that ninety percent will pass through a sieve with 40,000 openings per square inch. Although cement traditionally has been packed in bags, today most of it is transported in bulk by huge rail hopper cars or trucks (14).

During the City's operation, the mill produced approximately 900,000 barrels of cement under the brand name of "Monolith," an obvious reference to the monolithic mountain of limestone from which the prime ingredient was quarried. When the aqueduct was completed, Los Angeles continued intermittent production for various civic projects until 1920 when, because of increased labor and fuel costs, it leased the plant to private individuals. Before this happened, however, the mill operation was terminated and the facility closed down. Once again, the land was silent, but only for a while.

—EIGHT—

On February 6, 1920, three men signed a five-year lease with the City of Los Angeles to produce potash, which had been located three miles northeast of Monolith in the latter days of 1917 by P. H. Baker. Fred A. Ballin, president and principal owner of the Supple Ballin Shipyard and Pacific Marine Iron Works; Aman Moore, one of the first cement engineers in the United States; and Coy Burnett, a young, successful attorney, formed an association known as U. S. Potash Company. Later that year they obtained exclusive rights from a chemist named Olson, to a newly discovered plastic cement that was waterproof, and by the end of 1920 produced 43,767 barrels of the product.

In June 1921 Moore, who was the company's vice-president, sold his interest to Ballin and Burnett. Burnett, the secretary, became vice president; Ballin continued as president; and the company's name was changed. Monolith-Portland Cement Company was born. In just over two years Ballin sold his interest in the company and Coy Burnett was elected president, an office he filled until his death. The land and mill were subsequently purchased from the City for $450,000; through the years additional acquisitions, partly from the Jameson Corporation, increased Monolith's holdings to 14,000 acres.

From 1921 to 1923 periodic mill shutdowns enabled the company to make major improvements. In 1923 the three original kilns, which had been enlarged in 1921, were augmented by a new modern kiln which increased production capacity to 650,000 barrels per year.

The "Jameson" quarry was opened in 1922, located on Jameson Mountain, property which is still owned by the Jameson Foundation. A royalty per barrel has been paid ever since, adding considerable funds to the coffers of the foundation formed by Mr. and Mrs. Jameson many years ago. Improvements in quarrying methods occurred in 1926 when a "Glory Hole" operation was opened. A cone-shaped hole was dug vertically down from an upper level of the quarry with a tunnel running into the mountain to meet the bottom of the hole at the crusher level. Rock was then mined from the upper level, dumped into the hole, moved through chutes into rail cars in the tunnel, and hauled to the crusher.

The Monolith narrow-gauge railroad as it left the quarry. Plant superintendent Garrison is standing at left of engine — Circa 1920's (Barnett Hayes)

For over sixty years, beginning with Los Angeles' operation and continued by Monolith, the narrow-gauge railroad was the sole means of transporting rock from the mountain to the plant. At two-and-one-half miles, it was one of the shortest runs in narrow-gauge history. But at the beginning of 1973 the run ended. Progress intervened. The thirty-five ton Plymouth diesel electric engine which pulled three shifts of ore cars day-in and day-out, was replaced by a thirty-foot overland conveyer belt. With an ultimate load capacity of 1,000 tons per hour as compared to 175 tons per trainload, replacement was understandable. In April 1974 an amusement park near Newhall, California, purchased the engines, cars, and some of the track. "Old Grandma," an engine operated from 1929 to 1948 when she was retired, was sold to a private party in San Luis Obispo, California, for a yard decoration!

In 1940 the Jameson ranch properties were purchased by Monolith, which operated a cattle ranch for about ten years. When they ended their operation the land was, and still is, leased for grazing and farming.

In 1941 when the Federal government claimed first use of all production, Monolith cement was used in construction of the vast U. S. Naval Ammunition Dump at Hawthorne, Nevada. For two years nearly all of its production went into this project. In later war years most of the cement went to the U. S. Naval Base on Guam Island. In the ten-year period following the end of the war, plant production increased to 3,000,000 barrels, resulting in the highest level of employment — 500 men.

Monolith cement has been used in other major building projects. In 1926 it went into the building of St. Francis Dam in San Francisquito Canyon (15) as well as a state highway project between Ventura and Santa Barbara, and other major highway construction on the coast. In the early 1930's, with a depression reaching over the land, the company kept its head above water because of a contract to supply cement for the Boulder Dam project on the Colorado River.

—NINE—

In the heyday of the lime industry, bunk houses and kitchens were in close proximity to the stone kilns. True to form, when the City of Los Angeles built its mill, it also provided a home for the employees.

In 1909 when announcing the plant's opening, Mulholland commented, "The plant will give employment to about seventy-five men. A little village has been built near the works, where these men and their families will be comfortably housed. All the conditions combine," he added, "to make the jobs highly desirable for a certain class of workingmen."

Starting as a mere camp, over the months it developed into a small community. Logically named Aqueduct, it provided life's necessities. The City constructed all the buildings, including twenty-one dwellings of from one-to-six rooms each, and six frame tent houses. Seven bunk houses accommodated 130 bachelors. A kitchen and mess hall fed the hungry laborers, and a hospital building was erected to care for the sick.

Streets were surveyed; sewer and domestic water systems were installed; and an excellent artesian well supplied an abundant water supply to the community. The general needs of the families were provided by a privately owned store operated by Harry A. Marx, its first shopkeeper.

A schoolhouse was built for the community's children after the

VILLAGE OF MONOLITH
(Demolished 1975)

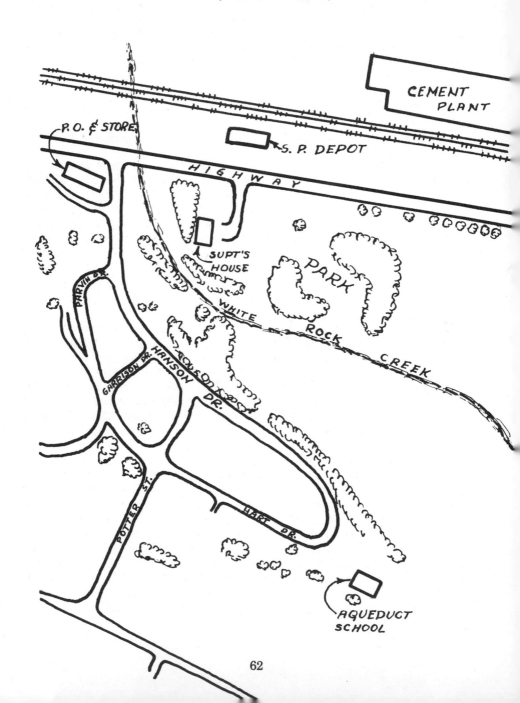

Aqueduct School District was formed on February 4, 1909. Mrs. Jean A. Durnal was the first teacher from 1910 to 1913 and in her first year's report she remarked: "The school building belongs to the City of Los Angeles. There are no blackboards . . . The desks and thirteen textbooks are all of the school property. They are in splendid condition." During that year the average daily attendance was twenty pupils, but it dropped to seven in 1913, when the plant closed down. Nevertheless, the school remained open and two years later the enrollment increased to an average of twenty-eight students each day. The peak enrollment of the Aqueduct School was in 1933-34 when it reached seventy-three students.

Although at a new location west of the town site, the Aqueduct School still educates the youth of the area; however, today many of the children are transported by bus from Tehachapi, as the enrollment from the eastern part of the valley dropped drastically. The school has been known as the Ala Monroe Elementary School since September 1965, honoring a woman who taught there, as well as at other district schools, for many years.

The village was called Aqueduct until April 28, 1910, when the United States Government changed the name of its post office to Monolith. Apparently they acquiesced to the forces of change instigated by the Southern Pacific Railroad which, by that time, was calling the plant's siding by that name. The post office opened October 19, 1908, with Marx as postmaster as well as shopkeeper. On October 11, 1899, a post office was established at Cameron Station, a few miles east of Monolith, with Joseph H. Stamford as the first postmaster. In 1923 after a few years of erratic service, the Cameron Post Office was permanently discontinued on October 15, when all mail was dispatched to Monolith.

When the mill operation closed in 1913, Monolith became idle, but not so much as to close the general store and post office, which continued to serve the families who remained.

And the years sped by. The peak population of the village was reached during the 1940's when an estimated 345 residents occupied the housing, attended the school, and patronized the general store.

On May 22, 1945, the last and longest-staying owner of the Monolith Store arrived. Ed Tompkins was a young man when he went to work for A. R. White. One year later, on July 15 he purchased the business and on August 8 assumed charge of the post office; his appointment actually became official in 1949.

During the early years of Mr. Tompkins' proprietorship once again the area experienced change. He saw a once thriving and busy community decline until, in 1972, only ten families lived in the slowly decaying village. In 1960 the plant initiated a policy of not renting homes as they were vacated; doors were locked, windows boarded, the face of the village slowly greyed with time and neglect. Employees no longer needed to live close to their work, as improved transportation and greater opportunities in nearby Tehachapi beckoned many Monolith residents to change their domocile.

By 1967 because of lack of business, the Monolith Cafe, also one of Mr. Tompkins' operations, closed. In May 1970 the completion of a major freeway through the valley immediately affected business at the Monolith Store. He "could see the writing on the wall," Mr. Tompkins told me one day. In the summer of 1972, the final decline of the company town of Monolith began. Mr. Tompkins decided to close the grocery. On September 30 the cash register rang for the last time as the last customer said a few words to Ed's wife, Helen, as she wrapped groceries. The doors were closed, forever.

And what of the few families who still lived there? Their future was decided, too. Undoubtedly quickened by the closure of the store, the company decided to end the community of Monolith. Its few remaining residents were asked to move. By the end of 1972, stillness reigned on the south side of the Southern Pacific tracks.

The Monolith Store in September 1972

—TEN—

One of the last residents to move from Monolith was Moses Garcia who, on a nostalgic Saturday in the summer of 1972, walked with us to the abandoned schoolhouse, speaking animatedly of the days he had spent there as a boy. Mr. Garcia was but one of many Monolith employees who either came directly from Mexico or traced their origins to parents who did.

In 1897 the town of Tehachapi listed only three Mexicans on its census. Out in the country there were a few others, the Californians, descendants of the Spanish conquest of the Pacific in the Eighteenth Century.

Today many residents proudly possess Spanish surnames, their arrival on the scene the result of internal strife and revolution in their homeland. When the Mexican Revolution began in 1910, an influx of Mexican citizens made their way over the border to escape the war. In November 1911 most of the labor force at Monolith was either Mexican or Austrian, and a new wave of emigrants into the Tehachapis also found employment with the railroad.

In the beginning the Mexican labor force also lived at Monolith, although probably because of economic rather than racial reasons, their homes were isolated from the rest of the employees as they lived in houses on the north side of the tracks, sharing a communal bath. Salaries for the common laborers were low and although they lived in poor housing, the women maintained immaculate homes for their families. As salaries increased they began to move into Tehachapi, where social segregation was never a major problem. It was because of economics that they first lived north of the tracks, or on less expensive land on East E Street. But as time passed and incomes increased, the Mexican families moved out into the town and some took an active part in the community's affairs. One of Tehachapi's beloved citizens was the late Stephen Valdez, Mayor of Tehachapi until his death in 1965.

It was only a coincidence that the original cement plant and the later reactivation of the industry by Burnett and his partners, merged in time with the Mexican Revolution's affect on its citizens. But it did, and provided a source of employment for hundreds during the years.

—ELEVEN—

On May 22, 1974, an advertisement appeared in The Tehachapi News: "MONOLITH TOWNSHIP FOR SALE. Buildings, garages, workshops, sheds, all types and sizes, some can be moved. Miscellaneous building materials, Cheap!" The town didn't disappear all at once. Driving along the streets in the spring of 1975 we still saw a few buildings, albeit in the worst stage of disrepair and decay. In only a few months, except for the few trees, also dying for lack of a good drink of water, the land would be flat once again.

As one aspect of an early industry ends, Monolith-Portland Cement Co. looks to the future. A $15,000,000 modernization program, partly instigated by air pollution control standards adopted by Kern County in the early 1970's, is a continuing activity. The three kilns have been shut down in favor of a new, modern one which began operation in the summer of 1974, eliminating seventy percent stack emission. This followed on the heels of improved crushing and screening equipment at the quarry, a part of the conveyor-belt installation. Another kiln is scheduled for the future, dependent on economic and business trends of the irregular national economy in the mid-1970's.

Mainly because of modernization the plant's employment force was down to 147 at the end of 1974. Yet the plant plans to maintain its productive usefulness even though the scene has changed materially over the years. It continues to be a major economic force in the area, with a

Village of Monolith in ruins — October 1974

January 1975 payroll of $197,000.

—TWELVE—

While not located within the Tehachapi Valley, a modern plant only twenty miles southeast at the edge of the Mojave Desert provides employment for 220, approximately fifty-three percent of whom are residents of the Tehachapis.

It wasn't the dry desert climate or panoramic view of the Mojave that brought California Portland Cement Co. to Kern County. It was lime. Since 1955 it has played a major role in the county's economy, particularly Tehachapi's. Its annual payroll for 1974 was in excess of two and three-quarter million dollars.

Cal Portland is one of three plants operated by the parent company. The first was developed in 1891 by the Murphy family in Colton; a second plant is at Rillito, Arizona, about fifteen miles east of Tucson. The Mojave plant was an expansion plan of the late E. E. Duque, who was married to a descendant of the original founders and served as a principal officer for many years. The local plant is sometimes called "Creal" honoring retired Chief Chemist Wilson Creal Hanna.

The production capacity of Cal Portland is 6,000,000 barrels per year. With another 100 years' supply of limestone, Cal Portland expects to remain a viable part of the economic community for a long time.

—THIRTEEN—

One other significant mineral discovery in the Tehachapis united two pioneer families, whose backgrounds prepared discoverer Jess Hicks and promoter John Cuddeback for the cattle business, rather than mining.

Hicks was a grandson of Mahala Hicks, who moved to the Tehachapi Valley, settling north of Old Town in the 1870's. She was born in Alabama in 1825 of a Cherokee mother and an Irish father named Mackay, a man of substance who kept a comfortable home and owned slaves (16). But wealth was of no consequence several years later when in its continuing zeal to possess land, one more bill was passed by Congress to allow white men access to Indian lands. The Indian Removal Act instigated by Andrew Jackson, forced the removal of over 14,000 Cherokees, supervised by American soldiers, to Oklahoma Territory during the winter of 1838-39, on the infamous "Trail of Tears."

Mahala Mackay and her father were in the march. They didn't stop in Oklahoma, however, but continued to Texas, settling on a ranch. Mahala was first married to Elias Burns, a law officer who died from pneumonia (17). The widow Burns then married James Ellington, with whom she traveled by wagon train to El Monte, in hand with their young son Tom, born in Waco, Texas, in 1851. Ellington, however, was killed at the Monte in a brutal murder in September 1854 (18).

It was after her marriage to Bob Hicks, a cattleman, that Mahala moved to the Tehachapi Valley where Tom had already settled. Tom Ellington was a cowboy, stage driver, saloon keeper in Old Town, and blacksmith and livery proprietor in Tehachapi. The Hicks Ranch was a few hundred yards north of the lake that graces the landscape in Golden Hills, called by the oldtimers Taylor Lake for a later owner. Today it is a rambling ranch on the east side of Tehachapi-Woodford Road.

The Cuddebacks, too, made their way to El Monte in the Gold Rush Days, but by a less torturous route. The heritage of the family originated in France where the family name appears as Caudebec. Long before they emigrated from France to Holland, from where they left Europe altogether for America, one of the Caudebecs performed an act worthy of knighthood. The family coat-of-arms is a crest of three fishes with laurel and olive branches, which denotes peace and victory. The emblem of the family later became the emblem of the town of Caudebec, located on the Normandy coast of France (19).

When the Caudebecs crossed the ocean during Colonial Days, they settled first on Manhattan Island, just after it was sold by the Indians in 1626 for $24.00 in beads. By this time the name had been anglicized to Cuddeback and when the Cuddebacks moved to a village on the Hudson River, the village became known as Cuddebackville.

Grant Price Cuddeback was born there and worked as a tow boy on the Erie Canal. A farmer when news of the gold discovery in California reached him, Grant made a quick decision, and headed west, joining a party of wagons led by Ira Thompson which, in turn, merged with a large company comprising forty-five to fifty wagons in Independence, Missouri (20). Also traveling in the train was the Royse Oatman family, which at some point on the trail left the company to continue alone. When they were attacked by Indians, everyone in the Oatman family was killed except two daughters who were captured, an event which has been fully documented in several histories.

The Thompsons, after reaching California, stopped in the Puente Valley, and it may be here that Grant Cuddeback left to proceed alone. In 1850 after losing most of his cattle, he packed his goods on the back of a horse and journeyed to the headwaters of the San Joaquin River. Menacing Indians, however, drove him away from the mines, and in a few months he returned to the Southland, settling alongside the San Gabriel River, near a clump of willows. Cuddeback is reputed to be one of the few Americans camped at what became El Monte when the first wagon train arrived there in 1851.

In February 1852 Cuddeback married Almira Hale, a descendant of Nathan Hale, a niece of President Franklin Pierce, and whose own descendants are related to Presidents William and Benjamin Harrison. Their first child, Moses Clinton, was born the following year, the first white child born in El Monte (21).

Cuddeback was active in regional politics, both at El Monte and in the Tehachapis. In July 1853 he petitioned for a public road from San Gabriel Mission to Los Angeles and San Pedro; in September he ran unsuccessfully for county assessor and was a candidate again in 1855. In August 1858 he was El Monte's delegate to the Los Angeles County Democratic Convention. And in February 1861 Cuddeback was appointed a Judge of the Plains by the Board of Supervisors with jurisdiction in any part of Los Angeles County (22).

Upon his arrival in the Tehachapis, Cuddeback ran cattle near Oak Creek Pass, wintering them on the desert away from the mountain snow. But he eventually took up land next to Tehachapi Creek, as it enters Tehachapi Canyon west of the valley. His wife died in the early 1870's, and he soon returned to Southern California, where he lived until his death in the early 1900's. The children were raised in the Tehachapi Valley by an aunt and uncle, Mr. and Mrs. Moses Hale, who lived next to the Cuddebacks on Tehachapi Creek.

There are several versions of how a now mighty cottonwood tree came to be planted on the homeplace. One is that Grant's son, Bill Cuddeback, was quarreling with a brother about who should have a twig they were playing with. Their mother, deciding to settle the quarrel once and for all, made the boys stick the twig in the ground — where it grew. Today only this now ancient 100-year-old cottonwood marks the spot where the first Cuddebacks lived in the Tehachapi Valley.

Although John Cuddeback, another son of Grant and Almira's, died some years ago, he is remembered by several oldtimers in the area as a man with a quick business sense; shrewd and stern, he knew how to turn a profit. One day, however, humor pierced the man's facade when he reportedly said to Jess Hicks, "You should have come direct to me, rather than go to my brother. We both would have made more money." It was 1916 and the source of the money was cinnabar. Hicks was a railroad man living in Keene, but during his off-hours he played prospector, roaming the hills in search of ore. One day as he was hiking northeast of Keene, Hicks found red rock on Cuddeback's land. Returning home, he tested the ore and found it was rich cinnabar.

Quicksilver had been produced in California for several decades, first discovered at the famous Almaden Mine near San Jose. Native Indians there had long used the red earth for body paint, but it was first mined by Mission Fathers who named the deposits after the old Almaden Mine in Spain.

Hicks, believing John Cuddeback too difficult to deal with, went to John's brother Bill, asking him to approach John with a deal. He did, and the Cuddeback Cinnabar Co. was formed, which included John and Bill Cuddeback, Kate Cuddeback Bonestell, and a fortuneteller. John's niece, Mrs. Bonestall, had visited the seer shortly before the discovery was made and was told she would obtain a great fortune from an unknown mineral, according to a popular story of the 1920's. Visiting her Uncle, Kate secured mineral rights to the holdings as he thought it was a big joke!

Near the original discovery, Phillip Fickert and John Durnal also located a small prospect on Cuddeback's land. It was principally worked in 1917 when a small amount of quicksilver was recovered in a six-pipe retort.

The stone dropped swiftly downward into the dark void; we waited in vain to hear its "kerplunk" as it reached the water we knew filled a deep shaft of several hundred feet. It was at this point that Jess Hicks first picked up the colorful rock. In 1973 the land had changed. All around us, in the narrow short canyon close to a busy freeway, were tunnels and exploratory diggings. The glory hole was filled with debris. Buildings of a recent vintage stood in quiet symmetry as if abandoned years ago. The original mine site is barely visible from the highway, although the scarred hillside above hints at the activity. Our guide that day knew the story of the mine better than most. Harvey Hicks, a brother of Jess's, had been at the mine from the first, and was with us as we roamed the ruins. He established its first camp, some yards distant from the mine, next to Tehachapi Creek. No sign of it is visible today as floods and time have destroyed the first primitive mill, where the original retorts were erected. The rock, mined above, was hauled by wagon and team down the short grade for processing.

Mr. Hicks told us how the rock was then ground into two-mash, and with crude oil heating a fire, passed through the burner. By this process the mercury was burned out of the heated rock, and as it condensed was "caught" above the flames and held in seventy-five pound steel flasks. Valued at $300 each when sold to consumers in Japan, the flasks made their initial journey by wagon and team to the rail siding at Keene; thence by train and ship to that distant land.

Within only a few months of its opening, in December 1916 the mine reportedly produced 150 pounds of quicksilver every twenty-four hours. In an era before the invention of the hydraulic drill, the muscle of men freed the rich ore from the tenuous hold of Mother Earth. Two men worked together: one held the piercing drill, while the other swung the heavy hammer, slamming it to its mark, breaking the rock.

There was lots of ore; miners were busy; but within a few years Jess Hicks sold his interest in the mine. By 1925 the other partners, too, made new plans. The next owners, Branson and Nicholson (at one time identified with the Yellow Aster Mine at Randsburg), reputedly agreed to pay $100,000 for the mine. They modernized: the rotary furnace, together with other equipment capable of producing 70-tons daily, was very impressive, but not the production. According to Mr. Hicks, the new owners would have served their profit-motive better had they left well enough alone, and forgotten their "new-fangled machinery." As the fires blazed and red rock flamed, the mercury did condense — into thin air. The furnace couldn't hold the quicksilver, as it is also called, and in this case, proved, for it quickly disappeared in fumes. And, too, the money for the mine may have disappeared as well. As the story goes, the original owners received their payment on a production basis!

Through the years lessees came and went, as the Cuddeback Cinnabar Co., although continuing the mine's ownership, discontinued production. Between 1927 and 1931 the Santa Ana Mining Co., managed by C. D. Holmes, recovered nearly 500 flasks. They improved the property, installed a small rotary furnace, and did considerable underground work. In 1936 the property was leased to the Walabu Mining Company, which later bought the mine; but since then only a small amount of quicksilver has been produced.

The property is now owned by John Broome of Santa Barbara, and the buildings which are visible from the freeway were a development of a more recent lessee, "Bud" Parker, who leased the property in the 1960's. Mr. Parker told me that although the ore was there, it was easier to transport it from elsewhere and mill it, which was what he did.

For several years there has been silence at the Cinnabar Mine down the hill; in the mid-1970's motion and momentum filled the air for a while, as once again men captured the elusive mercury but, once again, with ore brought in from another quarry.

Cinnabar, mercury, quicksilver. By whatever name, a source of riches, good stories, and many memories to those who knew the short, narrow canyon so well.

The Farms

. . . the valley has not been tried sufficient to prove whether the farmer may rely on being rewarded very amply by emigrating to and settling in it; yet it may be possible, and is even thought highly probable that "Tichipe" will, when properly tried, prove to be one of the best countries in California, for raising wheat, barley and Irish potatoes, but owing to the extreme cold weather which sets in early in the fall, and lasts until late spring, it is thought that corn could not mature after frost would overtake it. Nevertheless, be it as it may, there are large bodies of rich land, as yet unlocated, that spread out over a scope of country from six to ten miles in width, by twenty or thirty in length, not covered by Spanish claims, as in many other portions of the country, but is without doubt Uncle Sam's property.

We have good, cold, running springs of excellent water in almost every portion of the valley, sufficient for irrigating our farms. We have splendid timber, and a sufficiency to answer every purpose of farming, building, etc.

Excerpt of a letter from "A Miner in
the Tay-ee-chay-pah Valley, California,
In the Los Angeles Star,
March 15, 1856

In the summer twilight of a long August day we drove out of Cummings Valley on Banducci Road, pausing for a moment at a wide spot in the road near the crest of a hill. In the west a glorious scarlet-red sun was just settling down for the night behind a mountain; the sky was a blaze of fire and smoke, as light and cloud mingled in a kaleidoscope of color. Below, the historic Cummings Valley was still; no cars were visible on the distant ribbons of macadam; only scattered herds of range cattle and horses were seen moving over the landscape. The ground was a patchwork quilt of autumnal color where newly mown hay blended with uncut grain; and lines of fertile grass marked the boundaries of slow-moving water.

On a distant hillside the lights of Stallion Springs Lodge twinkled in the dusk. Over another hill to the northwest another historic valley welcomed a few travelers to secluded Bear Valley Springs. To sight and sound, on that late summer afternoon, the present seemed to be the past, as our awareness of earlier events crowded in to relieve the spectrum of the Twentieth Century.

In 1862 J. H. Brooks, a farmer in the Tehachapis, wrote to a Los Angeles newspaper: "Knowing that you take an interest in the production of our country I send you 4 specimens of wheat, raised by our best farmer, Geo. Cummings. These specimens are from a volunteer crop, this being the third crop raised from one seeding and 1 plowing.

"These specimens came from a field of about 80 acres, and it will average over 50 bushels to the acre.

"There are many persons, with families, hunting homes, and yet I know of no place more inviting than this valley. It is perfectly healthy — there are many thousand acres of the best kind of land, plenty of water of the best quality, and an inexhaustible supply of timber.

"There are now large saw and flouring mills ready to be raised, and they will both be finished and in working order, by the first of December."

The editor was so impressed with the wheat specimens he added his own comments: "The specimens of wheat referred to in the foregoing, may be seen at our office — they are most luxuriant, and for a second volunteer crop, astonishingly so. Tehachapi Valley is one of the most desirable locations for industrious families in the State — possessing all the attractions claimed for it by the writer. The climate is salubrious, the land is at a considerable elevation, and while there is abundant pasture all summer, the winter is sufficiently mild to afford feed for stock. Besides being in the highway to the new mines in Walkers' Valley, Mono, Esmeralda, thus affording a ready market for the production of the garden and farm — taken altogether it is a really desirable location for industrious agriculture."

George Cummings settled the land, but the ranch was actually developed by his son Edward G. Cummings who, according to the present owner, E. J. "Bud" Cummings, came to the country home from Los Angeles after the tragic death of his father in 1903 in a Bakersfield fire.

The man for whom the valley was named was more active in Southern California, the scene of his early triumphs, than in his valley. After landing in San Francisco in the summer of 1849, from an American schooner out of Austria, Cummings went right to the mines. Greed and excitement for the yellow dust were at white heat and fortunes were washed out of the rich placer deposits in a day. Cummings and a companion shared good luck; while mining that fall in Tulare County, they recovered $1,900 in five days. They moved on to Mariposa County, but were soon disappointed.

Enormous prices were paid at the mines for provisions. On one occasion Cummings paid $600 in gold dust for 200 pounds each of flour, beans, and rice — which apparently influenced him in the spring of 1850 to try farming. A rude hut was erected on the Merced River, but it was burned and his valuables, including some gold dust, were destroyed. He then planted a large acreage to potatoes, melons, and other vegetables, producing a fine crop. Potatoes were sold in the field for $75 per 100 pounds whereas the melons brought $8 to $10 each. Cummings was so successful that despite suffering from malaria which nearly reduced him to a skeleton, he farmed three years and made a good deal of money.

In 1853 Cummings became interested in stock raising and continued in that business on the Merced River. After he purchased land in the Tehachapis in the 1850's, which by 1899 included 3,300 acres, he raised and dealt in cattle and horses. He also owned a 160 acre ranch at Alpine Station in the 1850's and purchased a tract of about forty acres on Boyle Heights, where in 1875 he built a fine residence for his wife Sacramenta Lopez.

On his Boyle Heights property Cummings experimented in fruit growing; he planted 2,000 orange and over 1,500 deciduous trees, and added to the homestead until it included 1,300 acres. He subdivided thirty-five acres into lots on Aliso Street, valued at $1,000 each.

—TWO—

Although Cummings and his bride Sacramenta lived for a while in the Tehachapis, her preference for the city returned them to Los Angeles. In her marriage to Cummings, Sacramenta Lopez brought to her heirs a rich heritage.

She was a daughter of Francisco Lopez, who was born about 1820 in San Diego. His parents were Juan Lopez and Dolores Salgado. Juan was a son of Claudio Lopez and Maria Louisa Cota, his father figuring prominently in the early history of the San Gabriel Mission. Founded in 1771, the Mission was the center of what population existed in the region in the waning days of the Eighteenth Century, when Claudio Lopez, as a very young man, was a soldier, as was his brother Juan Francisco Lopez. In 1811 and from 1821 to 1830, Claudio was Major-domo of Mission San Gabriel, considered the most effective and famous assistant of Father Jose

Maria de Zalvidea, rated by his superiors as one of the best and most zealous of Franciscan friars, and priest, teacher, and manager of the Mission. Under his direction Claudio superintended the construction of many buildings, as well as the Mission waterworks. In 1826 Senor Lopez was Alcalde at Los Angeles.

Francisco Lopez was educated at the "Colegio de Mineria" — Mining College of the City of Mexico. For a while in the 1840's he taught school near Los Angeles.

After the founding of the Mission of San Fernando in 1797, thousands of acres of land came under the Mission's control to be used for ranch industries. With secularization of the Mission by the Mexican government in 1834, a civil administration took over the land management. In 1839 Jacoba Feliz y Lopez del Valle, daughter of Pedro Lopez (23) who was Major-domo at Mission San Fernando in 1837, and a niece of Francisco Lopez, petitioned with her husband Antonio del Valle, and was granted, El Rancho San Francisco, ex-mission ranch lands.

According to Francisca Lopez de Belderrain, another of Francisco Lopez's daughters, her father Francisco was a frequent visitor to his niece Senora Jacoba's ranch. And during one of those visits he made the first official discovery of gold in California! I have read many versions of the Lopez discovery, which was several years before John Marshall found gold in the trace at Sutter's Mill. Most accounts picture him as a vaquero connected with the San Fernando Mission, who one day, while searching for wandering cattle, fell asleep beneath an oak tree; when he awoke and picked some wild onions to munch on, he found gold flakes.

As Mrs. Belderrain wrote of her father: ". . . it is only fair to him that a glimpse be given into his true status and character," adding, ". . . he devoted his time to literature and history and was very fond of big game hunting in the mountains. He also took great pleasure in prospecting for gold . . . . In this way he spent his vacations. With his wife he would often spend a week or two at the Rancho of his niece, Dona Jacoba . . . In fact, he rented a section of the San Francisquito Ranch for his own stock. Often attired in a leather hunting suit, he would mount his horse, lay his rifle across the pommel of his saddle, and with his hunting knife fastened to his belt, would start for the mountains, to take a look at his stock and interview his vaqueros. He was always accompanied by a trusted servant, carrying his mochila containing prospector's tools. Each time he spied a cropping of rock having the appearance of mineral, he would dismount and break off bits of the rock, examine them attentively, then fill his mochila with the pieces to take home for more thorough examination — but invariably his prospecting met with disappointment (24).

"Don Francisco was a well educated man, of high ideals. He received his education in the City of Mexico, where he studied French . . . He was reserved and ceremonious. His appearance and manners were those of a caballero or gentleman of that period.

"One fine morning in the spring of 1842, when making one of his periodical visits to his niece's ranch, Don Francisco made preparations for an all-day outing in the mountains . . . . He wore a wide brimmed hat, a silk handkerchief around his neck and gauntlet gloves — chaparreras made out of bear skin, a pistol and hunting knife in their scabbards on a strong leather belt. His horse was a fine sorrel. The saddle was of brown leather, with big tapaderas covering the stirrups — a Mexican bridle, a rope made of horse hair of different colors, wound around the horse's neck, a rifle across the pommel of the saddle and a canteen with water hanging from the bow of the saddle . . .

"As he was bidding good-bye to his wife, she asked him to bring her some wild onions which grew in abundance in the canyons. After inspecting the stock, and taking a hard stroll up and down the mountains, he felt rather fatigued, and as the hour of noon had arrived, he selected a shady tree under which to rest and have lunch . . . He alighted from his horse and his servant spread a zarape on the ground, unsaddled his master's horse and placed the saddle on one end of the zarape, that it might serve as a head rest . . . After a lengthy siesta, Don Francisco awoke and suddenly remembered his wife's request. Taking the knife from his belt, he went to the slope nearby and began to dig up some of the wild onions. Noticing some yellow particles clinging to the roots, he examined them, wonderingly. He shook the earth from the roots, set them down and started to dig again with vigour."

Lopez had discovered gold. The date was March 9, 1842. He returned to the Rancho to tell the family. The next morning everyone rode to San Fernando Mission to share the news with his brother Pedro; that evening a rosary was said and a hymn sung. Afterwards they danced one or two quadrilles.

Lopez went on to Los Angeles to spread the news. Soon men began to arrive from as far away as Sonora, Mexico, to work in the gold fields. In November of the same year Abel Stearns, a friend of Lopez's, sent packets of placer gold with Alfred Robinson who traveled by ship around Cape Horn and eventually arrived at the United States Mint in Philadelphia. The approximately 18-3/4 ounces of gold dust was valued by the Mint at $344.75; it was the first gold from California to be handled by the United States Government. In the two years that extensive mining occurred at the Lopez discovery site, between $80,000 and $100,000 was mined.

In the spring of 1843 Lopez commemorated the anniversary of his discovery with a solemn high mass. Mrs. Belderrain described the scene: "A provisional chapel was therefore built on the very spot where the gold was first found. Ovens and enramadas or arbours were built and everything was made ready for the celebration. Several carretas were sent to the place the day before with the food supplies. The walls of the chapel were hung inside with richly embroidered shawls and the floor was covered with bear skins and those of other wild animals. The altar was built on the side of the hill, which had been leveled for the purpose. Three priests, two from San Fernando Mission and one from Los Angeles celebrated mass. Six altar boys and the whole choir from the Mission, eight musicians and ten singers, all neophytes, took part . . . It was a gala day."

You can visit the first gold discovery site today. Should you follow the route of the first pioneers and stage lines which left Los Angeles for the

Tehachapis, a side trip to tranquil Placerita Canyon, not far from Newhall, reveals a tablet marking the location, underneath the "Oak of the Golden Dream."

Francisco Lopez apparently never shared to any great extent in the thousands of dollars reaped from his discovery — but he went on to other ventures. On May 27, 1846, Governor Pio Pico granted to Francisco Lopez, Luis Jordan, and Vicente Borello, the six square league Rancho Los Alamos y Agua Caliente, a largely mountainous and timbered locale "with deciduous and live oaks and watered by flowing springs and small creeks running through hidden valleys still remote from civilization." The grant was later owned by General Beale and from 1873 to 1926 J. J. Lopez, a nephew of Francisco Lopez, was Major-domo at Rancho El Tejon (25).

Lopez also knew of a spring near San Fernando Mission from which the Padres carried oil in raw-hide bags to the Mission, where it was distilled for lighting purposes. During the 1850's he showed the location to W. W. Jenkins, W. C. Wiley, and Sanford Lyon, a few of its first developers. A major oil "discovery" was made there in later years; another developer was General Andres Pico.

After his marriage, Lopez settled on what became a part of Boyle Heights in an area lying south of First Street and west of Boyle Avnue and planted one of the first orchards and vineyards in the area on about thirty acres of land.

—THREE—

From their initial settlement of the Tehachapis in the mid-1850's, men grazed cattle. Open range and abundant grass enabled the large herds of fine beef to roam the plains and marginal lands of the natural mountain boundaries. During the 1860's, however, nature intervened. Great droughts in Southern California reduced the herds, so that the census of 1870 listed 670,000 head, as compared to an 1860 census of 1,234,000. The drought's effects were felt in the Tehachapis as well as elsewhere. Adding to the stockmen's problems was an easing of the Trespass Act of 1850 which had favored cattlemen until 1872. The Act had forced farmers to spend large sums of money to fence their lands, something few could afford. In 1872 the ramifications of the Act were eased and an influx of farmers into California helped pass a fence law which favored them. The free roaming herds were no more as the land was divided into farm plots, closed off, and the roving cattle kept out of the grain. "Nearly all of the cattle have been sold and driven away," commented a Tehachapi observer in 1876. "There are not any left except the few that can be kept on the farms. Nobody has made anything of late years in the cattle business up here. It has been expensive to keep them; and they do not then manage to keep more than two-thirds."

But the herds grew again.

It began as the range of Francois Chanac, a man of some mystery who is said to have ridden into the valley on horseback, with an Indian woman mounted behind. He came from San Diego, according to one legend, where he left a ship at the beginning of the Gold Rush. Another tale says Chanac rode through the country for the first time with George Cummings and, as did his friends, eventually claimed some land and settled down. Whatever way it occurred, Chanac began a cattle ranch on fertile ground in Cummings Valley.

Ross Hill arrived in Kern County in 1882. His initial operation was a spread comprising a modest 2,000 acres. As they entered manhood, his two sons Roland and Russell Hill, joined him. When his father died in 1902, sixteen-year-old Roland took over the ranch management, raising, in addition to cattle, horses and hogs, and eventually increasing the holdings to 14,000 acres.

Another decade passed. Appearing on the scene from Pasadena were three brothers: P. G., Donald S., and Charles W. Gates, owners of various businesses in several locations, including large lumber interests in Oregon, Alabama, and Louisiana. In 1912 the Gates brothers purchased not only the Hill Ranch, but also the Morris Ranch at Keene, and founded the Tehachapi Cattle Company. Roland Hill left the Cummings Valley ranch to oversee the combine's interests at Greenfield in the San Joaquin Valley. His brother Russell became the company's ranch manager, remaining with the operation for many years.

Their range was one of the most extensive in the area, extending at one time all the way from the Tejon Ranch boundaries to Caliente, including grazing lands in Tollhouse and Sand Canyons. They also leased the Cuddeback range northwest of the Tehachapi Valley. They ran upwards of 6,000 head of cattle at one time, at its peak on 130,000 acres of land. In addition to the cattle operation, the company farmed their own grain in Cummings Valley, as well as in Bear Valley, which was an excellent summer range, and also at Horsethief Flat.

After fifteen years, in September 1927 the 99,025 acre Tehachapi Cattle Company was sold to James Crofton for $718,804.53; Crofton continued to employ Russell Hill as foreman. When Crofton assumed ownership, the ranch headquarters had been relocated from the Cummings Valley "Hill Ranch" to its Keene headquarters. It was there that the next foreman, Walter Hicks, took over in 1946.

Hicks told me Crofton was "always in some sort of financial difficulties and soon began to dispose of his holdings. A little here, a little there, until in the early 1950's, it was all gone." Several owners took over. The Tollhouse range was purchased by L. E. "Boy" Williams of Caliente, the son of a pioneer Kern County settler and a successful cattleman in his own right. The Bear Mountain range was purchased by Jimmy Rogers, now of Bakersfield, who is a son of motion picture star Will Rogers. Crofton's ex-wife Vera assumed control of the range now known in part as Alpine Forest, a land development of the 1970's. And the Hill Ranch was sold to Rex Ellsworth, who is better known for his stable of racing horses than his cattle enterprises. Benquet California purchased that ranch in October 1969 for its subdivision Stallion Springs, at a cost of $3.4 million.

During the 1890's cattlemen usually drove their stock into the desert where, in the spring, the otherwise seemingly barren land became a paradise for hungry cattle. John Durnal and his partner Harvey Spencer,

An early day branding scene on the Hill Ranch in Cummings Valley. Ross Hill is second from left, Roque Leiva is fourth from left — Circa 1890's (Joe Leiva)

Another branding scene at the Hill Ranch. The cowboys are (left to right): Bill Chappell and Faye Adams on horseback, Duncan Monroe kneeling in right foreground with Dan Chappell kneeling directly behind him, and Fayrel Chappell on horse at right (Bertha Goings)

who ran a Tehachapi saloon, grazed an average of 1,200 head of cattle on 12,000 acres of mountain range. Together with Dick Shackleford, several of the Brites, and John Cuddeback, they moved their combined herds numbering seven to eight thousand head, into the desert for a month or so of lush grazing.

John Cuddeback's "Diamond Bar" was another large cattle ranch. Over the years he increased his holdings to many thousands of acres west and north of the Tehachapi Valley. His daughter Alzada Cuddeback ran the operation until the late 1930's or early 1940's, when it was sold. After several owners, including the Chilsom interests of Arizona cattle fame, part of the ranch became the Oak Knolls land subdivision, known today as Golden Hills. The Broome Ranch, owned by John Broome of Santa Barbara, with its headquarters at the site of an old CCC camp adjacent to the railroad loop, also belonged to Cuddeback.

In the Eastern Tehachapi Valley, where the Tehachapi Cattle Company grazed in Sand Canyon and its peripheral canyons, the Jameson Ranch operated an adequate spread. Although better known for his lime and oil interests, J. W. Jameson also ran large herds; his foreman for many years was Victor Phillips of Tehachapi.

A reduction of beef prices in recent years, as well as short feed created by a lessening of the annual rainfall, has influenced some large, as well as small, ranchers to end their cattle production. Several operations, however, still exist on their own ranches or on leased land, including the Ben Sasia, John Broome, and "Bud" Cummings Ranches, and a few smaller operations. But there is no doubt that much of the land is now gone, subdivided for city folk who seek respite on recreational lands of large corporations.

—FOUR—

All the Chanac Ranch foreman said was, "If you want to see a magnificent sight, I'll show you one." Instantly, a visiting newspaperman in 1892 accepted the invitation. The reporter's comments are a vivid portrait of life then, seen from a wagon driven by a pair of highstepping trotters and a journey through the valleys. He described:

"A ride of about eight miles through as fine a grain section as there is in the state, where a crop failure is unknown, brings one to the stately home of the late John Brite, now occupied by his son William." Brite Valley, from its initial settlement by its namesake, remained the land harbor of that family, and their good friends as well as relatives by intermarriage, the Wiggins clan, for several decades. Dry farming was their mainstay after the decline of the first cattle herds.

"After a sumptuous repast," the writer continued, "as we happened to arrive about dinner time, we continued the journey through Brite's canyon filled with mineral springs, in which sulphur predominates.

"Here is where Dr. Peery of Tehachipa erected a costly hotel, intending to make it a sanitarium for tourists and invalids, but the scheme was found to be impracticable and it was taken down and re-erected on the next lot to Doctor Peery's villa on Curry Street in Tehachipa, where it is now being used as a hospital and for patients desiring the Bi-Chloride of gold cure, for which treatment this eminent physician is famous.

"Passing through this canyon, which is two miles in length, we emerge into Cummings Valley. The magnificent ranch of Dr. A. C. Alberts lies at the head of it on the left, while at the right is the great Dobyns ranch. Further up to the right is Daniel Davenports place, which lies at the head of Bear valley.

"The ranch of Gabe Brites lies on the left about a mile further on and then we speed onward for about two miles through the richest grain fields that can be found in California.

"Wm. Clark, who owns half of the rich school section, has his residence . . . . Across the road is the Cummings valley school house, of which Mr. Skilling is principal, on the land formerly owned by Parson Hickey, while a mile northward, nestling among a beautiful grove of trees, is the residence of the famous Rev. John Hickey. A mile further on to the north is the charming villa of Elijah Stowell, adjoining which is the ranch formerly owned by Wm. Kaiser, but recently purchased by Wm. Brite.

"Still we speed outward for another two miles and come to the ranch of Michael Pierce, who came in the early days, and may be ranked with one of California's pioneers.

"The great ranch of Pete Bernamayou lies one-half mile to the left and from which this year he baled over 400 tons of hay, which sold for $12 per ton, and harvested 3800 sacks of wheat and 2600 sacks of barley from about 800 acres of land. Another mile brings us to the ranch of Lulu Cronin, to whom Chanac gave in fee simple the greater part of his possessions, while laboring under a fit of alleged temporary insanity.

"Another mile brings us to the old home of Francois Chanac, recently deceased . . .

"To the eastward lies Cummings Valley, its golden stubble dotted all over with flocks of sheep and cattle, while the shepherds, in picturesque attire, lazily attend their flocks. Bands of cattle and horses browsing in their well earned rest after the harvest, formed a pastoral scene of contentment and plenty."

—FIVE—

The memories linger on — especially in the minds of a few oldtimers, men in their eighties and nineties, who remember vividly their life on horseback out on the range. Only a few may have owned the large ranches; more than a few made them possible. They were the cowboys; with lariat in hand, kerchief tied around their neck, head shaded from sun or rain, and their string of horses. One of the fabled few was Antonio Leiva, whose descendency from an early California family labled him a vaquero.

It had been a long drive. Men and horses had been on the trail for many days, when at last they climbed from the San Joaquin Valley into the mountains. Entering Cummings Valley, they continued eastward, past the Kiser place in Brite Valley, into the desert beyond. As the vaqueros kept pace with the sea of horses, Antonio Leiva studied the beautiful

81

countryside and promised himself he would return.

They had left San Francisco one day a century ago on a long ride to deliver horses to the United States Army at Salt Lake City. The journey was finished, time passed, but one day Leiva came back. The mountains of Tehachapi were his home for the remainder of his life.

These pastoral lands were home to others of Leiva's heritage. Nineteenth Century census records of the Tehachapi region list only a few of Spanish descent; almost to a man, they were vaqueros, who worked the ranches in Cummings, Brite, and Bear Valley. Men were not cowboys then; they were vaqueros, as the Californian, whether of Spanish or Indian ancestry, rode the range as compadre to his Anglo counterpart, for spreads which covered the land from horizon to horizon.

Leiva and his four sons were such men. Antonio first appears on the census lists in 1880 with his eighteen-year old Spanish wife Piedad, and their two children: Roque, the eldest son, and Mersaid who died young. For a while they lived near the Chanac Ranch, but his inability to "prove" the land because it was a railroad section, forced him to look elsewhere. In an unnamed defile going southward into the Tehachapi Mountains, west of tree-shrouded, cloud-capped Cummings peak, Leiva located his homestead and built a sturdy cabin. By this time another son, Jack, was born, and soon Doro and Joe joined the boys, and Ernie, Rowena, and Clara joined their brothers. Others were born: they died too soon, in a fatal epidemic about 1900 which also took their mother.

Soon after settling in the mountains, Antonio earned his place in history with General Edward Fitzgerald Beale, owner of the monumental Tejon Ranch. Beginning as a cowhand, his knowledge and prowess soon proved his abilities as a vaquero. For thirty years Leiva was the cattle boss on Beale's ranch. Only every three or four months did he return to provide his children with the funds necessary to sustain their lives. Then back to Tejon he rode, ever faithful to his job.

As his sons became teen-agers, they joined their father at Tejon, and in later years other ranches in the Tehachapis employed one of them, or all at once, as vaqueros. Roque rode at Tejon first. In his later years he worked for the Tehachapi Cattle Company, moving with the outfit to Pacheco Pass, but returning to the Tehachapi Valley in 1947 when he was too old to continue as a vaquero.

Jack was at Tejon for a while. Mrs. Beale lived in Los Angeles, but periodically, with a lady friend or two, she went to the ranch for a few weeks of country living. "Old man Lopez," according to Joe Leiva, the only son still living, "would send Jack with them on saddle horses because he knew the country so well."

As the years passed, Antonio slowed down. He remained at Tejon, however, until one day in 1922, in his eighty-fourth year, he became ill. He boarded a train at Bakersfield and arrived in Tehachapi; within a week the vaquero was dead.

In that same year Jack Leiva left the range to open a gasoline station which he owned for fifty years. In September 1972 Bartlett's Richfield Station was sold, the oldest Richfield station in California. Doro, who had also ridden at Tejon, worked at the station most of the time and Joe continued in the cattle business, also working at Monolith. "It's interesting how we got the name for the gas station," Mr. Leiva told me. "No one knew what to call it. At that time lots of Bartlett pears were being planted by the Tehachapi Fruit and Land Company and someone suggested we use that name."

Although the family left the forty-acre homestead with its cool spring in 1903 so the children would "benefit" from a town upbringing, almost one hundred years later the homestead is still owned by Antonio's heirs. In the 1930's the original house, which had fallen down, was replaced by a cabin, which still stands, as does the history of the vaqueros, some of whom were the Leiva boys.

—SIX—

Especially along the coast in close proximity to its chain of Missions, Spain influenced California's history. But in the Tehachapis, except for the momentary passage of Francisco Garces in 1776, and perhaps a few Spanish and Mexican soldiers who traveled through the region, the European influence began with the American incursion of the 1850's. While he did come later, however, the Californian was in the Tehachapis, usually as a vaquero or farmer. The Leivas were but one of approximately two dozen Californian families listed on the census records for the years 1860 through 1880.

When Lt. Cooke arrived in San Diego to assist in the conquest of the west, although he blazed a new route, he also journeyed over and near terrain which had been explored during the period when the American Revolutionists were trying the patience of the English Lords. On a windswept knoll known today as Point Loma, overlooking the modern harbor at San Diego, I stood one day and with the mind's eye swept back through time to watch as the soldiers of Spain began their conquest of Califa (26). As I blotted out the monuments of this century, looking down at the whitecapped waves racing toward shore, I pictured Juan Rodgriguez Cabrillo entering San Diego Bay on September 28, 1542, establishing Alta California's possession by the Spanish monarchy. Sixty years later he was followed by Sebastian Vizcaino, who sailed into the bay in 1602.

Spanish exploration of New Spain was slow; not until 1769 did a land expedition march forth from the Spanish port at San Diego. The Governor of California, Don Gaspar de Portola, was at the forefront, as the party searched for suitable mission sites on its journey to Monterey Bay. Two years later on Sepember 8, 1771, the Mission San Gabriel Arcangel was founded. Captain Juan Bautista de Anza, a son of the frontier and commander of the Spanish fort at Tubac, with Garces, Father Juan Diaz, and a christianized Indian, Sebastian Tarabul, who had arrived in Tubac claiming he had crossed the desert sands, made an overland exploration and opened a desert trail northward to the Mission in 1774.

Anza's successful land journey fired the imagination of new frontier politicans; soon he led a second expedition of colonists for New Spain on the journey. They left Tubac on October 22, 1775, and marched northward. Amongst the colonists were two families: Dona Maria Feliciana Arballo de Gutierrez, widow of Jose Gutierrez, and her two daughters, Tomasa, aged six, and Estaquia, aged four. The Gutierrezes shared a tent with Santiago de la Cruz Pico, a soldier-recruit, and his wife and their seven children.

The Anza expedition arrived at San Gabriel Mission on January 4, 1776, where the colonists dispersed, some to San Francisco, some remaining at San Gabriel, and others going to San Diego, to begin their new life. In 1789 one of Santiago Pico's sons, Jose Maria, married Estaquia Gutierrez. They were the parents of several children, two of whom, Pio and Andres, played major roles in the Mexican political and martial period of California, leading battles, leading politicians, and in the end assisting the American Government as it took control of the new state of California in 1850.

Sculpture of Cabrillo's Caravel at Cabrillo National Monument, Pt. Loma, California

The Twentieth Century marriage of Edward G. Cummings to a daughter of the Sais family, which farmed in the western Cummings Valley, brought to her heirs the Pico heritage, as she was a granddaughter of Andres Pico who, as a soldier, took an active part in the uprisings against the Monterey government (27). In 1839-42 he was lieutenant of the San Diego Company, and in the latter days of the Mexican Government of California was in command in 1846 at the battle of San Pasqual with Lt. Kearny, who opened the Southern Route, as well as in subsequent battles with the Americans. He also met with John Fremont (28) at Cahuenga on January 13, 1847, to sign the treaty which ended the Mexican-American War in California and led to California's acquisition by the United States. During the early American government, Pico assisted the United States in various matters of law and acted as a bridge between the two countries. He later engaged in some mining and land management; in the 1850's he owned considerable acreage of the former San Fernando Mission lands. H. H. Bancroft described him as a "brave, reckless, coarse-grained, jovial, kind-hearted, popular man; abler in several respects than his brother, Don Pio, but not overburdened with principle."

Several years ago the family of John Yorba — he married Ernie Leiva — attempted to prove their descendency from another early-California settler. In 1769 Pedro Fages commanded the Spanish sea forces to California and was the lieutenant of the Catalan volunteers on that expedition. Antonio Yorba, one of the volunteers, was the grantee in 1809-10 of the Santiago de Santa Ana Ranchos near Los Angeles.

After the arrival of the Anza expedition at San Gabriel Juan Francisco Lopez, a soldier of the guard at the Mission and a brother of Claudio Lopez, fell in love with the widow Feliciana Gutierrez and married her. He was soon transferred to San Diego where their several children were born. Feliciana was remembered by Father Font in his diary account of the expedition. She so impressed him one evening, he recorded her daring, if disapprovingly, in his diary on December 17, 1775: "At night with the joy at the arrival of all the people, they held a fandango here. It was somewhat discordant, and a very bold widow who came with the expedition sang some verses which were not at all nice, applauded and cheered by all the crowd. For this reason the man to whom she became attached became angry and punished her." She was the grandmother of Andres Pico.

As the years passed the Anza Trail became dim in memory and actuality because it was little used. Then Mexico achieved independence from Spain. Land grants to soldiers and settlers renewed interest in the overland route from the interior. In the 1820's, while chasing horse thieves in the desert northeast of San Diego Presidio, Lieutenant Santiago Arguello actually discovered what in another twenty years became the Southern Emigrant Trail. Arguello suggested to the authorities in Mexico that the road through San Felipe Valley was a much better way to Alta California than the old Anza Trail which was being considered. Eventually his route did in fact become part of the official mail route from Sonora, Mexico, to California, although it was only a poorly marked horse trail, and was not well known.

Although the American gold discovery at Sutter's Mill helped influence thousands of Americans to travel the Southern Trail, it also brought thousands of Mexicans into the gold fields, following the old Sonora Road, the Anza Trail, and the Southern Emigrant Route. In 1849, 6,000 Mexicans crossed the Colorado River, and 1,000 a month in 1850, headed for the California gold fields. And long before Tehachapi was settled, men and events merged to form a base for its history.

SEVEN

As the Spanish-Californian is identified with the early cattle industry, the French, and Spanish and French Basques, are identified with the sheep industry. They met in the Tehachapis.

Sheep were introduced to California by Franciscan Padres on their first incursion to Alta California in 1769. A few American families drove large bands into California soon after it became a state, beginning a new agricultural industry. In 1876 Colonel Stoneroad drove 10,000 head from Merced County, California to Puerto de Tuna, New Mexico, passing through the Tehachapi Valley. Another large drive occurred in 1877 involving Stoneroad, Captain Clancy, Hugo Zaber, and three other men: McKellard, Robinson, and Clancy, along the same route. In that same decade, Basques employed by San Joaquin Valley sheepmen began their yearly migration. Each spring they herded their flocks on the "long trail" from the valley to summer meadows in the Eastern Sierra Nevadas, on their way passing through the Tehachapis by way of either the Tehachapi Valley, or by Walker Pass. It is from this journey through the mountains that the road known today as the Sheep Trail evolved.

The track was also used by early Cummings Valley residents traveling into the San Joaquin Valley. According to Vance Brite, when Jeremiah Shields was second district supervisor in the 1890's, money was raised to construct a road into "the plains" following the "track" that had been there earlier. Ranchers along the route participated in the road work as it transgressed their land. After it was completed in 1896 under county supervision, it was declared a public highway and designated County Road No. 159, or the Comanche Point Road. However, Brite said "it was a waste because few people used it," adding, "The Fickerts did, about twice a year to go shopping." But the sheepmen continued to follow the trail.

Reports of the fertile grasslands and prairies in the mountain valleys of the Tehachapis filtered into the San Joaquin Valley. About 1872, permanent sheep ranches were located here when sheep were introduced as a grazing animal. There had been some earlier attempts to establish permanent herds, but hostility on the part of intractable cattlemen prevented development. In fact, as late as 1878 intermittent hostilities occasionally occurred between the two factions.

The father of Tehachapi's sheep industry is Antone Pauly, who grazed large flocks which at one time numbered over 3,000 head. This was in addition to his cattle business. Pauly wasn't a Frenchman, but the son of a prosperous German merchant, who arrived in the United States in the early days of the Civil War and in the Tehachapis about 1869. During the last decade of the Nineteenth Century several Frenchmen did, however, add to the local industry. M. Mouleot mined fourteen years in Calaveras County after he arrived in San Francisco in 1854. When he came to the Tehachapis in 1870 with little profit from his ventures, he worked for both Chanac and Cummings for another fourteen years, after which he engaged in his own sheep business. Pierre Duhart came to Kern County in 1894. He built a comfortable residence in Tehachapi and grazed sheep over the surrounding area until 1905, when he moved to Bakersfield. Jean Baptiste Capdeville, a native of France, immigrated to the States in 1888, and first came through the Tehachapis in 1892. He returned in 1902, and finally settled permanently in 1909. After he moved to Kern County in 1894, at various times he managed flocks of 4,000 to 7,000 head.

After 1895 large bands of sheep regularly passed through the mountains or were shipped to market by rail from Tehachapi pastures. In May 1898 three Frenchmen with flocks totaling 1,000 head sold them for $10,000. In July 1899 four carloads of sheep were shipped from Tehachapi by rail: thirty-eight to San Francisco and two to Los Angeles.

The Monroe Ranch at Cameron Canyon was a colorful sight each spring, especially during the 1890's when sheep by the thousands were brought in for shearing, both from the San Joaquin Valley and on the northward trail from Southern California. The Monroes kept several shearing pens and one of their daughters, Mrs. Elizabeth "Babe" Powell, remembers the excitement of those days when she was a very little girl.

Shearing sheep near Tehachapi — Circa early 1900's (Ed Wiggins Collection)

Everyone was busy including the seven "Chinamen" hired by her mother as cooks. Her Dad even kept a small store to supply the "necessities" to the shearers, who were usually Mexicans and Indians. "Once let them get into town and you didn't know when they'd be back," Mrs. Powell recalled. "It was hard work and the shearers quickly looked for an excuse to relax."

G. Mendiburu immigrated to California in 1908, and soon started a sheep business in Kern County. He acquired quite a bit of land in the foothills of the Southern Tehachapi Valley where he dry farmed as well as grazed sheep. At the time of his arrival, the only other sheep-owning land owner in the area was J. P. Ansolabehere. With other sheepmen of the Southern San Joaquin Valley both men continued the yearly migration to Mono Lake in the Eastern Sierra Nevadas, driving bands of 2,000 head and more up the historic "long trail," grazing along the way. The Mendiburu holdings were sold several years ago; some of the property is now part of another land subdivision, a Boise-Cascade development known as Mountain Meadows.

The historic sheep drives ended in 1970, according to Joe Mendiburu, when the last one was made. So much of the land was absorbed by subdivisions, and new owners were not receptive to grazing, he explained, adding, "Labor became hard to get." Also, by the 1970's the nation's sheep population had dropped from a peak of sixty million to a 1974 census of sixteen million. Today sheep are transported in modern trailers pulled by modern trucks. Sheepherders, though, are still found in the Tehachapis late each spring and on through the summer, grazing their flocks, their loyal dogs ever at their beck and call. Most of them, however, come up from the Antelope Valley, grazing leased land after the harvests, clearing the stubble for the landowners.

At least they don't cause a major problem of many years ago. In the spring of 1916 the Tehachapi Women's Club vociferously complained about the nuisance when bands of sheep passed through the principal streets in town. Imagine the laundry problem created by dust, the odor permeating the houses, they said! But there was no solution according to the Board of Trustees, as there was "only one street leading in and out of town at either end." In 1928 the problem persisted; the Town Marshall was instructed to see that herders used the outlying streets, principally Mill. Finally, in the summer of 1933, the sheep still raising clouds of dust

Sheep drive on Curry Street — Circa 1916 (Ed Wiggins Collection)

and creating bad odors on their way to the stock corrals at the railroad tracks, a sign was placed at the southerly end of Mill Street, directing the sheepmen to use it, as they had been using Pauley Street.

Not all French and Basques were sheepmen. Farmers moved into the country while in town businessmen participated in the economy. One of the earliest French hotels in Tehachapi was the Basses-Pyrenees on F Street. In 1895 Jean Pierre Martinto, for several years a sheepherder, bought six lots. In addition to the hotel he had a livery barn and a stone and lime handball court. When he retired in 1908 the new owners changed the name to Martinto's Hotel. In the early Twentieth Century there were a few other French hotels and restaurants, and another handball court on H Street near the depot.

—EIGHT—

Until 1969 when the beautiful valley known as Bear, twenty miles west of Tehachapi, became a multi-million dollar land promotion, it was synonymous with another of Tehachapi's pioneer families, the Fickerts. In recent years Bear Valley was the Fickert Ranch. A large spread, embracing thousands of acres, the ranchouse was located at the northern end of the valley where the land begins to climb into the surrounding mountains.

A vast plain spreads over the valley floor. Scattered barns and long-abandoned ranch sites in out-of-the-way places, dot the landscape. Completely surrounded by mountains on three sides, and a high ridge on the fourth, the valley seems isolated from the rest of the Tehachapi country. Streams in wet years rush down onto the valley floor; snow covers the land in winter, wildflowers in spring. Tall pines and spreading oaks flavor the landscape with scent and shade. Birds and animals abound. It is a land that exudes an aroma of history; it is spiced with stories and seasoned with memories.

The arrival of the white man in the 1800's produced a variety of stories about the bear — the giant grizzly was usually the star. ''Old Clubfoot' is the principal hero of several tales; he was as ''big as an ox, with part of his right paw chewed off.'' He made a yearly pilgrimage into the Kern County mountains, including the Bear Mountain region, from his winter home in the San Bernardino Mountains. Many early settlers saw Old Clubfoot as they traveled through the country. In 1879 miners on their way to Los Angeles reportedly met him. He never offered to fight or retreat; just stood his ground as the nervous men detoured. That was the last reported sighting of the mighty giant.

Only a few years later, however, another grizzly, also called Clubfoot, roamed around Bear Mountain, as well as other areas of the Tehachapi Range. Two different stories explain his demise. One says he was hunted down and shot by Jerky Johnson, a colorful character of the Old West tradition who earned his living at the turn of the century hunting the mountains.

The other story attributes Clubfoot's death to a different act. A reporter for the San Francisco Examiner, Allen Kelley, was assigned the task of finding, capturing, and bringing back alive, a giant grizzly bear. In 1889, after five months roaming the Tehachapi Mountains, Kelley found Clubfoot and successfully transported him to San Francisco where he lived at the zoo until 1911. Kelley admitted, however, that he "elaborated to suit the exigencies of enterprising journalism" and that he distorted facts beyond recognition when writing of the exploits of his hunting safari. Perhaps that accounts for his version of the demise of old Clubfoot: ". . . in his old age, he grew weary of being killed and resurrected;" according to Kelley the bear in his frenzied death drive, broke into a physician's office, drank a bottle of chloroform, and asphyxiated himself with the dregs of the container.

At about the same time the main valley in the Tehachapi Range was settled, men also found their way into the isolation of the valley that eventually became known as Bear. Various men are credited with the earliest visits, including Peter D. Greene, who was associated with John Geldon, George Milliken, and Dade Holton, in planting a barley crop in 1859, and building structures. Raised for hay, rather than grain, early farming was secondary to the stockmen who had first possession of Bear Valley, and the first farmers were only transients. Two other men were permanent settlers in 1864: Thomas H. Godwin, later a Constable at Old Town, and B. Tungate (29), both of whom built cabins. Godwin first settled in Cummings Valley where in the late 1850's George Cummings bought his property.

Late in 1869 with his wife and two children, Fred W. Fickert left the mines at Havilah and a mining career, for the pastoral life of farming in fertile Bear Valley. Fickert was from Prussia where, at the age of fifteen years, a "restless and ambitious youth" became a sailor. For five years he sailed the seas, until in 1850, as provision master of a vessel sailing from Hamburg to New York, he arrived in the United States. Within a month, Fickert again boarded a ship, embarked for California by way of Cape Horn. He joined the thousands of goldseekers who sailed to the West Coast, landing at San Francisco. His wife Mary Glynn Fickert, a native of Ireland, also immigrated to New York. In 1860 her family sailed to California, cutting many miles off the journey by using the land route across the Isthmus of Panama to reach the Pacific Ocean.

The journey to California by land may have been the most direct route — it was also the most difficult. The hazards of Indians, disease (cholera epidemics were the most serious), lack of water and forage, added to the vicissitudes of the land clipper. The sea clipper, however, provided a different experience and while neither Fickert nor the score or so of other Tehachapi pioneers left a record of their sea voyage, much has been recorded about the journey by others. The Argonauts on the Eastern Shore were the most frequent sailors. They either rounded the Horn in a several months' journey of 15,000 miles, or went by steamer to Panama and by way of the Isthmus crossing, reduced their travel to about half.

Although the Isthmus route was much shorter, it was very hazardous, passing through malaria-plagued jungles and over a land wracked at that time by revolution. It was a 6,000 mile journey by sea; 3,000 miles from

New York to Panama and 3,000 miles northward again to San Francisco, the usual destination. Until the completion of the Panama Railroad in 1855, the journey across the Isthmus from Chagres to Panama City was a "horror." It improved somewhat after the first horrendous days of the gold discovery, when small side-wheel steamers made the run up the Chagres River; only a few travelers continued to ride in the native bungos from Chagres to Gorgona. Then all walked or rode on mules to Panama City, which was a five-day journey.

Passage around the Horn was provided by the Pacific Mail Steamship Co., which began service just before the California gold discovery and was not much better than the Isthmus route. Built with three or four decks, the side-wheel vessels carried small masts as well, sometimes setting sail. Larger ships employed seventy-five to 100 men — officers, seamen, and servants. Staterooms usually consisted of three narrow berths and there were three classes of passage — first cabin, second cabin, and steerage.

At least two stops were necessary to replenish supplies and make shipboard repairs: at Rio de Janeiro and Valparaiso, favorite ports along the route. The journey up the West Coast, after the harrowing experience of rounding the Horn, was quite difficult as ships ran counter to the prevailing winds.

Fickert remained in San Francisco only a brief time, proceeding directly to the mines. Like many others, he hoped to dig out his fortune from the quartz ledges in water courses of the mountain regions. He explored several northern counties, and in 1863 claimed discovery of the "Sierra Gordo" mine, located it, and formed a mining district. Owing to serious Indian outbreaks he was compelled for the safety of his family, to abandon the Cerra Gordo in Eastern California. It was left to others in later years to reap millions of dollars from the claims of the world-renowned mine.

In 1865 Fickert moved, first to Kernville and later in the year to Havilah. He decided after only moderate success to abandon mining and traveled over the Tehachapi Range, explored the country, and visited Bear Valley. Its beauty, fertile soil, and adjacent grazing country, attracted his eye and he decided on a location. First he purchased a squatter's right to 160 acres of agricultural land held by James Wiliams. This was the first of many land acquisitions; by the time the family was finished they owned the region.

Calhoun Field was settled by Ezekial Ewing Calhoun, a Justice of the Peace at Old Town in the 1870's. His holdings of about 6,000 acres was the largest single purchase Fickert made. Calhoun was in Havilah after gold was discovered there; then he moved his family to Bear Valley where he attempted farming. Calhoun's wife, Laura Davis, was a daughter of Mrs. Hulda Williams Snell, the second wife of James Williams of Old Town.

With a knowledge of law, in 1866 Calhoun was an active promoter of the new county of Kern, appearing often in Havilah urging the adoption of resolutions favoring local government by the area's citizens. When the State legislated the county later that year, Calhoun was elected its first District Attorney.

One of the Calhoun daughters, Eleanor, became a famous actress in

Europe and married Eugene de Czernucki-Lazarovich, a prince of one of the Balkan countries. "A few months ago I revisited California, my native State," the Princess reminisced in her memoirs published in 1915, "after having been absent from it in Europe since earliest girlhood with the exception of a few short visits years ago. I went again to the Sierran valley of my infant days, to find no house there, as the ruins of the one we lived in had been carried away . . . . in childhood I used to strain my eyes, hoping to see a solitary horseman — my father — returning after weeks of absence" (30).

Bland Field was the home of native Californian Tully Bland, who was born in Los Gatos in 1859, ten years after his parents joined the Gold Rush to California. Bland was one of the fabled vaqueros who rode for Miller and Lux as well as Carr and Higgins, well known San Joaquin Valley cattlemen. He became a freight conductor when the railroad came to Tehachapi, but after two years settled in Bear Valley to raise crops, stock, and children.

Bland's wife was Sarah Hart, a daughter of Moses', who, with his brother Issac (both of them sons of Josiah Hart's), was also a Bear Valley settler. Issac first saw the valley as a member of the government survey party of 1855 and then spent several years mining in the Kern River Valley before settling in Bear Valley about 1869. His job with the surveying crew had been marking and building mounds at the section corners. Moses settled at Oak Creek in the late 1850's and located a farm in Bear Valley in the 1870's.

Louis Fickert, a cousin, followed somewhat in Fred's footsteps. He, too, was born in Prussia, sailed the oceans, searched for gold, and finally settled down to farm about 1870 in Bear Valley. Joseph Fountain (or Fontaine as the name is also recorded), also ranched in the valley. At one time he was county supervisor from the second district. There were others — all of them the true western type of man, almost right out of the pages of a Zane Grey novel: tough, imaginative, adventurous, imbued with the spirit that settled the West.

Fred Fickert has been described by some oldtimers who knew him as a loner for whom business came first, "tough and hard." Ben Sasia, a Bear Valley native, once commented about the Fickert family's talent in acquiring land. The owner of a fine farm owed a $600 bill at Galinger and Waterman, one of Tehachapi's mercantile stores. That particular owner let one of the Fickerts know that if they paid the bill for him, the farm was theirs. The Fickerts did pay, taking ownership of the farm, and today the farm is the location of the clubhouse at Bear Valley Springs.

In 1875 fifteen land owners had six sections planted in grain. That year Bear Valley's crops were in a "prosperous state of cultivation, . . . all the land occupied by families." "The farm of F. Fickert has sixty acres of barley, wheat and oats," commented an observer. Other farmers of the time were Lewis Fickert, A. H. Butts, Mr. Hosac, John Nead, T. Flanagan, Mr. Hart, J. Glenn, a man named Wilson, T. T. Martin, J. Hart, E. E. Calhoun, Mr. Bigham, N. Hart, and a Mr. Smith, who altogether had 1,230 acres planted in grain.

Two ladies lived at the Fickert Ranch throughout their lifetime. Louise

Fickert, who was born in Havilah in 1866, and her sister Nellie, born just after the family moved to Bear Valley, watched the ranch unfold before their eyes. Neither of them married. When, in December of 1959 they both passed away, it was the end of an era in many respects. Nellie, at 91, died first, followed within two weeks by Louise, who was 96. Their nephew, Marshall Fickert, continued the management of the vast ranch until it was sold by the heirs in 1968, lacking only one year of being a century old.

Bear Valley is now owned by Dart Industries which purchased it in the early 1970's and is a major subdivision known as Bear Valley Springs. Behind a guarded gate a few hundred homes have been constructed, a country club was built, and recreation has taken the place of farming and

The Fickert family prepares for an automobile excursion in a 1911 Winton. That's Fred Fickert on the left. Their family home still stands, but has been remodeled for modern living — Circa 1911 (Darrell and Louise Stevens)

stock raising.

For many years access to Bear Valley was a distinct chore as no definite roadbed marked the way. Wagon tracks, swinging and swaying across the hills, marked the way. In 1877 a county paper called the supervisors' attention to the "fact that the large and prosperous community of Bear Valley is without a road." But it wasn't until the late 1880's that the Board advertised for bids to build the "Bear Valley Road . . . to be 9 feet wide, solid grade, with the necessary turnouts."

Fickert, who met with the supervisors in 1889, commented that Bear Valley was in the "direct descent from the Garden of Eden, but perhaps a little too thickly settled." He believed a great need was a "squait" and sidetrack, as the hauling distance was so great from the valley to the railroad that the distance precluded much profit when its products were marketed. That year an increase in grain production occurred and Fickert insisted that with reasonable railroad encouragement a large amount of good land could be added to cultivation.

Once there were enough children in Bear Valley so that it had its own school. From the 1870's until the turn of the century education as well as farming ·and cattle was a product of the settlers. While most of the families left the area with the passage of years, the schoolhouse survived. After Fred Fickert purchased the land on which it stood, the schoolhouse was moved adjacent to his ranch house. Today it is a tourist attraction at the Town Center of Bear Valley Springs.

Records for this district are very scanty, but it may be the same as the Fitzgerald School District, whose boundaries embraced the southerly portion of Bear Valley, where the schoolhouse had originally stood. This district was formed May 7, 1872, and in its first year of operation had an average daily attendance of twenty-three pupils. Gradually the attendance declined until in 1898-99, its last year of operation, the attendance was down to seven a day.

The first district clerk was Ezekial Calhoun; one of its early teachers, in 1880-81, was Miss M. E. Mauldin. One year when John Hickey was the teacher, he had some minor difficulties with a trustee and "vacated his professorship," causing the school to be temporarily closed. On October

Bear Valley Schoolhouse now located in the Town Center at Bear Valley Springs

94

5, 1900, the district lapsed and its territory was annexed to the Cummings Valley School District.

That district was also established in the 1870's when an influx of families caused formal education to begin on July 11, 1873. During its first year, although it served a "sparsely settled rural valley," the average daily attendance was twenty-four pupils.

Bad weather and poor buildings were a handicap of the Cummings Valley School for many years. A teacher's report in 1906 complained: "The attendance this last term has been quite irregular, on account of stormy weather. The children cannot well drive as far as they are obliged to and let their teams stand all day during bad weather." A 1908 report noted, "The schoolhouse as well as the outbuildings are in very bad condition . . . Most barns would furnish better protection from wind than the present building."

In 1910 a new schoolhouse was built at a cost of $3,160, replacing the wood building. In 1956 the Cummings Valley School District was annexed to the Tehachapi Union School District.

John Hickey, a native of Ireland who arrived in Illinois as a child in the 1850's, is the first known school teacher at Cummings Valley. At the conclusion of his sophomore year he left the university at Mount Pleasant, Iowa, moving to Kern County in 1875. First he taught school for three years in Bear Valley, and then came to Cummings Valley. Although he resigned from teaching, he continued as a school trustee for twelve years, also serving as an itinerant preacher and assisted in forming a congregation of the Methodist-Episcopal Church. In 1908 Hickey moved into Tehachapi and was one of the town's incorporators as well as its first mayor after the regular municipal election.

—NINE—

Agricultural mechanization arrived in the Tehachapis in the late 1880's. The mechanical monster known as the Iron Horse, however, was responsible as early as 1872 for an upsurge in farming even though the rails didn't reach the area for another four years.

With the knowledge that freighting was increasing through the Tehachapi Pass and as the construction of the Southern Pacific Railroad continued down the San Joaquin Valley, families from the Los Angeles region began to settle the vast, virgin lands of the Tehachapis. Freighting created a large hay, barley, and flour market, and oxen and horses needed to be fed. In February 1873 the valleys of Tehachapi, Cummings, and Brite, did extensive sowing, eight times more than the previous year. And in June all of the surplus crops were sold to the Owens River freight teams.

In 1875 settlers continued to move to the region at a rapid pace. Throughout the seventies and eighties natural rainfall and snowpack assured the major ingredient necessary to the production of dry farmed crops. The boom peaked in the final decade of the century.

The Tehachapi regional wheat production between 1870 and 1900 was a scene in the larger agricultural act when wheat was the most profitable crop in the state, and California was the largest grain producer in the nation. California produced a hard, dry, and unusually white wheat that was particularly popular on the Liverpool Corn Exchange in England.

In August 1889 seventy carloads of grain destined for the tidewater area and Eastern market were shipped by rail with only one-half of the crop harvested. Harvesting continued unabated through the rest of the year. In September the annual shipment was up to 700 carloads, and by December most of the available land in the region had been taken up by settlers. The addition of farm lands continued into the 1890's, when yields, prices, and rainfall were high.

Mechanization came when Elijah Stowell of Cummings Valley introduced the combination reaper-thresher which he bought for $1,500 in June 1888. The next year R. R. Taylor bought a new combined harvester and thresher, making the cutting of his 1,200 acres a busy, but so much easier operation.

Until the development of the combine, separate operations necessitated a long harvest. Cyrus McCormick's reaper replaced hand tools in 1831, bringing the first mechanization to the farmer's ancient craft. In 1860 in California the spout and draper were attached to the McCormick reaper: two drapers were used, one above, one below, until the grain was in a wagon running alongside, all motivated by horse power. In 1885 a header wagon was developed to run alongside the header and receive the heads of wheat.

The combine was introduced in the San Joaquin Valley in 1868, when wheat growers built and perfected the machine. By 1888, the year of Stowell's purchase, it was used almost exclusively. In 1891 more harvesters were imported into the Tehachapis and the following year almost a score of farmers utilized the combine in their threshing.

An eloquent picture of the machine's function is painted in Frank Norris's "The Octopus," in which he writes:

"The sprocket adjusted, the engineer called up the gang, and the men took their places. The fireman stoked vigorously; the two sack sewers resumed their posts on the staking platform, putting on the goggles that kept the chaff from their eyes. The separator man and headerman gripped their levers.

"The Harvester, shooting a column of thick smoke straight upward, vibrating to the top of the stack, hissed, clanked, and lurched forward. Instantly, motion sprang to life in all its component parts; the header knives, cutting a thirty-six foot swath, gnashed like teeth; beltings slid and moved like smooth-flowing streams; the separator whirred, the agitator jarred and crashed; cylinders, augers, fans, seeders and elevators, drapers and chaff-carriers, clattered, rumbled, buzzed, and clanged. The steam hissed and rasped; the ground reverberated a hollow note; and the thousands upon thousands of wheat stalks, sliced and slashed in the clashing shears of the header, rattled like dry rushes in a hurricane as they fell inward and were caught up by an endless belt, to disappear into the bowels of the vast brute that devoured them . . .

"All that shrieking, clamoring machinery, all that gigantic organism, all the months of labor, the plowing, the planting, the prayers for rain, the years of preparation, the heartaches, the anxiety, the foresight, all the whole business of the ranch, the work of horses, of steam, of men and boys, looked to this spot — the grain chute from the harvester into the sacks . . . at this point, the labor of the rancher ended. Here, at the lip of the chute, he parted company with his grain, and from here the wheat steamed forth to feed the world'' (31).

Harvesting grain in the Tehachapi Valley — Early 20th century (Ed Wiggins Collection)

Throughout the 1890's the acreage under cultivation increased as did the yield, although fluctuating moisture began to worry the farmers. In the summer of 1891, 15,000 acres were harvested: one-third in wheat, the rest in barley — with a yield of ten to twelve sacks per acre. Wheat sold for $1.25 a bushel and barley went for $1.10. A year later the sown grain acreage was doubled, and at least forty sacks were harvested from each acre. An 1892 observer remarked, "Tehachapi is a peculiar town. A few years ago it was only a cattle range. Now it vies with the metropolis of Kern in its endeavor for honors. The fact is Tehachapi has the backing of about 60,000 acres of the richest land in the State and a most perfect place in summer." Summer fallowing had been introduced a few years earlier, and in 1892 almost all the farmers realized that particular method of farming would reap the same amount of grain or more. So heavy was the harvest late that summer, that "long lines of teams constantly pour in from Bear, Brite and Cummings Valley. There is hardly room at the

Tehachapi warehouse to store away the grain," which was destined for the Liverpool Exchange.

In 1893 conservative estimates placed the land sown to wheat and barley at between 90,000 and 100,000 acres. Fourteen combined harvesters and twenty-five headers of from twelve to sixteen foot sweep, worked the fields. Each harvester required twenty-six to thirty horses for locomotion, and the headers about six. Six hundred horses were often used in the fields. While some of the harvest was sold, a large quantity went into storage waiting higher prices. During Cleveland's administration the price per bushel dropped to $1.01 (the highest price had been in 1876 when it reached $1.92, perhaps contributing to the boom in Calfornia agriculture). In the spring of 1894 growth was reported to be more promising than ever before. "By careful estimates just made there are in the Tehachapi country taking the land lying south of Caliente and north of Cameron, 83,000 acres sown this season to wheat and 24,000 acres to barley, with the harvest estimated to reach a record of 107,000 acres." In the immediate Tehachapi region 60,000 acres were included in this manificent yield.

It was only a matter of time before an industrious individual recognized a potential which he put to work. In the summer of 1895 J. A. Moore, president of the Tehachapi Trading Co., began to construct a flour mill in Tehachapi. Finally a home market was to be provided for nature's bounty. The mill cost $15,000 and employed the latest in improved machinery. It was ready for business in January 1896.

Each year as the decade counted down, production continued unabated, and the prices fluctuated. In 1896 hay sold for $8.00 a ton and the increase in mining discoveries and production on the desert called for more local marketing than ever before. By 1897 a change in the precipitation was noticed; lower snow packs and rainfall began to worry the farmers, though they continued to be satisfied with their annual yields. That summer a scribe wryly commented, "News is scarce and so is the money. We are still waiting for the promised prosperity."

In 1899 the Tehachapi Times complained, "The promise of a good season next year does not help the people this one. The absence of both rain and the fabled wave have done much to put many prominent citizens on the special to Oxnard. What we want here is more rain and less prospect for it." In August, although the harvest was good, very little grain was shipped. The growers appeared inclined to store it, waiting the prospect of better prices. If the railroad was the boom to the wheat farmer, it became his nemesis, as the monopolistic railroad maintained exorbitant freight charges affecting the Tehachapi region as well as the San Joaquin Valley.

And then, as summer faded into fall in the last year of the century, the boom busted, and the influx of families only twenty-five years earlier reversed itself as a number of farmers left the Tehachapis to live elsewhere. Stopping in Bakersfield as they journeyed north, two parties told an editor, "These people go on account of the successive drought, but their places will be filled by others when the seasons are more favorable and the mountain town will again become the bustling point it has been in the past.''

Nevertheless, as the centuries turned, grain farming continued. In 1907 Kerr and Jones were hailed as the most extensive farmers in the region, with 2,500 acres under cultivation. But in three more years a newspaper reported in December that 4,000 acres of land had changed hands in just the past few months. Dry farming was on the wane, giving place to orchards of apples and Bartlett pears.

—TEN—

As dry years and a depressed grain market caused the extensive fields of the 1890's to decline, a pear tree promulgated a new farm economy in the early Twentieth Century, and as with wheat production, fruit followed the state trend.

In its "Progress and Oil Review Edition" of February 28, 1911, the Bakersfield Morning Echo described the change:

"It is generally believed that the year 1910 marked the beginning of an era of development of the lands adjacent to the town of Tehachapi that will, within a few years, make this as highly productive a section as lies within the boundary lines of our justly celebrated state. The invasion was started when B. M. Denison last year sunk a 13 inch well casing, developed a bountiful supply of water, installed an up-to-date pumping plant and set 40 acres to Bartlett pear trees."

Burt M. Denison is the "father" of this region's modern fruit industry. He came to Tehachapi as the Southern Pacific Company's station agent in 1888, but soon entered other endeavors. With Dan and Jack McFarland in the 1890's he established the Oak Creek Lumber Company, operating a saw mill and box factory. Great quantities of lumber were produced and shipped from the factory; at six o'clock each evening, three immense wagons pulled by a large tractor, arrived at the Tehachapi depot loaded with lumber for shipment outside the valley. By the close of the decade a combination of depleted lumber in the vicinity of the mill and exorbitant prices for wood owned by others, made it unfeasible to continue the operation and it soon ended.

Denison was also one of the original incorporators of the California Pine Box Company, manufacturers of orange crates. Also in the 1890's, he owned a grocery business in downtown Tehachapi and established a general store, moving into the new Pauly building in September 1896, considered one of the finest stores in town. He also had a hay and grain yard and a large grain mill, and in 1897 built a new warehouse west of the stock corrals. In February 1898 Denison built a brick building in the Irribarne Block on G and Green Streets, purchasing 200,000 bricks from Mrs. Pauly.

And then, a pear changed the skyline. In his own back yard, each fall Denison gathered a good yield of pears from two prolific trees. A man of some vision, he sold his store about 1909, and with the proceeds and in partnership with C. O. Lee, bought forty acres just outside the town's limits and planted the area's first commercial orchard. His $8,000 investment was such a success that in time he increased his orchard to 120 acres. As Denison waited for his first forty acres to produce, he planted the rows in between the trees to cabbage, pink beans, onions, and potatoes. He also bought a one-quarter interest in a canning factory at Burbank, where several carloads of "T-HACHA-P" pears were canned each year; the brand eventually was patented by the Tehachapi Fruit Growers Association.

The pear is another result of the Gold Rush. After David Elliot arrived in California, he took one look at the rich, black delta soil around Sacramento, and changed his mind about scrambling for gold. The year was 1853. Elliot was thinking about pears when he saw the rich soil, and the orchard he planted on Sutter Island in the Sacramento River, now the oldest known Barlett orchard in the country, is still flourishing. The original trees were ordered from France and made the long sea voyage of 10,000 miles in tubs of their native soil to be transplanted in California — and they grew. The fruit became famous to miners and passengers on the Sacramento River stern-wheel riverboats; at times hungry men reportedly paid as much as an ounce of gold, worth $20.67, for a single pear!

Elsewhere in California, by the late 1860's the Santa Clara Valley was a colorful spring palette of flowering apricot, plum, apple, and pear trees. In the 1870's the growth of Southern California's citrus industry continued the fruit explosion in the state.

Although Moses Hale has generally been regarded as the first orchard planter in 1880, when he set out apple trees on his farm in Tehachapi Canyon, in 1876 William P. McCord, a Bakersfield nurseryman filled "some large orders of fruit trees to be planted in the valley." Soon others followed Hale's efforts and in the fall of later years the area was a rich harvest as families throughout the region picked fruit for their own use. In 1889 Fred Fickert promoted Bear Valley as a "natural Eden for apples and pears." He complained, though, that choice peaches didn't thrive well (as later farmers also realized), but grew in an abundant quality for preserves. But, as he also said, "When a 3 year old apple tree produces 1,000 pounds of choice apples it is a sign of a pretty good country for that sort of fruit."

Another early orchardist was Joseph Kiser, whose heritage is worthy of comment. His grandfather Jacob Kiser immigrated to America from Germany, and fought in the Revolutionary War, as did his son Jacob, who also fought in the War of 1812. Jacob Junior was a farmer in Pennsylvania where, in 1829 his son Joseph was born. He arrived in California in 1852, mining and raising stock in various sections of the state. In 1863 Kiser came to the Tehachapis in search of gold, but four years later settled a ranch in Brite Valley. Today the ranch is the site of another 1970's land development, Enchanted Lakes. Each spring flowers still bloom on the few apple trees remaining in the Joseph Kiser orchard. One outlet for his fruit was the Southern Pacific Railroad, which supplied apples to its Harvey Houses.

W. H. Knapp, who in 1876 was a railroad telegrapher at Summit Station, later acquired 480 acres adjoining Tehachapi and also planted 180 fruit trees.

In 1890 large quantities of trees were shipped to Tehachapi from Fresno nurseries, as more farmers turned their attention to fruit and vine cultivation. An early result of this change in agriculture was an increase in windmills and tanks necessary to produce water for irrigation. Some wells were "coming in" at only ten feet below ground level.

On G Street in 1891 two fruit stands sold their produce to area residents as well as travelers. In 1893 a local market offered three cents a pound for the "finest apples to be found in the state."

Cherries entered the market in 1894, when J. B. Phillips' orchard, which had been planted to 600 trees in 1890, came into full bearing. He sold fruit from his farm northwest of Old Town for ten cents a pound; his black Tartarian cherries were described as "simply perfect." In 1895 he added other fruit: apples, pears, peaches, apricots, currants, and gooseberries.

In Cummings Valley rancher Elijah Stowell planted a small orchard of Bartlett pears in 1890. Four years later the trees were so laden with fruit that "six or eight props for each tree are necessary to prevent the limbs being crushed to the ground."

The absence of a steady grain market in the 1890's increased the farmers' interest in fruit. In November 1895 a resident suggested, "From present indications it will not be long until the farmers of Tehachapi valley will cultivate more apples than heretofore. Our valley is a grain producing country," he added, "but for the past two years, in the absence of a reasonable market for grain, a few farmers have cultivated apple orchards to a good purpose. As yet it is not known as a fruit producing locality. But here are a few facts worth mentioning. Moses Hale . . . . Last year he sold the entire output for $700. James Brite from Kiser's old place, realized over $500 from a young orchard of eight acres. Louis Buhn has an orchard of six acres near old Tehachapi that brought him between $500 and $600." A month later the same person said, "Several other farmers are talking orchards . . . Those who have apple orchards in Tehachapi, Cummings, Brite and Bear Valleys, will realize lots of good money from the sale of this fruit as the mountain apples are always in demand and bring at present 3 cents a pound delivered at the Southern Pacific Railroad depot."

As grain production decreased, apple production increased. In the winter of 1898 the California Nursery Co. of Mills, California, shipped to its agent John Irribarne 1,200 fruit trees. An astute observer said, "Our farmers know a good thing when they see it. There is more money with less expense in winter apples than any other farm product."

The success of Denison's pear orchard is attributed to several factors. Obviously trees had been planted in the Tehachapis for some years; however, Denison realized the advantage of a commercial market and the importance of a constant water supply to nurture the trees. In conjunction with his first plantings, he sank the well at a cost of $3,700 and installed the pumping plant. "There is an abundant and never failing supply of water," reported a Bakersfield paper in 1911, "of the purest and best quality for domestic and irrigation purposes in the entire Tehachapi District, mostly within 80 feet or less of the surface." By 1900 five pumping plants were operated for irrigation only, each producing 225 to 600 gallons of water per minute, under constant pumping and during the

Burt Denison in his brother Lon's orchard south of Tehachapi — Circa 1920 (Dr. Lon Denison)

driest seasons, in no way affecting the water supply. No one believed the supply could ever be affected. The Southern Pacific Company, for instance, ran its pumping plant constantly day and night in 1910; since 1903 they had produced an average of seven million gallons of water per month "without in the least affecting the level or supply of water in their own or in nearby wells." Many pumping plants were installed as a result of the increasing interest in fruit production, and "they can have no effect on the water supply of this district."

In September 1910 Bartlett pears were shipped to Los Angeles, fetching six cents per pound. Value was increasing. In the spring of 1911, an additional 500 acres of deciduous fruit was planted.

In 1911 with much of the region's land changing owners because of the reduction in grain farming, non-resident land owners also began to plant trees on their property. About 5,000 acres of land adjacent to town was immediately affected, although it didn't produce a quick cash return, as an apple crop takes twelve years to break even and pears seven.

One of the largest promotions involved landed interests of several non-residents, including Carle Turner McKinnie, who arrived in the valley in 1910. With his associates he purchased 1,600 acres adjacent to the town and organized the Tehachapi Fruit and Land Company, Inc. with himself as president and manager. Under his direction the company began irrigating, using its own pumping plants, and resold 1,000 acres, 500 of which they planted to Bartlett pears and winter varieties of apples.

Although "Fruit" is first in its corporate name, "Land" has even

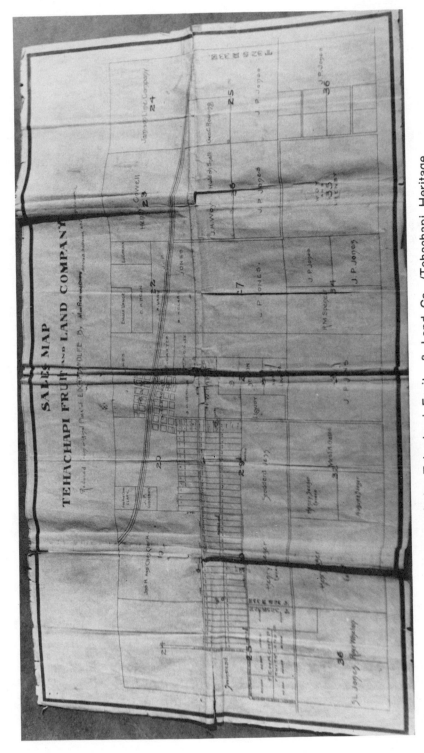

Sales Map of the Tehachapi Fruit & Land Co. (Tehachapi Heritage League)

greater significance. Fruit was the gimmick, land the profit, as the Tehachapi Fruit and Land Company, Inc. subdivided its property for resale in ten acre parcels. On August 14, 1911, the company filed a subdivision map in the County Recorder's office and opened a real estate office in the Clark Hotel. A printed brochure encouraged people to come "to the country."

Another land development, the Tehachapi Red Apple Tract, was located near the Catholic Cemetery and south to Valley Boulevard. The tract was owned by the Sharer Investment Company, which filed a subdivision map on May 17, 1913.

As a gimmick to entice people to buy land, some of the subdividers allegedly stored the Winter Pairmaine near cellar entrances. It is a very odiferous green apple that smells good, but looks bad. Nevertheless, fragrance influenced some people to buy land.

Another result of the orchards was the activation of Tehachapi's Board of Trade (the forerunner of today's Chamber of Commerce). The Board of Trade actively promoted orchards in 1915 and contributed to an interest in the area's fruit in the immediate years following. At the first annual Kern County Fair in 1916, the Board of Trade exhibited fruit; in fact, on October 27 all "business in town" was closed, so "everyone" could attend the inaugural event. A special train was added to the daily run so local school children could attend. Their promotion was a success, the Tehachapi booth won blue ribbons on forty-six premiums it displayed, and the most attractive exhibit was apples.

In 1917 Denison's "T-HACHA-P" brand was in keen competition with the Land Company's "Tehach" pears. The next year 1,800 acres of pears were commercially produced and 1,700 acres were in red winter apples. On April 12, 1917, the first Farm Bureau Auction sale was held, advertising they would sell "anything except land." By the end of the year an estimated 3,239 acres were planted to orchards. After 1918, however, very little land was added to production, perhaps an indication of the soon-to-become very apparent problem of non-resident farmers attempting to produce their land from afar, for in 1920 an effort was made to reactivate the Farm Bureau, as the original had ceased from lack of interest. The Farm Bureau was reorganized, but throughout the next forty years the Board of Trade, Farm Bureau, or Chamber of Commerce — call it what you will — had its up and downs, paralleling the periodic economic change in the region.

In the early 1920's the district leveled off in its agricultural production. In 1922, 30,000 acres were devoted to grain (a decided drop from the 100,000 before the turn of the century), and 5,000 acres were planted in orchards. Modern farm machinery harvested wheat, barley, and rye. From the railroad depot practically all the region's pears, apples, and cherries were shipped to New York and other Eastern markets, where they commanded high prices.

The business affairs of one man and his heirs, as they managed a vast acreage in the Tehachapi Valley, exemplifies the region's agricultural scene from the turn of the century until the depression years of the 1930's.

Senator John Percival Jones of Nevada, although well known in that state, Southern California, and in mining schemes throughout the West, is little known for his investments in the Tehachapis. When he died in 1912 he owned 3,926 acres, primarily east, south, and north of the town of Tehachapi.

Jones was born in Wales, raised in Ohio, and arrived in California in 1850 at the age of 21. He joined his peers with pick and pan, until a venture into politics elected him sheriff of Trinity County. After waging an unsuccessful campaign for Lieutenant-Governor of California in 1867, he moved to Virginia City, Nevada, where his activities in the great Comstock mines soon made him a millionaire. Once again Jones entered politics and was successfully elected Nevada's representative to the United States Senate. After arriving in Washington in 1873 and as a major consequence of his background, he introduced considerable mining legislation into Congress.

Also during the 1870's Jones was involved in a number of California ventures. Mining continued to interest him; he financially backed an enterprise at Panamint City, located in Surprise Canyon of the Panamint Range. After purchasing an interest in the San Vicente Rancho in 1874 from Colonel R. S. Baker, with whom he was also engaged in a cattle business at Tejon, in 1875 Jones founded the town of Santa Monica, expecting it to compete with San Pedro as a California port, and also to be the terminus for his railroad, the Los Angeles and Independence. From Panamint City to Santa Monica, Jones intended to transport his ore, and conversely to bring new life from the coast into Eastern California. (The railroad was completed only eighteen miles from the port and Jones' interest in Panamint City soon waned. (During this same period he also invested in the Big Blue Mine near Kernville.

Perhaps it was while Jones was connected with the Big Blue or running cattle at Tejon, that he first became interested in the Tehachapi Valley. In any event, on March 23, 1892, he was deeded most of Section 21, immediately adjacent to Tehachapi, by the Southern Pacific Railway. Within a few years he purchased land from Peter D. Greene, Lucas F. Brite, and Robert R. Taylor, among others, adding to his holdings and eventually owning all of Sections 15, 27, and 33, as well as a very large portion of several contiguous sections.

About 1900 Jones formed a partnership with Charles Kerr to run cattle and to farm. The cattle operation spread out on 29,000 acres of alternate sections of government land and property owned by John Cuddeback from Old Town to Caliente and in the mountains northeast, and was known as Kerr and Jones. The farming occurred on the sections owned outright by the Senator in the Tehachapi Valley under the business name of California Steam Farming Company (32).

In 1905 and 1906 they leased much of the Cuddeback property as range land and ran about a thousand head of cattle. Kerr managed the operation from Tehachapi, and Jones continued his life of comfort, managing other business investments from his home in Santa Monica.

When Burt Denison decided to plant his first orchard he bought the land from Jones in February 1910 for $2,000. (Jones had already sold some of his property: in 1903 to the Union Lime Company; in 1904 to Ferd Snyder; and in 1911, to the town.) He watched with interest as Denison planted his pears, as he planned to follow the lead of the Tehachapi Fruit and Land Company. In the summer of 1911, his son Roy wrote, ''As I talk with people in Los Angeles and elsewhere I find that the apple prospect at Tehachapi is getting to be pretty thoroughly advertised. Almost everyone seems to have heard of the apple industry there and I am sure that when the time comes to put our land on the market we should have no difficulty in selling it at good prices. In another year Denison's orchard will be bearing and we should have something to show people'' (33).

Unfortunately, Senator Jones died in November, 1912, and his personal plans for the Valley failed to materialize. In the course of administering his estate, however, the heirs incorporated the Ramina Corporation in April 1914, at the time considered ''one of the most extensive developers of the varied agriculture of the irrigated valleys of northern and southern California'' (34).

The corporation didn't waste any time assuming management of its Tehachapi investments. First it got rid of Charles Kerr. Robert K. Walton, an attorney and Ramina's first president, wrote one of the heirs in December 1914, that Kerr had misled Roy Jones as to the value of the cattle business. Adjacent cattlemen were critical of the partnership's animals and range, although Walton admitted, ''It is only an exceptional man who could manage 4000 acres of ranch and 50,000 acres of cattle range at the same time at a high stage of efficiency.''

The family assumed a measure of responsibility for Kerr as he sustained a serious back injury while handling a harvesting team which permanently incapacitated him, and so the family dealt less harshly with him than they might have otherwise. They finally bought him out after selling the cattle to ''two big cattlemen named Bowker and Benton'' for $30,000: $6,000 in cash and $24,000 in twelve units of a syndicate known as the Imperial Valley Farm Lands Association.

The new ranch manager, J. W. Jennings, developed the corporation's property. His initial observations describe not just the general condition of Ramina land, but much of the region's acreage, and why:

''. . . I found the condition of the ground throughout the whole to be in very bad condition, in so much that it has been continually plowed from year to year at a depth of from two to three inches, plowed in the same direction year after year, and having been plowed with the heavy traction engine which so compacted the ground that the life of the soil was practically destroyed. Also that the ground was left in such a condition that the flood waters during the rainy season of the year washed great ditches at a depth of from a foot to ten feet deep.''

Jennings began to improve the property and promoted the planting of extensive orchards. ''In order to place this land upon the market,'' he wrote the heirs, ''and have land that we can sell to the different buyers it is necessary that we should have some planted to fruit trees thereby enabling us to give the choice of planted or unplanted land.'' He added, ''I have every reason to believe that the future of the Tehachapi valley is the best of any in the state of California . . . I do not base my opinion upon my own knowledge of conditions, but from the fact that prominent men of Horticulture fame as well as Agriculture fame in the last few months have made a thorough investigation of the Tehachapi Valley and have gone on record that we have without question the best conditions for the growing of pears of any section in the Southwestern states. Also from the fact that the red apple as produced here is the very best in quality that is to be found on the market. With these conditions and from the fact that the opening of the Panama Canal, which prominent advocators leads us to believe the settlement of this coast country will be very large in the coming years and also from the fact that this opening of the canal gives us a foreign market for our fruit enabling us to get prices that no other country can compete with, makes it very essential that we should go ahead and carry out our plans that we have already started.''

This opinion was obviously shared by the Tehachapi Fruit and Land Co., as well as other orchard-land developers.

Ramina continued the grain operation and added additional resources which, by the end of 1915, included hen houses to raise its own eggs, so as to save grocery and meat bills. Using the area's newly introduced electric power, Ramina installed a separating machine to manufacture butter and sold some of it. High grade horses and mules were bred to obtain first class prices. Eleven thousand fruit trees were planted, expected to bear in two or three years. After trading for water rights in the hills it built a five million gallon reservoir and introduced irrigation to the ranch, both for itself and resale to others.

A lumber yard was constructed and the corporation also sold cement, buying on consignment by the carload, selling at a profit, and paying for the goods only after it collected the money. Ramina also installed a mill for cleaning and steaming barley, selling directly to consumers in Kern and Los Angeles Counties. An automatic system was installed which hoisted and distributed the wheat as well as cleaning and scouring it. In fact, ''. . . our little plant is equipped with the most up to date machinery in the United States and has already aroused great interest throughout the state,'' commented the president, adding, ''Most of the Tehachapi wheat has been sold for chicken feed and has never been considered a milling wheat because it was never properly cleaned and marketed . . . In addition our plant is capable of handling not only our own wheat but also that of our neighbors and the farmers in all the four valleys that have Tehachapi as their railroad shipping point. For this we will make a charge which will pay us a reasonable profit and in addition we will charge them for storing the wheat in our warehouse until it is sold.'' Ramina contracted with the Southern Pacific for a side track past their warehouse doors ''which will enable us to load freight cars full to the brim with loose wheat through the force of gravity. This is much faster than loading by hand out of a wagon and much cheaper.''

But the corporation's plans for quick land sales did not materialize. ''We have been unable to sell any of our planted orchard land or unplanted orchard land that we subdivided last spring,'' Walton complained in 1915. ''The hoped for influx of buyers has not materialized.

Things are improving, however, and there are some signs that the coming year will be better in that respect."

By 1916 Jennings had planted the Ramina property to 380 acres of orchard, 1,440 acres in wheat and 800 acres in barley. At the same time he commented on the neglect of neighboring orchards and a general set-back in the region. In 1917, after Roy Jones became the corporation's president, he became disenchanted with Jennings, accusing him of grandiose ideas for the Tehachapi properties as well as overextending the corporation's assets and investments. And so Jennings removed himself from the scene. But the business didn't improve. Although in 1922 they were ecstatic with the "biggest crop that has ever set up here, the estimate for the valley is from 100,000 to 150,000 boxes of fruit to be shipped and from our orchards the estimate is from 26,000 to 30,000 boxes," there was disappointment in most yearly crops during the twenties.

One pear grower, F. H. Rawley, experimented in 1925 with an innovation which in later years spelled the success or doom of orchardists. He owned a ninety-acre orchard and by a $5,000 initial investment purchased 8,000 smudge pots and 16,000 gallons of oil. The first season's smudge cost him $2,000; but he realized a full crop. In conjunction with smudging, that year L. J. Kanstein began a serious effort to arrange for an official weather station in the Tehachapi region during the frost-danger period. There had been no government station prior to then, although since 1912 daily records were kept by the local Santa Fe Railroad Agent and filed in the company's Los Angeles office. In 1927 an official weatherman began to come to the region each spring to assist the farmers, and since that time the weatherman has come each year.

Following Rawley's experimental smudging, Ramina put in pots during the winter of 1926, but one or two good years during that decade failed to support the operation. In 1930 when the area expected a good crop, several nights of blizzard conditions in May (a condition not heard of since 1914) ruined the fruit, and Ramina sustained a complete loss — despite smudging for several nights in succession. Jones lamented, "I simply cannot finance Ramina any longer . . . At present I have cut down the whole program to just one or two men who are trying to keep the place up with only the absolutely necessary work so that we may be able to offer it for sale or trade. But it would have to be a regular giveaway price because nobody any longer considers that pear growing at Tehachapi is a commercial possibility. All but two or three orchards have been abandoned."

Jones wrote to J. G. Bisbee who was president and manager of the Pioneer Fruit Company in San Francisco: "By the way do you know of anybody American or Jap who would consider the taking of our orchard on lease. We would make mighty interesting terms. We are sick of the worry."

The national depression, continuing late spring frosts, poor fruit — all contributed to the worsening Tehachapi Valley conditions. Finally in 1931 Ramina contracted with C. A. Willis to act as its agent and sell the Tehachapi property for $100,000, but Willis couldn't locate a buyer. Jones appealed in another letter to Bisbee, "Do you suppose you could find me a buyer for the orchard AT ANY PRICE . . . . I am dead sick of bothering with the whole thing. The stockholders are getting restive and are urging me to get rid of the property. We will make a price that would be an absolute find for anybody who wants an orchard . . ." But there were no prospects; "real estate is so dead that bargains are going begging . . ."

In 1910 Jones had watched the Denison orchard with interest; as Denison went, so did the rest. In 1929 he observed that "Denisons is an almost complete failure and Mrs. Denison has lost the orchard on her mortgage and is broke. . ." But in 1931 they were still picking; they "shipped 11 car loads and fell $200 short of getting back packing and freight and got not a cent for all their smudging and care during the year."

Inevitably, the lack of attention by absentee owners, together with other factors, took its toll on other orchards. Taxes were going up, as were expenses; some crops were lost; and the initial wells and water systems proved inadequate. Many of the orchards never produced at all, and only the most responsible owners fired pots and saved their crops. Finally, about 1930, trees began to disappear as the first of several major "pulls" affected, in a burst of final action, the great splurge of fruit production in the Tehachapis. And, as they failed to make tax payments, some land went into the county's hands.

It was all over, too, for the Ramina Corporation. In 1934 it turned over its property to the Mortgage Guarantee Co., but it wasn't until 1943 that the last of Ramina's equipment, which had been stored in the Denison orchards, was sold to J. G. Bisbee for $2,000.

Bisbee, as president and manager of the Pioneer Fruit Company of San Francisco, had been on hand throughout most of the orchard era, encouraging and guiding the orchardists, both individually and through the Tehachapi Fruit Growers Association. The association, with a 1928 membership of twenty-two, only nine of whom were resident owners, struggled along attempting to maintain what they had originally expected to be a major economic crop for the region. Pioneer worked with the association in all aspects of orchard management as well as shipping fruit from the valley from a shed near the railroad depot.

—ELEVEN—

In the summer of 1939 there was a noticeable drop in the water table of the Tehachapi Valley which began to affect city wells. By 1940 grain planting had so substantially declined it was no longer considered a major cash crop. Altogether about 16,000 acres in the four valleys produced grains of any kind. Contributing to the decline was the lack of adequate rainfall for almost all of the Twentieth Century and the farmers' failure to summer fallow, plus their failure to follow good farming practices as we know them today. Labor costs were up, rainfall was down, and many farmers looked for a more lucrative product.

This is not to suggest that grain disappeared completely from the scene. Marginal lands are still dry-farmed, and the mid-1970's are seeing new acreage turned to the plow, but at least farmers don't have a problem that existed in 1911 and 1913. The State Horticultural Commissioner urged the extermination of the Russian thistle in Tehachapi to prevent the town from being quarantined so that no hay or grain could be shipped out.

The lowest point in orchard acreage was 1947 when only 115 of the district's many thousanded acres were producing — including the original Kiser apples, and Denison's pears (now owned by J. G. Bisbee).

As early as 1929 Roy Jones noticed a change in the agricultural scene. With a number of orchards dead or already pulled, he began to "pin my hopes of the future not on pears so much as on onions, potatoes, and other things. We have a portion of the Y orchard about ten acres -- leased to the former agricultural advisor of Kern Co., and he is conducting some scientific experiments with seed potatoes . . ." In two years the "Y" orchard was completely pulled and planted in potatoes.

Coincident with the change in agricultural production was the arrival on the long road to Tehachapi of a new breed of immigrants, regional Americans migrating from one section to another.

The vicissitudes of the Dust-Bowl years in the mid-1930's and 1940's, coupled with the depressive economy, forced hundreds of families to uproot themselves from the soil of the Midwest and head to the West. They arrived at a time when their labor was needed in the farming of row crops, especially the acres of potatoes grown during the war years of the Forties.

They came by the hundreds, crossing the Western United States in their burdened automobiles, escaping the drought and the economy. John Steinbeck's "Grapes of Wrath" described the tattered masses, but they were not unlike many others who, for a variety of reasons before them, had sought a new life out West.

"All night they bored through the hot darkness, and jackrabbits scuttled into the lights and dashed away in long jolting leaps," penned Steinbeck of the Joads, the stars in his epic. "And the dawn came up behind them when the lights of Mojave were ahead. And the dawn showed high mountains to the west. They filled with water and oil at Mojave and crawled into the mountains, and the dawn was about them.

"Tom said, 'Jesus, the desert's past! Pa, Al, for Christ sakes! The desert's past!' " words which were shouted out many times through the years of migration on the long road.

" 'I'm too goddamn tired to care,' said Al.

" 'Want me to drive?'

" 'No, wait awhile.'

"They drove through Tehachapi in the morning glow, and the sun came up behind them, and then — suddenly they saw the great valley below them. Al jammed on the brake and stopped in the middle of the road, and 'Jesus Christ! Look!' The vineyards, the orchards, the great green and beautiful, the trees set in rows, and the farm houses."

The Joads drove on through Tehachapi into the San Joaquin Valley to achieve literary fame there through Steinbeck's best seller. But many other Midwesterners passed through and returned again, or came and stayed. And many are still here, their distinct dialect quickly revealing their origins; their hard work and close familial and regional ties binding them together.

For about twenty years a series of "row" crops were planted which dominated the agricultural scene. Potatoes were the first, planted initially for seed and sale to other areas. With the outbreak of the Second World War, however, a need for large quantities of table potatoes and the Government's promise of financial benefits, resulted in every available acre with water planted to the first major row crop.

In excess of 5,000 acres was cultivated, primarily with winter russets, and the Tehachapis had a new large crop acreage. Because the potatoes were handpicked, although a machine dug them to the surface, a huge force was required for the backbreaking labor. "All the locals who would work did, and the rest came in," recalled Brad Krauter, retired Kern County Agricultural Inspector. It was nothing," he added, "for 300 to 500 transients to hit the area."

Potatoes sold high and many of the growers during the peak period of the war years made good money from the crop. Some of them were farmers from the Southern San Joaquin Valley who came into the Tehachapis, not to live, but to plant. One observer of the time remembers some of the "biggest poker games in the state were located in the Tehachapi Valley then . . . It was nothing to see $5,000 in a pot."

Because the crop was so lucrative, repeated plantings on much of the same acreage caused the land to become infected with potato diseases. Potato farming, which had peaked during the war, gradually decreased until it trickled to just a few farmers having such crops in the mid-1970's.

Other row crops were also introduced, all of which fared well until the Tehachapi District found itself unable to compete economically with other areas. Sugar beet seed was first planted in 1946, when there was as yet little demand for it. Grown for Farrar-Loomis Seed Company in Hemet, California, the seed had high yield and brought good prices. Its peak production lasted about two or three years, when it began to wane, although it continued into the 1950's.

J. C. Jacobsen and Don Carroll, both of whom had farmed other row crops, first planted alfalfa seed in 1950. It had a profitable market and expanded throughout Kern County, although the Tehachapi region, for five years or so, was the center of the certified alfalfa seed industry in California. Shipments were exported to Canada as well as to other foreign countries.

According to Mr. Carroll, Tehachapi was a "clean area, alfalfa hay had not been grown to any extent, but although it was a successful crop for several years, it too declined in production when the price went down and economically the region couldn't compete with other areas."

A major reason for the constant switching of crops in the 1940's and 1950's, according to Mr. Jacobsen, was change in the market demand, as well as economics and the water picture. "Those who didn't switch," he explained, "didn't survive."

Yet another agri-industry begun in the 1950's was grass seed — fescue and Merion Kentucky bluegrass — with Claude Botkin, Jacobsen, Carroll, Grant and Marty Sullivan, Gene Mettler, and Frank Goodrick, as primary producers. The area soon established a reputation for growing quality seed, and sod growers in the East flew out to inspect the fields. They encouraged Jacobsen to plant sod grass which he began in 1960.

Sod grass continues successfully today although the firm is now owned by Nunes Turfgrass which, in 1975, had 300 acres planted, leased Jacobsen's original sixty acres, and contracted with Grant Sullivan for another seventy-five. According to Wad Young, local manager, further expansion is at a standstill because of the cost of buying imported water.

While grains, alfalfa, grasses, potatoes, and other row crops continue to be grown in the Tehachapi region in the 1970's, their economic impact for large numbers of farmers has diminished markedly. Of the many crops grown through the years, the one remaining today as a major economic contributor to the agri-industry of the region was also one of the earliest.

As the second half of the Twentieth Century began, Tehachapi agriculture was at a low ebb, this condition existing in much of California. Both Carroll and Jacobsen, innovative farmers in the district, believed still another new specialty crop was needed. After observing the yearly success of Bisbee's pears, they seriously considered planting that fruit. But they had also watched the monetary return from the five acres of peaches at the Linda Vista Ranch of Henry Hand's and his uncle's, Lance Estes, which began to bear about 1952. In 1956 Mr. Jacobsen planted his first orchard in both peaches and pears, followed soon thereafter by Carroll and Fred Patterson doing the same. Others joined them, and with proper care and cultivation fruit production has again become a viable economic factor.

In 1954, in an article for the December 23rd issue of The Tehachapi News, Roy E. Ballard, a Work Unit Conservationist, referred to the Tehachapis as "The Valleys of Seed," and some of his remarks picture a capsulated view of the end of yet another era in Tehachapi's agricultural history.

He wrote of "Marveling at the graphic scene of field after field of many species of plants being raised for seed production," and described them "Spread out like a patch-work quilt on the valley floor, and catching the sweet aroma of the alfalfa blossoms, wafted to his nostrils by the gentle breezes. and a few miles farther west, the thrill is repeated a second and a third time as Brites Valley and Cummings Valley come into view. . .

"The wide-awake landowners of this section, such as Claude Botkin, Don I. Carroll, Bud Cummings, C. and W. C. Handel, J. C. Jacobsen, Jr., Jake Ratzlaff, Ben Sasia, and Edward Schnaidt, have projected the task of seed growing to a point where it will gross an income of over a million dollars annually . . ."

Referring to the potatoes still being grown in the region, Ballard lauded, "Yields of over 400 sacks per acre are being produced . . ."

He was also impressed with harvesting techniques. "Man's ingenuity was really tested in harvesting the alfalfa seed. Result; the development of a special windrower, as used on the Henning Ranch, by which the alfalfa was cut and windrowed preparatory to threshing. On the Henry Kirschenmann Ranch, the next step in the process was being carried out.

"An interesting innovation was displayed on the Grand Oaks Ranch, owned and operated by Don I. Carroll. Special adjustments and extra attachments were applied to a standard grain binder to catch the shattered seed of the Akaroa orchard grass that would otherwise be lost in the reaping process. The gleanings thus gathered more than paid the bill for harvesting and threshing. After curing in the bundles, the seed was hulled by means of a stationary thresher. As shown on the Jacobsen Bros. ranch.

"Two methods of threshing were generally employed for Merion bluegrass. On the Grand Oaks Ranch, the bundles were placed in shocks to dry, then gathered and threshed by a stationary thresher. The Jacobsen Bros. applied a novel style. The bundles, immediately after cutting, were moved to a central location and placed onto a heavy paper that had been spread onto the ground. When sufficiently dried, a stationary thresher was brought to the site and the seed extracted from the husk. Any shattered seed being retrieved from the paper which had been placed under the bundles.

"Still another style of threshing was used by Ben Sasia on his ranch in Cummings Valley. He used a portable rig to thresh his sugar beet seeds. And harvested an astounding reward. An average yield of over 6700 pounds of seed per acre.

"The seed story does not end when the crop has been harvested and threshed," continued Ballard's explanation of the industry. "Then the process of cleaning the seed so as to prepare a high quality product for the market begins. To accomplish that task, two seed companies: the J. C. Loomis Seed Company and the Tehachapi Seed Company, have established plants in Tehachapi. After passing through the cleaning plant, the quality product is ready for market." Samples of the seed were also drawn and forwarded to the state agency for sampling for purity and germination test, after which the seed became a state certified seed which commanded a premium price.

A variety of conditions continued to affect the farmers during the 1950's and 1960's although they experimented, often successfully, with new crops which peaked and ebbed during that time. Real property taxes went up as did labor costs. The day when a man worked for $1.00 was in the distant past. General operating costs also went up; and the water table, predicted in 1911 to supply the area forever, dropped drastically. Some wells went dry. Land values in the region had not changed for many years and were at $275 to $300 per acres. Something had to happen.

In 1947 the Tehachapi Soil Conservation District was organized as a necessary advisor to the fluctuating farm industry. It was formed to solve "very urgent soil conservation problems on their farms and on a community wide basis." Three land use areas were involved: 17,500 acres of dry farmland, 9,500 acres of irrigated land, and 111,350 acres of potential rangeland. With Mr. Jacobsen as president of a board consisting of Al and Doris Bailey, and Sam Iriart, the District attempted to assist the farmers in its 138,050 acre area. In 1948 contour irrigation systems were laid out, surveys were made for land leveling, and other conservation matters were investigated and studied. Applications for assistance were

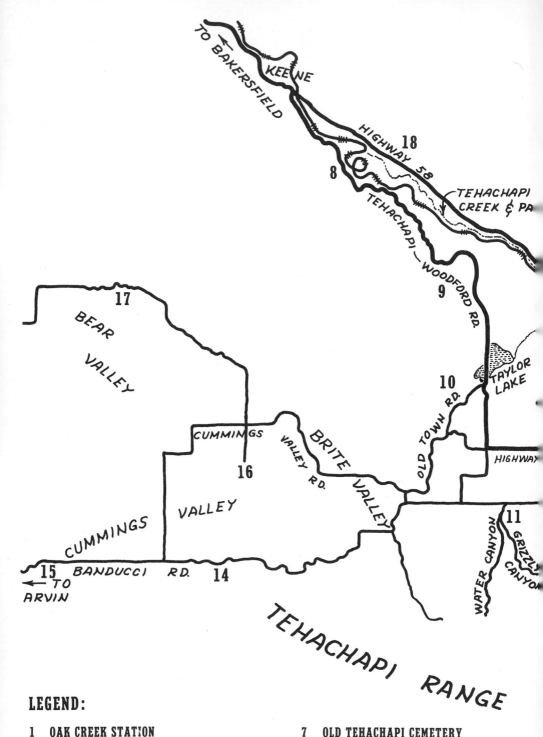

LEGEND:

1	OAK CREEK STATION	7	OLD TEHACHAPI CEMETERY
2	CAMERON STATION	8	TEHACHAPI LOOP
3	QUARRY RUINS	9	HALTER GRADE
4	LOS ANGELES — HAVILAH ROAD	10	OLD TOWN
5	MONOLITH VILLAGE	11	CHINA HILL
6	GREENWICH	12	PINE TREE MINE

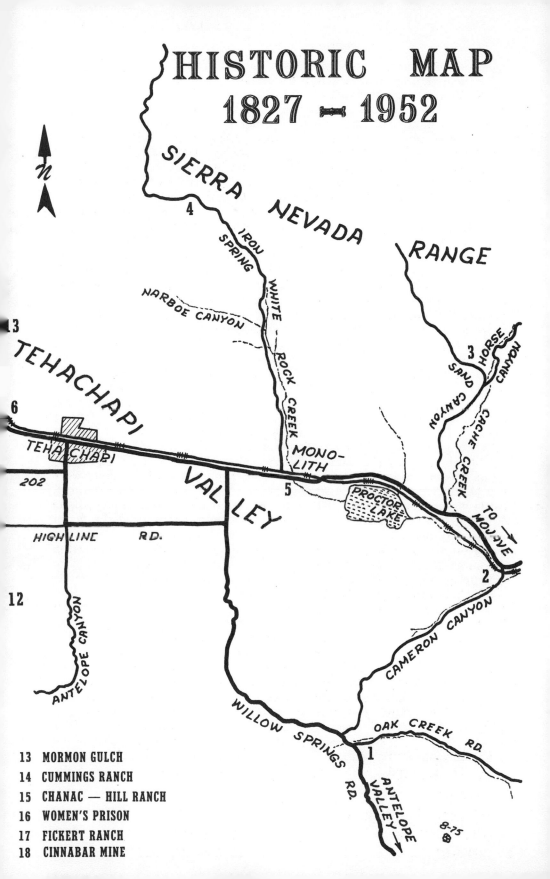

HISTORIC MAP
1827 — 1952

SIERRA NEVADA

RANGE

4

IRON SPRING

WHITE

NARBOE CANYON

ROCK CREEK

13

3

HORSE CANYON

SAND CANYON

CACHE CREEK

TEHACHAPI

6

TEHACHAPI

MONO-LITH

VALLEY

5

PROCTOR LAKE

TO MOJAVE

202

HIGH LINE RD.

12

ANTELOPE CANYON

2

CAMERON CANYON

WILLOW SPRINGS RD.

OAK CREEK RD.

1

ANTELOPE VALLEY

8-75

13   MORMON GULCH
14   CUMMINGS RANCH
15   CHANAC — HILL RANCH
16   WOMEN'S PRISON
17   FICKERT RANCH
18   CINNABAR MINE

received that year from owners of over half the district's acreage.

By the early 1960's, if agriculture was to continue as an economic force in the District, water had to be found. When the Soil Conservation District was formed, the farmers became keenly aware of water conservation. But it was not until 1963 that a small group of area farmers formed the Tehachapi-Cummings Water Conservation District and had preliminary reports prepared. However, during a time lag from 1963 to 1969, the assessed valuation of the District tripled and, at the same time, inflation increased prospective costs by about one-third over the original projections. This didn't deter the voters, though, who in 1971 approved a $6.5 million loan and a $2.5 million bond issue so the re-named Tehachapi-Cummings County Water District could finance a water importation project.

Ground breaking on June 17, 1972, at the Brite Valley storage reservoir site of the aqueduct system to bring Feather River water into the Tehachapi basin came none too soon. From 8,896 irrigated acres in 1957 farmland had decreased to 2,416 acres by the end of 1971. A basin overdraft grew from 3,000 acre feet annually to 9,000 acre feet, representing three billion gallons of water removed and not replaced by annual rainfall or runoff from the surrounding mountains.

In November 1973 the thirty-three mile pipeline with its four strategically located pumping plants carried the first water to the reservoir. By autumn 1974 the groundwater condition had already improved, according to district manager Robert Jasper, even though small domestic wells, the City of Tehachapi, and the Golden Hills Community Services District were allowed to continue pumping to avoid the high cost of treating imported water for domestic use.

With the future agricultural industry assured because of the aqueduct, let us look into history. It does repeat itself. Even in the 1800's there were dry years. The early 1860's were very bad — the grass never greened, cattle weren't fed. In July 1877 John Brite bought Hendrickson's China Hill placer mines for $2,000, but not for the gold. He wanted the water rights. An observer remarked, "It is Mr. Brite's purpose to utilize the water on his valuable farm nearby when irrigation should be required in the summer and to lease or run the mines during the winter."

Brite proved his knowledge of the land earlier, however, when he sought water in another way. He owned over 1,000 acres of enclosed land, much of it under cultivation, and lived comfortably with his wife and ten children in an adobe house, surrounded by a complex of houses and barns that made him one of the biggest ranchers in the region. In 1875 the "most interesting feature of his improvement," commented a visitor, "is his water supply. On the opposite side of the ridge that separates his premises from Cummings Valley is a fine spring noted for the purity and excellence of the waters." He explained, "This, by means of a tunnel 300 feet in length, runs through the country rock, he has tapped and brought out a fine stream for the use of his farm." It was gravity fed as wooden troughs carried the water downhill to the farm.

In 1973 I visited the spring in a fire truck! On the grounds of the

California Correctional Institution, with Fire Chief Laughlin as chauffeur and amiable guide, the truck struggled up a steep grade, where we parked and walked a few hundred feet to the spring, but the years have taken their toll, as Brite's spring, too, had dried up. A brick wall secured the entry to the tunnel through which the pure water once flowed. Chief Laughlin recalled that the Institution used the spring until the late 1960's when the county labeled it "contaminated" whereupon it became reserve fire water. The women's prison originally used the spring as a major source of drinking water; however, as its population increased, wells were drilled and new sources of supply augmented the "purity and excellence of the waters." Finally, one day in 1972, the spring that had watered man, beast, and crop for countless years (even the Indians knew that spot as evidenced by their ubiquitous bedrock mortars), the water ceased to come altogether.

Forever? We will never know, but one day after my visit, another tunnel of metal pipe was driven through the "country rock," carrying water where water once flowed freely, right through the tunnel that was. With one great surge inward and upward the Feather River water, in a last burst of energetic motion, came to Brite Valley, to irrigate a whole District.

The Town

Of the million and a half people living in California in 1906, over a third lived within a 75 mile radius of San Francisco. Subtract also those who lived in the population clusters of Southern California, and it became clear just how empty was the countryside and how isolated remained rural life.

Kevin Starr in Americans and the California Dream

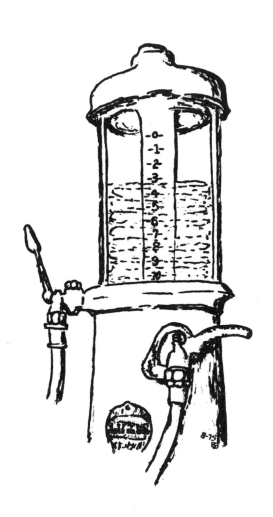

—ONE—

It's late at night. The sounds of day have diminished into the restful slumber of purple darkness. A town sleeps, as only an occasional barking dog, meowing cat, whirring tire of a midnight motorist disrupts the silent stillness.

Then, out of the distance, a new sound reaches across the plain. A piercing whistle strikes the darkness as the clackety-clack of car on track adds a melody to the strains of a passing train. For one hundred years, day after day, as year became decade and a century passed by on parade, the sound has been constant and the same.

The Southern Pacific Railroad arrived at the base of the Tehachapi Mountains in 1875. Construction of the line had been continuous since 1869 and the county's papers printed articles of hope and anticipation. In October 1873 the Havilah Miner commented, when ". . . the Southern Pacific will be completed to that point," referring to Tehachapi, "when a junction will be formed with the great Owen River country — Cerro Gordo, Lone Pine, Independence, Panamint and Death Valley. Then Tehachapi will be the liveliest place in Kern County, if we are not mistaken in our figures."

In February 1875 as the rails pushed forward, the Kern Weekly Courier remarked, "We found in Tehachapi and adjoining Valleys a larger population and more improvements than we had expected to see, but as the country is extensive it is still very sparsely settled and the band of men has done little more than make a visible impression; . . ."

In 1853 Lieutenant R. S. Williamson together with Lieutenants J. G. Parke and George M. Anderson as well as a crew of twenty-three men, surveyed and suggested the route through the Tehachapi Mountains. This group spent several weeks exploring the area before deciding Tehachapi Canyon was the most practical railroad route (35). As early as 1844 John C. Fremont, while traveling along what he named Pass Creek, now known as Tehachapi Creek, noted the canyon was suitable for a stage and railroad route.

Track laying was not difficult until the barrier of the Tehachapi Range was reached. The engineers were faced with the problem of rising 4,000 feet to traverse forty-six miles. So impossible did most people believe this to be, that Caliente was presumed to be the terminus of the railroad and a big land boom occurred there, but the engineers were not to be foiled by a mere mountain.

The Tehachapi Grade was conquered by Chief Engineer William Hood, who initiated a novel technique when, instead of surveying upward, he began at the summit of the Tehachapi Pass and surveyed a right-of-way downward, curving it with the contour of the slopes. Early one morning Hood is supposed to have staked out what is now known as the Tehachapi or Walong Loop, resembling two large circles drawn with a giant

119

A long Santa Fe Railway freight train is stretched around the Tehachapi Loop. Freight trains longer than 85 cars pass over themselves as they curve around the circle. (Santa Fe Railway)

compass, measuring 3,794 feet in length.

Eighteen tunnels were constructed between Caliente and Tehachapi Summit, aggregating 8,240 feet and 8,300 degrees of curvature, the whole on a 2.2 grade. Timbering of eleven by fourteen inch redwood was used in the tunnels, which were twenty-two feet high and sixteen-and-a-half-feet wide.

The material used in track laying included rails thirty feet long, six feet longer than usual, to give a smoother ride. Fish plates or joints were used instead of chair joints. Twelve inches of ballast was laid, with six inches under ties, although in an eight-mile section near Caliente, six feet of fill was required. The tracks were laid on ties of Mendocino redwood, 2,800 to the mile.

And once again Chinese laborers appeared in the mountains, this time as the monumental work force that built the railroad through the Tehachapis. About 3,000 workmen came from Canton, China, and when their job was finished the immigrants spread out over the county, many of them settling in Bakersfield, but others following their predecessors in the search for gold at abandoned mines and tailings.

After several months of construction the monumental ascent of Tehachapi Canyon's southern flank was finished and on July 10, 1876, the rails arrived on the Tehachapi plain. Two months later, on September 5, 1876 the rail link connecting San Francisco with Los Angeles was completed at Lang Station, north of Los Angeles and near present day Newhall. Such was the excitement of this momentous event that a special train carried invited guests southward, including a reporter for the Sacramento Daily Record-Union who telegraphed his dispatches en route.

"'I had no idea of the magnitude of the work,' said an eminent San Francisco banker, as he viewed the wonderful route by which we had ascended the Tehachapi canyon. Every little way from Caliente to the summit — a distance of 20 miles — some new and wonderful feat of engineering skill has been performed; here a chasm has been filled and there another is walled up with solid masonry; in one place, we are clinging to the face of a precipice and in another we are in a deep cut, whose precipitous walls rise upwards on either side to a great hight (sic).

". . . The track winds its way up the steep mountain in sinuous folds, that over-top each other in a succession of terraces; the broken mountains are repeatedly tunneled, and every artifice has to be employed to enable the engine to climb the steep grade . . .''

In Mojave the reporter looked at the last stage to Los Angeles "and the venerable coach was drawn up alongside the depot . . . On its side was painted 'San Francisco and Los Angeles.' The driver had a sullen, dissatisfied look, and showed plainly in every feature that he considered his coach and six the equal of any train on the Southern Pacific Railroad. What a contrast," exclaimed the reporter, "to our swift flying trip to Los Angeles is the slow, lumbering speed of the stage coach!''

One era ended as another began. In 1875 the Telegraph Stage Company connected the southern terminus of the Southern Pacific's construction at Caliente with Los Angeles via Tehachapi and Oak Creek Passes, switching over from the Tejon route it had been using. The Los Angeles-to-Havilah route by way of White Rock Creek fell into disuse only a few years before, as the county seat transferred to Bakersfield and interest in Havilah declined.

At least two roads entered the Tehachapi Valley from the west as the Telegraph commenced operations. The original Kern River Road, a mere wagon track in the 1850's down the canyon floor, fell into disuse in favor of the safer road from Old Town over what is known today as Halter Grade and down the contours of the mountain to Comb's Station, near the Broome Overpass of a Twentieth Century freeway.

In 1872 Anson Cross, freighting supplies to and from the San Joaquin Valley, made minor repairs to the wagon road so it would be at least passable for increasing team activity. In July 1873 Peter Greene opened a toll road from Comb's Station to Tehachapi Summit, following an easier grade on the slopes north of Tehachapi Creek, and located his toll house east of Comb's Station, but with the completion of the railroad, by 1878 it was little used, and the main avenue of traffic, besides the iron rails, was the road from Old Town.

"It was bright and early one morning in the winter of 1875-76 that the writer found himself one of a party which uncomfortably filled a big six-horse Concord coach that pulled out of Caliente up the long grade

121

toward the Tehachapi summit," wrote journalist George F. Weeks who was on the journey. "With the exception of the grading camps scattered along the line of the proposed railroad there was no settlement in all that distance, while even at the latter place there was scarcely enough to be dignified by the name of hamlet. The most vivid recollection remaining of that portion of the trip was a so-called 'dinner' eaten at Tehachapi — said 'dinner' consisting of 'Arizona strawberries' (which for the benefit of the uninitiated should be translated as just plain red beans), soda biscuits, yellow as gold and hard almost as cobblestones, stewed dried apples seasoned with flies, and black coffee, and for which a good hard 'dollar of our daddies' was demanded. The recollection and taste of that delectable meal abode with the eaters thereof, or at least one of them, for many days, and I never pass through Tehachapi to this day without still tasting the soda and the flies."

Weeks retained other memories of that journey, recalling: "As was always the case with a party of stage coach travelers in those days, it did not take long for all the passengers to become on the best of terms with each other, and a right jolly party they were. Stories were told, jokes cracked, and a stage of familiarity was reached which may be described as that wherein one and all were almost ready to confide to the others what their real names were when at home east of the Mississippi, and what had been the moving cause for their more or less sudden immigration to a healthier clime . . . ."

Weeks described a crusty old salt, a "forty-niner" who took note of his recent arrival in California by indicating Weeks' failure to carry any blankets. The Argonaut explained: "Well, you're the only one of the outfit that didn't have any, and I spotted you at once for a tenderfoot. If you'd lived in California six months you would have known better than to have started on a stage ride that would keep you out all night without taking some blankets along to keep yourself warm." The wisdom of that remark became apparent later.

"Some time after leaving Tehachapi the road passed through a range of hills and then down their flanks into a vast apparently level plain." They were on the "Mojarvey desert" headed for Los Angeles.

When correspondent Weeks rode the stage through the Tehachapi Valley, Peter D. Greene was engaged in founding another community in the valley, which he called Greenwich. In 1875 Greene constructed a large building located at the summit of the pass, which housed a saloon and post office. There was also an express and telegraph office, and a hotel and bar operated by Adelia Ward. The Los Angeles Stage kept a relay of horses at Greenwich, as it was adjacent to the toll road Greene built.

Greene anticipated the railroad depot of the Southern Pacific Company being established at Greenwich when the tracks arrived in the Tehachapi Valley, but the Southern Pacific had other ideas and located Summit Station a mile eastward. By the beginning of 1878 the buildings were moved to the new town and Greenwich disappeared.

Some years later after traveling from the Owens Valley to Mojave to board a train for Bakersfield, Mary Austin described some problems in riding the stage:

"If one happened not to know enough to engage in advance the seat beside the driver, the trip was rather a horror, crowded into the stuffy interior between 'oldtimers,' liquor salesmen, mining experts, an occasional stray 'girl' from the local bawdy-house, or one of those distressed and distressfully pitiable 'lungers' of whom you had the grace only to hope that he wouldn't die on your shoulder."

There were still other thought-provoking instructions for the would-be traveler wherever he went:

"The best seat inside a stage is the one next to the driver. Even if you have a tendency to seasickness when riding backwards — you'll get over it and will get less jolts and jostling. Don't let any 'sly elph' trade you his mid-seat.

"In cold weather don't ride with tight-fitting boots, shoes, or gloves. When the driver asks you to get off and walk do so without grumbling, he won't request it unless absolutely necessary. If the team runs away — sit still and take your chances. If you jump, nine out of ten times you will get hurt.

"In very cold weather abstain entirely from liquor when on the road; because you will freeze twice as quickly when under its influence. Don't growl at the food received at the station; stage companies generally provide the best they can get.

"Don't keep the stage waiting. Don't smoke a strong pipe inside the coach — spit on the leeward side. If you have anything to drink in a bottle pass it around. Procure your stimulants before starting as 'ranch' (Stage Depot) whiskey is not 'nectar.'

"Don't swear or lop over neighbors when sleeping. Take small change to pay expenses. Never shoot on the road as the noise might frighten the horses. Don't discuss politics or religion. Don't point out where murders have been committed especially if there are women passengers.

"Don't lag at the wash basin. Don't grease your hair, because travel is dusty. Don't imagine for a moment that you are going on a picnic. Expect annoyances, discomfort, and some hardship."

Perhaps his impressions of the countryside were gained while he whipped the horses across the Tehachapi Valley in the course of several years staging in the Tehachapis. In 1877 William Hamilton who owned the Telegraph Stage Company for a short period during that decade, made his first purchase in the Tehachapis, buying property near the salt lake from the railroad. In 1879 he purchased two other properties at the lake — from John Hendrickson and John Narboe.

Hamilton's reputation as a stageman of thirty years' experience was known throughout the West. Beginning in 1850 he had whipped horses in Oregon and Nevada, and prior to his involvement in the stage lines of Southern California, he owned a line of stages between Colfax and Grass Valley in the Northern Sierra Nevada Mountains.

In 1898 the famous Major Benjamin C. Truman reminisced about his longtime friend William Hamilton, when Truman wrote for the Overland Magazine: "Short, stout, jolly Billy Hamilton is known as one of the oldest and best drivers upon the Pacific coast . . . . He could handle the 'ribbons' with any of them for thirty years, . . . Billy was fond of his 'tod' when not driving. For twenty-five years he made more money than he knew what to do with, and he literally threw it away. He was generous to a fault and has loaned more twenty-dollar gold pieces in his life than he could ever get back than you could put in a peck measure. I have ridden with Billy in the Sierra, through the Mojave desert, and over the Coast range, and considered him one of the most delightful whips in the world. He weighs 190 pounds and is sixty-five years old, and although he has struck bed-rock pretty closely a number of times, he was often helped out by Leland Stanford and Charles Crocker, (who never went back on any of the forty-niners who had done them a service), and now owns a pretty ranch in Kern county, where he resides when he is not at the Palace Hotel in San Francisco, playing 'cinch' for half bottles of Extra Dry.''

Eric Francis, a former Wells Fargo employee, recalled, ''Then we had the famous Bill Hamilton of Stage Coach fame, bald as a billiard ball and most profane: . . .''

Hamilton's reputation followed him wherever he went. The Los Angeles Star praised him in December 1873 as ''A noble, generous, industrious, honest man among men; he is known as a prince among his fellows, and just as good, kind and humane to a horse or a dog as he is to a man or woman!'' In that city, too, he had a reputation for heavy drinking; some said he was able to drink the entire town of Los Angeles under the table and still possess an appetite for a full course dinner washed down with goblets of Verv Clicquot.

During the important days of the Independence and Owens River mining in the late 1860's and 1870's, Hamilton held all the important mail contracts to that area. In March 1873 the Star reported that Hamilton and his partner Roberts were ''running the largest piece of staging in the world.''

At his death in San Francisco, while Hamilton had lost his fortune, he had many friends. Wealthy men, notable in the building of the state, arranged for his last rites and the burial of one of California's noted stagemen.

If the culmination of rail construction in California in 1876 was the end of staging on some major routes, it did not entirely doom the stage to extinction. Localized travel between small communities, avenues where no rail transportation existed, continued to be served by the stage-and-six.

As the Nineteenth Century closed and a new day dawned, staging continued. The late Victor Phillips, born in 1887 near Cambria, arrived in the Tehachapis in the early 1900's. He enjoyed a rugged life as a whip at an early age, and loved to talk about the past. When he was about sixteen, Mr. Phillips drove a public stage for Bennett and Wallace on a route from Caliente up the creek by the same name to the Piute Post Office, located at the base of Piute Mountain. The trip took about six hours, leaving Caliente at nine in the morning, stopping at Millerville for lunch, and arriving at the post office at about three in the afternoon. Mr. Phillips couldn't recall any ''movie-style stage robbers; the only trouble I had was carrying drunk miners back to the diggings at Piute Mountain.''

In 1974 ninety-year-old Duncan Monroe, a contemporary of Phillips', recalled how he had driven the stage when he was a boy of ''about nineteen" from Mojave to "18 Mile House." On a bright winter day as we drove along the desert macadam north to Mojave, Mr. Monroe suddenly said to me, "That's where it was," and pointed to a bare alfalfa field next to the road just south of Cinco. From 18-Mile House Mr. Monroe's brother Ed drove the stage to Randsburg. He laughed as he recalled the one time Ed was held up and the "United States mail was stolen," referring to the U. S. Mail Stage Line Co. which operated between Randsburg and Mojave.

Mr. Monroe's father was a victim of the notorious bandit Tiburcio Vasquez, when Vasquez and a compadre robbed the stage at Freeman's Station near Coyote Holes, down on the desert. The bandits first stopped a traveler on the road, bound him and left him on the ground. According to Mr. Monroe, the traveler was his father Donald who, after releasing his bonds, went to the station and untied the robbery victims.

"Sinks of Tehachapa, Ca." as photographed by Alex Gardner during an 1867-68 surveying trip for the Kansas Pacific Railroad. This later became known as Cameron's Station (Home Insurance Co. of New York)

Donald Monroe was another Argonaut who found his way to the Tehachapis. A native of New York State where he was born in 1839, he arrived in California twenty years later after a sea voyage that took him across the Isthmus of Panama and up the coast to San Francisco. From there he went to Sierra County for several years and arrived in the Tehachapi Valley about 1865. He farmed, raised stock and, in the early

1870's, drove a stage between Havilah and Los Angeles, and Havilah and Santa Barbara.

Soon after the Southern Pacific was completed, William Sawyer, his wife Eliza, and their two daughters, arrived at the railroad siding of Cameron; however, within a year Sawyer passed away and the widowed Eliza married Donald Monroe. Her two little daughters also died, but she and Donald raised their own family of six children. Mrs. Monroe was born in 1843 in New Orleans, Louisiana, and while she was still a baby her parents, the Theriots, moved to St. Paul, Minnesota, where she remained until the Civil War; and after her marriage to Sawyer they moved to Los Angeles.

The Monroes bought a stage station. George Wash Cameron and his brother Alexander mined in the Tehachapi Valley in the 1860's, and Wash later settled at the junction of the canyon that took his name and the road to the desert. There, as the Eastern California trade picked up in the late 1860's and early Seventies, he operated a station for stages and freighters. Until 1914 when the stage station was destroyed, it was the Monroes' home.

—TWO—

Completion of the tracks into the Tehachapi Valley brought the long anticipated Iron Horse, but not to the town of Williamsburg. Located as it was at the foot of Black Mountain, the commercial center of the Tehachapis was four miles too far from the depot. The town born in 1869, the same year as the railroad began, tried for a while to ignore the ominous growth of a new community next to the tracks. By 1885, gasping for breath as families and merchants moved to Summit Station, as the new town was first called, little remained at Old Town to invite continued life. And so, as the railroad gave life to one town, it brought the demise of another.

Beginning in 1876 new Tehachapi began to grow, its initial birthpangs and adolescence guided and controlled by the same company that birthed the town, the Western Development Company of the Southern Pacific Railroad. By Acts of Congress on July 27, 1866 and March 3, 1871, several railroads were awarded grants-of-land in alternate sections in the amount of 12,800 acres per mile along their proposed rights-of-way, the federal government retaining the sections in-between. All along the track of the Southern Pacific, odd-sectioned lands came under their control which added up to approximately sixteen percent of California's federally owned lands. This was the case at Summit Station, which was part of the railroad grant.

The development company began to convey its property in 1877, both at Summit and throughout the four valleys. The usual fee for grant-land was $2.50 an acre, although the price varied according to its quality and situation. Four methods of payment were available: payment in full at time of purchase was the first method; the other three were long term options with annual interest of seven percent, but regardless of the option

126

MAP

OF THE TOWN OF

TEHACHAPI

KERN CO. CAL.

S½ OF NW ¼ N½ OF SW ¼ - SEC 21

T 32 S R 33 E

M.D.B & M.

Surveyed 1885

Scale 200 Feet to One Inch

FILED OCT 5 1892
N.R. Packard Recorder
By H.L. Packard Deputy

selected, the entire payment in every case had to be made within five years.

Many settlers were used to land company schemes as they were an integral part of the opening of the frontier as it moved westward until it could move no more. Much of the West was opened up by speculators who followed explorers and trappers into the wilderness. With vague maps they sold farms and homesites on a frontier they had never seen. Many of Tehachapi's original settlers or their ancestors, were in Kentucky and Missouri in the Eighteenth and Nineteenth Centuries when vast areas were opened to settlement by these development companies.

Although surveyed in 1885, the original map of Tehachapi was not recorded until 1892 at which time property owners in the town and throughout the Tehachapis took legal title to the railroad land. That many years passed before the final patents to the Southern Pacific were approved by the Federal Government, on December 1, 1891, and the railroad conveyed the property to Western Development Company on February 6, 1892.

Sometime between 1876 and 1885, the development company platted the town; the original street names remained the same; and streets today honor area residents, nearby locales, and national figures. The company obviously anticipated growth to the south as, by using letters for bisecting avenues, it left out the first two of the alphabet, beginning with C Street.

Along the line of the Southern Pacific's tracks, especially in the fertile San Joaquin and Tulare Valleys, settlement by wheat farmers on valuable railroad land was fraught with grave consequences, as they farmed alongside the tracks. The years between settlement and filing of the federal patents were tumultuous and violent. In the lore of the Tehachapis, however, that situation did not exist. The reason may be that the canyon up which the railroad climbed, the "dry plain" across which it moved after reaching the valley floor, wasn't the obvious vast fertile land at lower elevations. Passenger rates not pro-rated for shorter distances and freight rates almost equaling those from New York to San Francisco were the two major complaints of area residents and agriculturists.

This continuous disaffection and persistent complaints of the lower valley's farmers did affect the Tehachapis, however, when in the 1890's a second railroad initiated service through the mountains. Highly discriminatory local freight rates by the Southern Pacific, as well as the line's alleged monopolistic tendencies and domination of political life (according to the farmers), resulted in a committee of shippers in June 1893 attempting to establish their own railroad from Stockton to Bakersfield. Organized as the San Francisco and San Joaquin Valley Railroad, but popularly referred to as the "people's railroad," they were off to a slow start because of fear of retaliation. In January 1895, however, another comittee meeting showed some signs of progress as vast sums of money were raised to construct the line. A half-million-dollar donation came from Claus Spreckels, the leading sugar refiner on the Pacific Coast. Large donations by his two sons, as well as contributions of both money and land by metropolitan areas, which were also affected by the Southern Pacific's freight rates, resulted in the beginning of construction at Stockton on July 22, 1895 and the line was completed to Bakersfield on May 27, 1898.

In the meantime, the Atchison, Topeka, and Santa Fe Railroad had entered California at Needles, extending its line to Mojave by way of Barstow and also to Los Angeles. It was no surprise to the owners of the "Valley Road," or to observers of the competition swiftly cutting into Southern Pacific, when Santa Fe began negotiations to purchase the competing line, assuring the owners it would be preserved at all costs.

Once again the awesome Tehachapi Mountains had to be crossed in order for Santa Fe to compete with the Southern Pacific. Historians differ as to the next scene in the power play. The railroads suggest a mere agreement between the two companies for Santa Fe to use the Southern Pacific's track. Considering the keen competition between the lines, that answer is too simple. Early Kern County residents call it a case of blackmail. With Santa Fe threatening to build a road it had already surveyed, the Espee decided it better make an agreement and exert some control. On the other hand, Wallace Smith claimed in "Garden of the Sun," it was "covetousness." Espee wanted a branch road from Demming, New Mexico to Guaymas, Mexico, which was controlled by Santa Fe. Santa Fe wanted a route over the Tehachapis. However the route resulted, an agreement was consummated between the two companies on January 16, 1899, and ever since 1900 both lines have utilized the 67.38 miles of track between Kern Junction and Mojave, where the Santa Fe once again rolls on its own track.

By the time Santa Fe joined the parade the character of the trains had materially changed. Rail traffic through Tehachapi Canyon, across the valley, and into the desert was intensive and consistent from the beginning, and certainly more of an adventure than the modern engines and cars which pass this way today.

A Southern Pacific C-4 engine on the Tehachapi grade near Caliente in 1911. Note the coal fuel in the tender. This engine was built by Schenectady in 1901 (Ed Wiggins Collection)

The original engines burned wood or coal, as their ten wheels pulled the cars up the great ascent from Caliente — only sixteen air miles from Tehachapi, but 2,734 feet higher, crossing Tehachapi Creek seven times on the way. All along the line, at the many sidings that were constructed, small mountains of wood cut from the nearby mountains waited to feed the hungry boilers. Central Pacific's No. 222, built at the Schenectady works, an American Standard engine, was one of the first engines on the tracks, as was the C.P.'s No. 108, a Rogers plant 4-4-0, built in 1868 and

"El Gobernardor" — Circa 1890's (Southern Pacific Company)

named the Stager. Other engines on the Loop Route were named the Runner, Rusher, Rambler, Roller, Pacer, and Courser.

"Cook Hogs" were introduced in 1880, twelve-wheel engines weighing 120,000 pounds. This was the largest engine operated on the Tehachapi Grade until 1895, when a twelve-wheeler weighing 155,000 pounds went into action.

No engine equals the majesty of El Gobernador, who for a few short years provided helper service on the mighty climb up the mountains. When a train met him coming up, it hurried to a siding to let him go by as no one wanted to face this giant engine head-on. The 4-10-0 weighed 217,000 pounds and came to the tracks in March 1884. Created at the railroad's shops in Sacramento under supervision of general master mechanic A. J. Stevens, and named for Governor Leland Stanford (36), El Gobernador was acclaimed as the heaviest and most powerful engine in the world at the time. With its complement of twenty-four cars, the heaviest capacity was 40,000 pounds, it did the work of two "Cook Hogs;" its engineer and fireman were handpicked and specially trained.

El Gobernador had one major problem; it could only travel during daylight. And the ride down the hill was dizzying because it was backwards; it was too unsafe to turn the engine on the mountain or switch it to a siding. Daily, for over ten years El Gobernador conquered the mountain, until one day in 1894 it became "impractical," partly because the boiler furnished insufficient steam. The twelve-wheeler arrived on the scene and El Gobernador was broken up for scrap. The monster that defied the mountain was, in the end, defied by the mountain.

Tehachapi's early growth was a natural evolvement, slow and steady, not spectacular. In fact in August 1878 a complainant remarked, "Our railroad has not been to us a source of prosperity. Thousands of acres of land are still vacant."

But certain events occurred, both nationwide and statewide, to influence the arrival of new families. The collapse of the Los Angeles County land boom in the mid-1870's caused by decimating droughts, motivated many families to move northward, some to the four-valley Tehachapi system. In 1884 Benjamin Cummings Truman, one of California's chief publicists, trumpeted a call for a million "Well disposed, industrious people, who desire to better their conditions in life, to come to California and help to settle her vast territory . . . ." Potential settlers were given every consideration and encouragement. An advertisement assured "Persons who wish to buy from either the central or the Southern Pacific Company, can obtain a land-seeker's ticket, with a voucher for the cost of the ticket, which voucher will be accepted by the company as part payment for the land selected. Both companies publish instructive pamphlets for free distribution to people seeking homes in California."

During the 1880's, when another land boom affected the Los Angeles area and particularly the San Fernando Valley, an attempt was made to use the Southern Pacific as the thread along which a row of settlements would be built. There was even a halfhearted attempt in 1886 to promote Tehachapi, but the land was not as well situated for colonization and settlement as the San Fernando Valley flats, and promoters satisfied themselves instead with stressing Tehachapi's "resort possibilities."

As part of its nationwide promotion of rail travel, in 1884 Adams and Bishop published "The Pacific Tourist, a Trans-Continental Guide of Travel from The Atlantic to the Pacific Ocean" (37). One of the recommended tourist attractions was the Southern Pacific route through the Tehachapi Pass, which emblazoned, in part:

". . . the tourist will prefer to see for himself and his attention will be divided between the work and the scenery of the canon. The latter is not majestic, like that on the American River, but quite picturesque and often grand.

"Leaving Caliente, the Tehachapi Creek is lost sight of, and the road winds around among the hills."

As he began the climb up the mountain the passenger read of Bealeville, a small station honoring General Beale. Then, "After leaving Bealeville the road passes around Clear Creek Canon, one of the most formidable pieces of work on the mountain, having in it tunnels 3, 4, 5, and 6; and as you enter the canon, you see on the left the road ascending the opposite wall of the canon more than a hundred feet above, and it is only three or four hundred yards across the canon!

"The old road to Havilah and Kernville appears like a trail on the hills beyond Caliente, and the new road may be seen following up the canon of Caliente Creek.

"Oaks are now becoming more numerous and beautifying the hillsides. The old stage-road to Los Angeles is seen far away and above on the right.

"The scenery now grows wilder; the rocks in the canon are sharper and more forbidding, and piled higher and higher. In the narrow canon there are rocks frowning from above, and rising up from the crooked defile of the creek 700 feet below.

"An occasional pine is now seen, and as the altitude increases they will become more numerous.

"As one looks back down the canon, he may see the top of Breckenbridge (sic) Mountain. It was hid at Caliente, but has now crawled up into view. The old stage-road is crossed and recrossed, and at length the railroad crosses the Tehachapi Creek itself. Off to the right we have a pretty view of Bear Mountain, a peak of the Sierras. It is snow-crowned late in the spring.

"The track then curves, making the 'Twitty Creek Bend,' from which, in clear atmosphere, one may look out over the wide expanse of the San Joaquin Valley, off hundreds of miles towards San Francisco

"We recross the Tehachapi Creek, just as we approach

"Keene. It is a small station. Around it there are many points of interest in the mountain scenery, but the view is not extensive or sublime."

Although it was of little moment to the tourist-railroader, Keene has served a community for as long as Tehachapi Summit. When the Southern Pacific reached this point in 1876, isolated ranches dotted the terrain. It was the establishment of a rail camp in the shadow of three dominant peaks, however, that began the community which celebrates its one-hundredth birthday in 1976. On May 29, 1876, when one of the first passenger trains stopped there, the station was called Wells. Madison P. Wells, known to his friends as "Matt," was a cattleman living on Tehachapi Creek. When he announced for Sheriff in June 1875, a Bakersfield paper proclaimed, "Mr. Wells is considered in every degree competent to perform the duties of the position to which he aspires." Perhaps it was "Matt's" friends who honored him, but within a week the station's name was changed.

James R. Keene was a San Francisco financier, president in 1875 of the San Francisco Stock and Exchange Board. It was his name the Espee impermanently gave to the station; even the station's name was changed. Apparently there was some confusion between Keene and Kern, the name of the county, as well as the name of the junction near Bakersfield where the Southern San JoaquinValley office of the Southern Pacific was located. To allieviate the confusion Keene Station was called Woodford for a time, while the same community that grew up around it was known as Keene, although it, too, was sometimes called Woodford — it's still confusing, a century later. Woodford is still perpetuated — in the name of the winding road that hugs the mountainside in its meandering route from Old Town down the hill. Such a small community to have had three names, which today is definitely known as Keene.

It's really by way of the Tehachapi-Woodford Road that motorists from the east, cherishing scenery and solitude, should approach Keene. Magnificent views of the Loop are offered at more than one vista point. Flowers in spring, snow-covered hills in winter, distant grazing cattle in summer, and even a spritely waterfall in a wet year — are worthwhile attractions.

It was alongside Tehachapi Creek that the camp began, and where, until the end of 1972, the symbolic yellow buildings of the railroad could be found. On a foggy day in December, while driving the modern freeway I saw with sadness that the buildings were in the hands of the wrecker; before they disappeared completely I returned and spent some time just standing, looking, and photographing.

Keene was once a busy rail siding. The tall, golden grass growing on the hillsides was good feed for thousands of cattle; Keene and its environs was headquarters over the years for several cattlemen who shipped from the spur. After the 1916 discovery of cinnabar on John Cuddeback's property it, too, was shipped from the station.

Its pleasant winters and comfortable summers; its elevation above the winter fogs of the San Joaquin Valley; its situation at 2,700 feet above sea level: all provided Keene with an ideal climate for people afflicted with chronic pulmonary infection. Hence, Stonybrook Retreat, a treatment center, was built there, where the first patients were admitted on December 1, 1918. In 1923 the hospital had its own school, and in 1929 Kern County opened a preventorium for children susceptible to pulmonary diseases. By 1951 the facility had grown to a 170-bed sanitorium and was self-sufficient.

Although the patients were removed to Kern General Hospital in Bakersfield in the late 1960's, the rambling buildings still remain inhabited as the headquarters for Cesar Chavez's United Farm Workers organization.

A school district was formed at Keene on March 6, 1883, with Miss J. B. Gregory as the first teacher, and Madison Wells the first district clerk. The first year an average of 6.36 pupils attended the school, which was located on a flat of ground next to Tehachapi Creek, just east of the freeway overpass that crosses it today. The highest attendance was in 1934-35 when there was an average of sixty-eight pupils, thirty-two of whom were at Stonybrook.

During the 1912-13 school year "railroad bums" were the teacher's principal problem, as she complained, "The fence is very dilapidated and greatly in need of repairs. The trustees intend to have it fixed this summer and also a windowpane through which many I.W.W.'s enter for a night's repose."

The original schoolhouse was destroyed in a water spout some years ago, and for a long time school was continued in a schoolhouse near the railroad buildings. After it was condemned and for a short period the children were educated in a rented building. The school was permanently closed and children from Keene are now bussed into Tehachapi, with which Keene merged on February 26, 1954.

The general store and branch library were active locales. The library, too, is gone, and the store hangs on from one owner to the next. At its most social time in history, some years ago when its one hundred or so citizens were more than half railroad people, the weekly movies, pie suppers, and holiday parties, were looked-forward-to by all. There is still a post office, which continues to serve a populated community of about 150 people, as well as outlying ranches and gentleman ranchers.

But, back to our 1880's rail tour.

After enjoying the ride around the Loop and "passing tunnel 11 the train has reached

"Girard. It is a small station. The old stage-road comes near, but it is down in the bottom of the canon. It looks as if the summit was close at hand, but it is nearly nine miles away. The open country is an indication of its approach, but numerous spurs of troublesome rock must yet be pierced with tunnels.

"At length the tunnels are all passed and the canon begins to widen, showing the near approach of the summit. The road is no longer in Tehachapi Canon, but in Tehachapi Valley.

"The stage and railroad are side by side.

"At last the station called

"Tehachapi Summit is reached. About two miles to the right is the old town of Tehachapi, with about twenty houses. It is on the old stage-road, but the new town will eventually outrival it."

—THREE—

"Leaving Greenwich is leaving the habitable world," commented a reporter in January 1876. "Here are the last vestiges of vegetation and life. Beyond all is barren and inhospitable and desolate." And yet, east of Greenwich is where Tehachapi grew, from a rail camp to the four-valleys' commercial and population center. Tehachapi wasn't, strictly speaking, a desert town, situated as it was in the semi-arid mountains, although in the minds of early Mojave Desert settlers the community was closely associated with the towns of Mojave and Randsburg. Out of the desert and mining camps during the last three decades of the Nineteenth Century came disillusioned Argonauts to join the original settlers — miners and cattlemen; and from the settled cities of Los Angeles and San Francisco merchants, as well, joined the growing community — growing not just in numbers but cultivation.

What was needed to serve the population over the years appeared: hotels, saloons in great number, a post office, general merchandise stores; blacksmiths manned their shops; livery stables opened for business; and a lumber yard provided wood for the first buildings.

According to Peter Greene, Justice of the Peace during the growing years of Tehachapi Summit, there was a healthy condition of progress in the region by 1888. Land had doubled in value and the areas of cultivation were constantly increasing. Building continued in and about Tehachapi. Grain crops were large and quality above average. Everywhere there was the appearance of thrift and prosperity.

The production of lime and building stone, employing a large labor force, circulated a great deal of money. Moreover, the land owners, in addition to their fine crops, struck a bonanza by supplying fuel to the Los Angeles market. Cord wood in 1888 sold for $5.50 on the ground, the forests being extensive and accessible. "It is not uncommon for 20 cords of wood to be made from a single tree," claimed a citizen. John Brite took advantage of the forests to supply his lumber mills. In July 1889 his saw mill turned out several thousand feet of lumber daily, most of it for local use.

The growth pattern continued in 1889 as two new warehouses were constructed to accomodate the continuing manufacture of goods, and several smaller buildings were built. A Bakersfield paper reported, "Tehachapi holds the air of the enterprising little town she has always been in spite of hard times and warm weather."

The Nineties are best described as the years of recognition, with the population at last aware of its solid foothold as a necessary adjunct of the region's life. An influx of "city" folk brought stability to business and culture to the community, as the changes that occurred in the final decade have served and will serve the Tehachapis for years to come.

Prosperity continued and Judge Greene commented on a region he saw grow from a wilderness into one of the "most prosperous sections of the state. Its exports largely exceed its imports and as a consequence the people are becoming exceedingly prosperous." In 1890, 1,490 full carloads and part carload lots of goods were shipped from the railroad depot. In 1891 the total exceeded 1,600.

Lime and lumber continued extensively, as did the manufacture of building material. The valleys grew all of its own produce. It was only natural that so "desirable a region should attract a large immigration and accordingly it is rapidly filling up with people. The town of Tehachapi is growing rapidly. A large hotel is soon to be built," it was reported in April 1891.

By 1893 the physical character of the small Western town of Summit Station, now known as Tehachapi, changed, assuming the settled attitude

The Vance residence on northwest corner of D and Curry Streets was one of several homes that gave the thoroughfare the name "Nob Hill" — Circa early 1900's (Ed Wiggins Collection)

of its residents as the material wealth of the region continued to produce and benefit. It had long been the fashion of the wealthy growers of the Tehachapis to build "town houses," a custom initiated a few years before by John Irribarne, a native of France and upon his arrival in Tehachapi in 1886 a leader of the community — building the first warehouse adjacent to the railroad in 1889. Irribarne also erected an expensive residence on Curry Street, which soon became a favorite locale of "charming villas," referred to as the "Nob Hill" of Tehachapi. As Old Town disappeared, some homes were also transported to the new town, mounted on logs that rolled across the dusty road as teams dragged them along (38).

Architectural change occurred when wood frame buildings of the business district were replaced with stately brick. As early as 1890 H. N. Jacobs used brick for building from his own yard where he employed Chinese recruited from Los Angeles. In May 1891 Antone Pauly began to manufacture bricks at his yard north of the tracks. Building a hotel west of town he demonstrated to other businessmen the propriety of brick over wood. Slowly the Old-West frontier aspect gave way to a sense of solidarity typified by brick.

With growth and an attitude of prosperity, and all that money flowing over the counters, guidance and control of finances was only a matter of time. The man to do the job was already on the scene. Isador Asher, born in Prussia in 1861, came to America in 1876. He clerked in a Los Angeles business, arriving in Kern County in 1880. Until 1885 he worked for Hirshfield Brothers and Company at Old Town. Then he began his own business in Tehachapi. It was a successful merchandise store in new quarters in 1892, occupying a prime location on G Street, a few doors east of Green. Asher built a fine brick building, 50 by 100 feet in size. A wide gallery ran along three sides of the spacious salesroom where large quantities of general stock were shelved. There was also a basement under the entire store, where surplus stock and heavy wares were stored — transported when needed on the first floor by a freight elevator. The various sales departments were connected by cash cars, propelled on wire by a "push" system.

At the back of the store was Asher's office and the cashier's desk. And here was the location of the original and first Bank of Tehachapi. An important date in the commercial history of the town is October 11, 1892, when the bank was incorporated with Asher as the president, his store clerk Albert Ancker, cashier and manager. There was a board composed of L. Harris, H. A. Blodgett, and H. Hirschfield. The bank's authorized capital was $100,000 of which the paid-in capital was $10,000, a small but auspicious beginning (39).

Asher evolved naturally from his role of businessman to banker. Banking practices were largely governed by the banker's knowledge of an individual and his standing in the community as well as his reputation for industry and integrity. A loan was usually based on those assets rather than tangible security — certainly a benefit to the population, many of whom may not have been possessed of personal wealth, but were rich in integrity.

During the peak grain production period of the 1890's, several of the

Brites modernized their operation by purchasing combine harvesters. Asher, in his role as merchant-banker, backed them financially in their purchase, as he reportedly "backed everyone."

STATEMENT.

The proposed office will be called _Tehichipa_ (_Tehichipa_)

[*The name of the candidate for postmaster should not be applied as the name of a post office. It is preferable to have some LOCAL or PERMANENT name, which must not be the name of any other office in the State; and you should aim to select a name not appropriated to any office in the United States.*]

It will be situated in the _S.E._ quarter of Section _36_ _inch_, Township _12 North_,
Range _13 West_, in the County of _Kern_, State of _California_.
It will be on or near route No. _14832_, being the route from _Los Angeles, Cal._
to _Havilah_, on which the mail is now carried _three_ times per week.
The contractor's name is _Tomlinson & Co_

Will it be *directly on this route?*—Ans. _Yes_

If not, how far from and on which side of it?—Ans. _On the Route_

How much will it INCREASE the travel of the mail one way each trip?—Ans. _none_

Where will the mail leave the present route to supply the proposed office?—Ans. _does not leave_

Where intersect the route again?—Ans.

What post office will be left out by this change?—Ans. _none_

The name of the nearest office to the proposed one, on the same route, is _Rovena Or_
its distance is _Fifty_ miles, in a _Southerly_ direction from the proposed office.

The name of the nearest office on the same route, on the other side, is _Havilah_
its distance is _50_ miles, in a _North West_ direction from the proposed office.

The name of the nearest office to the proposed one, off the route, is _Kern River_
distance by the most direct road is _60_ miles, in a _North_ direction from the proposed office.

State the names of the other offices near the proposed one, their directions and distances from it by the most direct roads.

Ans. _There are none unless it be San Berno which is 100 miles and Kernville about 70_

The name of the most prominent river near it is _Kern_
The name of the nearest creek is _Oak Creek_
The proposed office will be _60_ miles from said river, on the _South Side_ side of it, and will be _On Oak Creek_ from said nearest creek, on the _North_ side of it.

If it be a village, state the number of inhabitants.—Ans. _No_

If not, state the number of families within two miles.—Ans.

Also, the number of families within one-half the distance to the next office.—Ans. _150_

A *diagram, or sketch from a map,* showing the position of the proposed new office, with neighboring river or creek, roads, and other post offices, towns, or villages near it, will be useful, and is therefore desired.

A correct map of the locality might be furnished by the county surveyor, but this must be without expense to the Post Office Department.

ALL WHICH I CERTIFY to be correct and true, according to the best of my knowledge and belief,
this _16_ day of _December_, 186 _8_ _P. D. Greene_

I CERTIFY, That I have examined the foregoing statement, and that it is correct and true, to the best of my knowledge and belief. _Geo. Gleason_ Postmaster of _Ravena City_

An 1868 application for the first official post office in the Tehachapis, which was located at Oak Creek Station (The National Archives)

In the 1890's the post office finally became respectable. The United States Government appointed Peter D. Greene in 1869 postmaster at the stage station at Oak Creek, calling it "Tehichipa." In 1875, in an effort to establish his community Greene was again appointed a postmaster, of Greenwich on December 2nd.

Tehichipa was next approved as a post office in the spring of 1877 when Old Town received an official appointment of Edward Green as its postmaster. That location was discontinued October 20, 1885, when all mail went to Greenwich, which was really Tehachapi. Although Greenwich as a viable population center ceased to exist in 1877, the postal name applied to Tehachapi until April 18, 1893, when to end the confusion since neither Old Town nor Greenwich existed, the name was officially changed to Tehachapi. At the same time Charles A. Lee was appointed postmaster, having served as Greene's deputy since his appointment in January 1890. Before that Lee was employed by the Southern Pacific Railroad Company, but a near fatal accident resulted in amputation of his right leg and crippled his left hand.

In 1891 while Greene was postmaster, he personally erected a building to house the post office exclusively. It remained there until 1898 when it was moved to the rear of a lot adjoining Burt Denison's brick building, as it was more centrally located in the downtown business district.

Another form of communication, the telegraph, became respectable on January 5, 1895, when new telegraph offices were opened. The Pacific and Atlantic Telegraph Company started stringing lines along the route of the Butterfield Stage Line in 1860; later Western Union consolidated that line with its telegraph coast-to-coast. As the Nineteenth Century closed a correspondent pridefully reported in an 1897 Bakersfield paper: "Our Town, Tehachapi, is prosperous with its soil so deep and rich, with inhabitants 642 . . . . We have 3 stores of general merchandise, one hotel, one lodging house, one drug store, 2 churches, 1 schoolhouse, 3 blacksmith shops, 1 butcher shop, 1 grocery and gents furnishing store, 2 barber shops, 1 lodge room for secret societies, 3 boarding houses, 2 grain warehouses, 1 lime warehouse, one opera house, one ice house, one bank, one post office, one express office, 2 telegraph offices, 2 justices of the peace, 2 constables, 2 night watchmen, 2 notary publics, 3 carpenters, one tinker, 2 physicans, one attorney, two livery stables, 4 feed lots, 1 harness and one shoemaker shop, 3 restaurants, one flour mill and ten saloons."

—FOUR—

As the Twentieth Century began the hopes and aspirations of the citizens of the Town of Tehachapi blended into a concerto of occasionally harmonious action. Throughout the previous decade calls for an improved water works were met with a languishing lack of applied effort. Elsewhere in the state gas and electrical power were becoming a reality. The remoteness of the Tehachapis, coupled with the lack of a governmental agency to initiate action which would bring modern conveniences to the community, precluded anything but vociferous comment by word of mouth and print.

In 1907 the estimated population of 613 enjoyed the advantages of two churches, a three-room public school, four "department" stores, a bank,

Looking south on Green Street from G — Circa 1902 (Ed Wiggins Collection)

Looking north on Green Street just past its intersection with F Street — Circa early in second decade of 20th century (Darrell and Louise Stevens)

Tehachapi Hay & Grain was founded in 1905 by Herman Weferling, Phil Marx and Albert Ancker. This is a Circa 1914 view when it was located on Robinson and E Streets (Ed Wiggins Collection)

Looking north on Green Street on a winter day in 1918. In the brick Masonic Temple at the right foreground the early Town Hall meetings were conducted (Herbert N. Force Collection)

a drug store, livery stables, blacksmith shops, hotels and lodging houses, and a weekly newspaper. An Opera House (located above Asher's Store) provided entertainment. Forty-five thousand acres of land were sown to barley or wheat. Ten passenger trains in addition to numerous freight trains passed over the rails each day. Was progress stalemated in Tehachapi? No, but the voices of status quo, blending with a fear of excessive taxation, spoke louder than those which called for incorporation.

"The question has often been asked lately, 'What advantages are to be derived by a town from incorporation?' " began the editor of The Tehachapi Tomahawk in a 1904 lead news item. "The principal advantage, to my mind, is that of self-government. The state laws relate to the government of any barren section of land, with a single inhabitant, almost as much as they do to a town of any population that is not incorporated. The same can be said of the ordinances passed by the county supervisors. It is obvious that in thinly settled districts, especially in towns, conditions will arise that require legislation which cannot be acted upon at Sacramento and many laws now in force become null and void, as soon as a town is incorporated, so far as that particular community is concerned. This is because the local board of trustees are more capable of meeting the legislative requirements of their immediate vicinity, by their proximity thereto, than are the representatives and senators who assemble at Sacramento.

Three years later in June 1907, The Tehachapi Tomahawk encouraged: "Incorporate for the welfare of Tehachapi. The advantages of incorporation become more apparent as the time passes merrily along. City ordinances could regulate upon what streets traction engines could pass and they could be taxed for those street's maintenance; a city ordinance could say in what sections of the town hay barns, warehouses and barley crushers could be erected and operated and not have them scattered indiscriminately through the residential district and adjacent to the public school buildings; and there are many other things than that to keep a 'town' from going ahead which a 'city' ordinance would regulate in the interest of the community."

The strong and cohesive voice of progress finally resulted in an election in 1909 to decide on the future course of growth. Would Tehachapi incorporate? Yes! On July 24, 1909, the "Town of Tehachapi" was legally established when sixty-eight eligible voters appeared at Chormicle's Hall to cast their votes at the polls. When the ballots were counted, thirty-six had voted for incorporation, twenty-three against.

The original town boundaries had by now expanded and included 329 acres. Antone Pauly, who had acquired 1,750 acres through homestead and purchase during the 1890's, sold portions of his holdings to J. A. Haralson, S. Heineman & Company, Isadore Asher, and J. M. Jackley, all local businessmen. What has become known as the Pauly Addition, was recorded as an addition in August 1895, extending the western boundary two blocks and adding Pauley Street and Mill Street, on the corner of which a flour mill was then in business.

To the east, the original Hayes Street boundary line had been extended to include open space all the way to what is known today as Dennison

Road (40).

Government was established, to be administered by the five members of a Board of Trustees who were T. P. Sullivan, a former roadmaster for the Southern Pacific Company; J. M. Jackley, owner of a harness and shoe shop; L. E. Kessing, an innkeeper; John Hickey, farmer, teacher, and preacher; and Phil Marx, cashier at the bank, assisted by a Clerk, Treasurer, and a Town Marshall.

On August 17, 1909, at 7:30 p.m., the Trustees held their first meeting in the Bank of Tehachapi, at which Marx was elected president of the Board (the title Mayor was not created until 1930). The Trustees' discussion centered around general matters of procedure: ordinances fixing the time and place of regular meetings; the bonds for Clerk, Treasurer, and Marshall were read for the first time.

What was the first major legislation to be considered? An ordinance regulating the straying of "domestic animals" and a tax on dogs, which was eventually set at $1.00 for males and $3.00 for females. (In September a Deputy Poundmaster was appointed to assist the Marshall.) In the 1890's the county had appointed a poundmaster for the Town, but in 1897 the paper complained, "It would not be out of place for the poundmaster to get a move on and protect our trees and yards."

The need for a public dumping ground was also considered, and the first Marshall, C. V. Bernard, was appointed at a salary of $25.00 a month.

Two days later, on the 19th, the Board met in the Kessing Building on G Street, again to discuss general matters of procedure. They also saw a need to draft an immediate liquor ordinance. Before 1909 was over, other ordinances were passed relating to municipal licenses, vagrants, and establishing a Board of Health.

The Trustees continued meeting in the Kessing Building, establishing committees to handle general town improvements and making their appointments. C. V. Reed was the first Town Clerk, at a salary of $20.00; C. A. Lee was the Treasurer, receiving one percent of all monies collected and paid out; and Charles Heath was the Town Recorder.

On April 11, 1910, the first regular municipal election was held with seventy-four votes polled. Kessing, Hickey, and Sullivan were returned to office; Ferd Snyder, a lime man, and Henry S. Downs, a shopkeeper, were elected in place of Jackley and Marx.

The Trustees adopted their Common Seal in August: "The Summit of a High Mountain, at sunrise with a minerature (sic) Railroad running across the Summit. On the Margin of which Seal shall appear the words Town of Tehachapi, Kern County, Calif., Incorporated August 13th, 1909."

In December new quarters were obtained when the Trustees moved into the "southwest corner room of the Masonic Temple," where they continued to meet for many years proudly referring to the location as the Town Hall.

(It was with an attitude of deep community pride that the Board held its first meeting in a new City Hall on May 10, 1932, constructed on three lots at the corner of F and Robinson Streets. The building cost $5,728 to build, and remained unchanged except for alterations as growth necessitated,

142

until a major remodeling took place in the late 1960's.

If, in the early years of its existence, the Board of Trustees was overly involved in general citizen complaints — if you had a problem, see your trustee — by the mid-1930's the meetings were quite standardized in procedure. Various departments had been systemized to handle matters that for some time came directly to the Trustees.

It wasn't until 1946 that the Town became a City. The Board of Trustees had discussed this change in 1937, but at the time saw no real advantage and tabled the matter. An Act of the State Legislature in 1946 changed the Town's official name to "City of Tehachapi," and made the Board of Trustees a City Council.)

With government firmly in hand, in slow procession modern improvements were provided. The first act of consequence was to create a park. In September 1910 Phil Marx was offered, and accepted, $750 for Block 33 and two adjoining lots. Over the next three years some improvements took place. The planting of trees was delayed, however, because there was no ready access to water, but some were planted by the spring of 1912. In 1914, to allieviate the watering problem. C. V. Barnard was allowed to plant a hay crop in exchange for watering the trees. Louis Boden also watered them, using a tank wagon which he filled at a fire hydrant, hauled to the park, and watered each tree with a bucket.

An additional 160 trees were planted in 1915, and in 1920 there were more trees planted as well as other improvements. By 1925, however, the condition of the park deteriorated; it was unsightly and neglected. Not until the summer of 1935 did the park become an attractive area for recreation when a W.P.A. project installed a sprinkler system, planted lawn, erected comfort stations, and constructed a simple bandstand for Sunday afternoon concerts under the trees.

(In 1958, in an election spearheaded by Mayor Steve Valdez, the Tehachapi Recreation District was established to provide a "more balanced recreation program" to the area, and to build a municipal swimming pool. It took ten years to build the pool and today, in addition, the District manages and maintains the city parks, ball parks, a rodeo ground, and is developing camping and picnicking areas at the Brite Valley Reservoir.)

The water problem that worried the park management, also plagued the community for years. As early as the summer of 1878, the railroad proposed bringing water to Tehachapi from the mountains by means of pipes; at the same time they wanted to organize a fire department. But in the 1890's there were still continuous calls for the town to establish a water department. In fact, the Tehachapi Water & Light Co. was incorporated in 1892 to supply the town with water, but to no avail.

Meanwhile, Dave Clark, owner of a hotel and butcher shop, installed a gasoline motor at his well and distributed piped water to much of the business district. The Venator & Davis City Meat Market also had a deep well and pumping plant from which they sold water as well as ice, of which they could produce 3,000 pounds daily.

In January 1911 the Trustees began to seriously consider a water plant which culminated in a contract to dig the first Town well in April.

Completed in August at a depth of 258 feet, it was capped and ready to use. The next step was to construct the system. Voter approval provided for a pumping plant, reservoirs, pipelines, water mains, and fire hydrants. By May 1913 forty-one applications for taps had been received and in June, sixty water meters were purchased, followed in 1914 with another eighty. The old individual water wells themselves were being filled in during September.

An era of windmill pumps had ended. According to Sherm Chitwood, everyone had trouble with water even though windmills in yards pumped wells, drilled only to thirty to forty feet and provided all that was necessary. If someone didn't have a well, they bought water by the bucket from a neighbor. But it also meant outdoor toilets, and one of the immediate effects of the water system was to introduce indoor plumbing. (Additional bond issues in 1946 and 1955 provided for new city wells and the replacement of wooden mains.)

The Tehachapi Water Works — Circa 1914 (Ed Wiggins Collection)

The matter of obtaining property for a community dump was discussed at several meetings during 1910, but not until January 1911 was a deed for the dump ground finally approved. It was first located where the Northside Park is today. A caretaker was on hand and got the salvage. Before the dump was created, most refuse was thrown into outhouses, holes in yards, and garbage became slop for animals, as almost everyone had a few chickens and a cow in their yard. But the newly designated dump had already been used as a disposal site and was a problem from the beginning with rubbish being burned and the gate in need of repair. The site remained a public dumping ground where the townsfolk brought their own rubbish until garbage collection became a business in the 1930's. Collection was started by two men in 1934, and in January 1935

Edwin R. Jones took it over. Private collection continued until 1944, when the cost of operating the system became prohibitive and the City turned the operation over to its Department of Water and Streets (41).

The streets also concerned the Trustees. They were dirt. Of necessity watered in summer to keep the dust down, in winter the quagmire created by snow and rain caused a deplorable condition that over and over again caused the complaint "something has to be done." Summer sprinkling was a daily chore, accomplished by a wagon drawn by a team of horses, and periodically the roads were graded. In 1917 gravel was spread on Green Street with the intention of doing the same thing on other main streets in town.

There were wooden sidewalks in the early days, and in winter, boards were sometimes laid across the streets. In 1909 the sidewalks were so dilapidated and dangerous that the Trustees passed another ordinance, regulating their repair and removal.

Finally, in 1927 a project was started to install sidewalks, curbs, and gutters, but it was not completed until an improvement district was formed to force it through — over much objection by cost-conscious property owners. The cost of improvement was $2.50 a foot and the property owner could pay cash or carry a ten-year loan with interest, which in the long run proved to be the expensive way.

The town finally began to oil its streets in 1929, influenced by the increased automotive traffic and the statewide highway improvements that had been taking place all through the 1920's. At first only nine blocks were oiled, but at least it was the beginning to a welcomed project. Another nineteen blocks were oiled in 1933, and there were few tears shed in the summer of 1939, when the old sprinkler tank was sold because it was no longer of any use to the town.

Even before the Trustees considered a lighting system, one of a sort existed. Kerosene lamps cast a fluttering glow in home and business, augmented by the light of wood fires in winter and sunshine in summer. Coal oil was used to light street lamps at night, one of the varied duties of the Town's night watchman. Using a pulley system, the large lamp and shade were pulled down the pole, filled, and the chimney cleaned.

Carbide and gas lights were installed by some property owners in 1911, and eight were installed on downtown streets. Again, they were maintained daily. A hand cart was purchased by the Trustees so the maintenance man could easily carry his supplies to fill the globes each day and return at night to light the mantles.

Thomas Alva Edison's invention of the incandescent electric light, and his first operation of a complete electric lighting and power system, heralded a new age for mankind. Scientists had been learning how to turn electric power into light all through the Nineteenth Century; and although in 1878 a few arc lights were in use in the United States, they were too large and glaring. In that year Edison developed the incandescent bulb, a slender rod in a vacuum or near vacuum of glass, heated to incandescence by electric current and prevented from burning out by the absence of oxygen.

George Westinghouse of Pittsburg, while visiting Edison's plant in

145

Menlo Park, New Jersey in 1880, spotted a flaw in Edison's system: the short range of direct current produced by the generators. In 1886 he patented a transformer which reduced voltages in electric circuits, thus concentrating high voltage and that same year established the Westinghouse Electric Company. In the fall he produced the first alternating current system which supplied power that could be carried further and also more cheaply than direct current.

Shortly after the turn of the century, certain activities on the Kern River occurred which eventually brought electrical energy to the Tehachapis. In a gesture intended to provide power for the streetcars of their Pacific Electric Railway and Los Angeles railway systems, Henry E. Huntington and William G. Kerchoff's Kern River Company, a subsidiary of Pacific Light and Power Company, began constructing a hydroelectric generating plant on the river, five miles downstream from Kernville. Water rights for the plant had been secured in 1896 by the Kern River and Los Angeles Electric Power Company, a predecessor of the Kern River Company. (A powerhouse had earlier been built there, in 1897, by Kern County industrial pioneers to provide electricity for Bakersfield.)

Construction materials for the plant were transported by rail mainly to Caliente, where they were transferred to heavy wagons for the long haul over the mountains to the Kern River Valley. Often following stage roads, freighting on the Caliente grade tested the mettle of more than one man.

Victor Phillips relished describing his early teens, when he hauled

Hauling a turbine to Borel from Caliente Station on the Caliente Road in 1912 (Southern California Edison Company Historical Photograph Collection)

freight for his father. One job necessitated hauling cement for the power plant over the mountains from the Caliente railroad spur to the Kern River Canyon. There were no large trucks with multiple horsepower to carry the loads, a driver behind the wheel. Large wagons did the job with six-to-ten horse power pulling the loads and Mr. Phillips, as driver, mounted on the back of the left wheelhorse. There was no power steering wheel either. With a single jerk line attached to the bridle of the left leader, young Phillips controlled his team. A gentle jerk turned them right, a steady pull turned them left. Between jerking, pulling, and voice commands, the teams made their way over the early roads, often carrying one-ton loads in the wagons.

Upon completion of the new Borel hydro-plant in 1904, named for. Antoine Borel, an early partner of Huntington and Kerchoff, the transmission line to Los Angeles was erected. Following in part the mountainous route of the early Los Angeles-to-Havilah stage, the 60,000 volt wood pole line was briefly the world's longest high voltage transmission line. It extended from the Borel powerhouse, 126 miles across the Tehachapis, through the Antelope Valley and over the Santa Susanna Mountains to the Kern Substation on Mission Road in Los Angeles. As the line passed through the Tehachapi Valley, its proximity made electric power practical, except for the lack of a cohesive power to bring it all together.

In 1910, to provide electrical power to the City of Los Angeles' plant at Monolith, two substations were built there. The Monolith Substation of 450-kilovolt-ampere capacity served the village, while the Monolith Cement Substation of 1,500-kva capacity served the plant.

Monolith Sub-station in 1916 (Southern California Edison Company Historical Photograph Collection)

147

Meanwhile in Tehachapi the first official comment about the installation of an electrical light plant was made at a Trustees' meeting on September 2, 1913, by a Mr. Erricson; his "advice was noted."

In February 1915 the Trustees began to seriously discuss providing electricity to the town via the Pacific Light and Power Company's transmission line. One month later they passed a resolution describing the Town's intent to "acquire, construct and complete an electric system for estimated $8,000 and to have electricity for a bonded indebtedness." At the election on April 12, 1915, the unanimous need for power expressed itself with 113 casting their votes in the affirmative, overwhelming the eleven who voted no.

Celebrating the inauguration of Tehachapi's electrical lighting system with a street dance on July 31, 1915 (Tehachapi City Hall)

Although other bids were received from Los Angeles concerns, they exceeded the bonded indebtedness; the bid of Pacific Light and Power Company was approved and Tehachapi became a "resale customer." In May the proposed right-of-way for the high-tension line was selected: from Sullivan Spur (just west of Monolith) to the town, along the old narrow-gauge rails to the Los Angeles aqueduct plant, to a substation where the City's garage is now. From there the lines were strung to the customers. Street lighting posts were ordered for downtown; two and one-half acres of land was purchased from the Ramina Corporation at Sullivan Spur on which to locate the switch and transformer houses; and two licenses were issued for wiring private homes — to Davidson Bros. and Waterman-Galinger Co.

Electric power had its problems. The street lighting system used an excess of current, necessitating instructions to the night watchman to turn off all lights on moonlit nights, except the circuit on Green between F and G Streets. Also, because it was inconvenient to collect light and water bills door-to-door, an office for the Superintendent of the Light and Water Department was opened in the Bank of Tehachapi.

Tehachapi's first civic scandal was a result of electric power. Frank A. Lathrop, a consulting engineer and purchasing agent who had assisted the Trustees throughout their negotiations with the Power Company, was charged with embezzling $3,291.55 of the Town's money in 1915.

A lack of sufficient electric current in 1918, because it was too expensive, caused the Trustees to reduce their rates to "permit free use of current for cooling and power purposes."

The Southern California Edison Company, which had merged with Pacific Light and Power in 1917, expressed an interest in purchasing the Town's system in 1923. Receiving no affirmative response to their $7,648.12 offer, Edison installed lines parallel to the Town's system, and solicited business at the same wholesale rate it was selling to the Town. Needless to say, the Trustees considered these "unfair methods." Realizing they couldn't prevent Edison's competition, in June they reconsidered selling the system to Edison; although five years passed before it occurred, when in August 1928, they accepted Edison's offer of $23,500 and with voter approval sold the system. Money from the sale financed the new City Hall in 1932.

In the 1890's some residents discussed importing gas with a San Francisco firm, but to no avail. While the Trustees were divesting the town of the electric business, in the fall of 1926 it began negotiating with Midway Gas Company, which was planning to supply gas to Monolith-Portland Cement Company (42).

Natural gas was first used commercially in California in 1906 by the Santa Maria Gas Company. Gas, manufactured from oil, had earlier replaced the coal, wood, and "asphaltum" used to manufacture gas, as was done in Los Angeles. Natural gas had three distinct advantages: it had twice the heating value of its predecessor; it was much easier to handle; and it was substantially safer.

The gas supplied by Midway was produced at its "west side" field in the Southern San Joaquin Valley where in the Buena Vista Hills, great natural gas wells were first plumbed in 1909. The construction of the line was a monumental challenge. An eight-inch 187,947 linear foot pipeline, capable of furnishing 10,000,000 cubic feet of gas per day, was constructed from a point north of Wheeler Ridge on old Highway 99, across the southern end of the San Joaquin Valley, and up the mountainside. Its base cost was $287,998.75. Modern construction men express admiration of the ability to lay the mountain line using manual labor and without modern equipment. After cresting the mountains the line crossed over Cummings Valley, entered Brite Valley about where the old Brite house is at the corner going into Brite Canyon, came into the Tehachapi Valley, and went on to Monolith. (To this day Bear Valley does not have natural gas, although there are two thirty-inch pipelines belonging to Pacific Gas and Electric Company. A lack of users there has precluded connections.)

Voter approval of the Trustees' action came in December 1926, and in the spring of 1927 gas permits were issued. The first district foreman, Frank Wilson, did all the work: he took care of service calls, installed meters and read them — until eventually an increase of business necessitated the addition of a serviceman. In 1928, its first full year of operation, the gas company's operating revenues was $12,026.87.

Most townspeople were eager to tie into the line. Everyone was burning wood, until it began to get scarce. Some coal was also imported from Utah, but it was expensive at $20.00 per ton. Some people also bought a kerosene burner for wood stoves.

It wasn't until the late 1930's that the final utility project was developed and another vestige of the past disappeared. While a sewer system had been discussed by the Trustees as early as 1917, it wasn't until 1937 that action took place. Meanwhile there were continuing problems of waste water running down streets, cesspools and septic tanks flooding and having to be dug deeper or filled in and another put down, as modern pumping equipment didn't exist. In 1921 when mosquitoes were quite a problem, the blame was laid to cesspools, but the only action taken by the Trustees was to pour in kerosene or crude oil. They talked about a sewer.

An election for a bonded indebtedness to finance the system was finally held in February 1937, and the immense interest in the project resulted in an overwhelming vote of confidence with 220 voting for the project and only twenty-one against. In October the Federal Government offered the Town a grant not to exceed $25,364 to assist in the project.

When the sewer was completed, though, there were still problems. In 1939 there was a complaint before the Trustees that some residents still had outdoor toilets, and even in the 1940's a dozen residences had not yet been connected to the system as the tenants walked the "outside mile." As recently as 1951, some old cesspools were still found in town and filled in.

One other modern convenience came to Tehachapi during the developmental years, although it was not a result of governmental action. When Alexander Graham Bell, on March 10, 1876, asked his assistant in the next room, "Mr. Watson, please come here," the Bell Telephone Company was born.

The first interconnecting telephone exchange on the Pacific Coast occurred in San Francisco in February 1878, another a couple of months later in Oakland. In the Tehachapi Valley, far removed from the big commercial cities of the north, a primitive system was also inaugurated that year. According to an 1878 Visalia Delta item, a telephone was in full operation between Tehachapi and Old Town. Tehachapi's operator was W. H. Knapp, while young Paul Narboe operated in Old Town. Oral tradition claims a private telephone exchange was developed in Tehachapi in 1894 with a few subscribers, and sold to the Sunset Telephone Company in 1898.

The earliest exchange system developed in California supplied a separate wire from a central station to each subscriber, who was furnished with a transmitting and a receiving telephone, a signal bell, and a signal button to call the operator. All of these wires terminated at the exchange in a large switch and annunciator.

In 1901 Sunset Telephone-Telegraph Company, which was formed in 1883 for the express purpose of constructing and operating long distance lines, arrived in the Tehachapi Valley and began supplying service. James Brite was one of the first town customers to have a phone installed in his shop. Tehachapi's first "telephone girl" was Mattie Turner, who received a commission as her salary.

The system was modernized in 1906 when post holes were dug for the phone line, part of which had been strung along barbed wire fences. Again in 1910 another up-dating occurred when the Board of Trustees permitted the Pacific Telephone and Telegraph Company to install a new system. Further improvements were made in 1919.

By 1925 sixty subscribers enjoyed the benefits of telephone service, which was available for twelve hours each day and provided by two toll lines. That year the operators began to receive a regular salary instead of the straight commission. In 1926 William and John Robison built a house on F and Robinson Streets for the exchange, with apartments for the operator so she could be reached at night. Twenty-four hour service became a reality in 1928, when both day and night operators were employed.

The old and obsolete "crank and cuss" system ended with the 1952 earthquake. Within four months of the disaster Pacific Telephone Company constructed a $125,000 dial system, replacing the last two operators, Mrs. Ada Lee McLaughlin and Mrs. Violet Hamilton.

—FIVE—

A number of events transpired at about the same time, which changed the character of the town's law enforcement. In constructing the new City Hall, a jail was provided. Finally, after years of continuing deterioration, the original wooden jail was closed. It had been located in the two hundred block of East H Street between Robinson and Davis, and as early as 1912 complaints were made about its condition. From time-to-time, repairs were made, occasionally with county assistance. In 1916 two electric lights were installed. But in 1924 the jail was deemed a health hazard — there was no water, toilet nor ventilation, and no fire protection. Finally in 1934 the old jail was dismantled.

About this same time the Town experienced its second civic scandal, when Marshall P. N. Luca was charged with embezzlement. He resigned in 1932 and was subsequently arrested, tried, found guilty, and resided for a while in the State Prison at San Quentin.

After incorporation and the appointment of a Town Marshall, the Marshall was busy enforcing the Town's ordinances. The first, approved September 19, 1910, provided for the punishment of a variety of misdemeanor offenses. Any house of assignation, prostitution or ill-fame, the interior of which was not entirely protected from gaze by wire screen, lattice, blind or other device, was guilty of a misdemeanor. To "carry, concealed upon his person, any pistol or firearm, slingshot, dirk, or bowie-knife, without written permission from the president of the board of trustees'' made a man a lawbreaker. Willingly or maliciously breaking or destroying windows from any occupied or unoccupied house, or outhouse; engaging in any sport or exercise having a tendency to frighten horses; riding or driving any horse or other animal immoderately or beyond a moderate gait; tieing any horse or mule or riding, driving, or leading it on any sidewalk; or riding a velocipede, bicycle, motorcycle, or tricycle immoderately or beyond a moderate gait: all of these acts were considered misdemeanors. If a person was found guilty and imprisoned in the town or county jail, and refused to labor or did not labor on the public streets or works where required, he was guilty of another misdemeanor and the Town Marshall could "feed any refractory prisoner or prisoners on a diet of bread and water during that time."

To protect the townspeople from night crimes, in 1910 Dick Williamson was paid $10.00 a month to be a Night Watchman; the following year he was appointed a Deputy Marshall.

The passage of an ordinance in September 1930 created changes in the police department, when for the purpose of acquiring workmen's compensation insurance, a policeman's duties were detailed. At the end of the year the Chief of Police, as he was more often being referred to, established traffic ordinances and bought ticket books.

All tools necessary to enforce the law were provided by the officer, as in 1941 when then Chief of Police H. W. Kirkbride installed a red light and a siren on his own car, which was used in the course of his regular duties. It wasn't until 1950 that the City bought the department its first new police car. Finally in 1944, recognizing the need for additional assistance, the Town of Tehachapi Police Department was formed, providing special police officers. The first special officers included Oscar Piper, Harold L. Schlotthauer, Charles Hicks, Dick Crowell, Clyde Brite, and Douglas Kingsbury. Nevertheless, in 1946, a group of twenty citizens appeared before the City Council with a petition expressing the need for an additional full-time police officer and, as a result, a second policeman was hired on February 4.

In the 1940's a too-frequent change in police department personnel took place. Illness, suggestions of personal gain, charges of incompetence, misunderstandings, caused one man after another to join and then leave the Tehachapi Police Department. Not until 1958 when William Mantoth, who had been employed at Monolith-Portland Cement Company and joined the force in 1954, became the Chief, was a sense of continuity established.

With Mantoth's elevation to Chief, the force increased in size, from the Chief and Night Watchman to four officers. Police Academy Training was initiated and brought modern enforcement and protection techniques to the City, an educational system which continues to the present.

Chief Mantoth was fatally wounded in 1968 when he was shot while attempting to arrest a man on charges stemming from an alleged rape and kidnaping. Although this was the only occasion in the town's history of a fatal assault on an officer, Mantoth was not the first peace officer in the

152

area killed in the line of duty.

That happened 100 years ago when knifings and shootings were so numerous that Old Town acquired quite a bit of notoriety, all of it unenviable. A much-publicized murder in October 1876 resulted in one of only two legal (!) hangings in Kern County. (In 1880 a state law required all executions be performed at the state penitentiary.)

Constable Thomas Godwin shot and killed a man who, with his friend James Hayes, was "breaching the peace." Both men had resisted arrest. Hayes decided to avenge his friend's death, returned to Old Town, killed the Constable, and was summarily arrested by other peace officers.

His trial was held at Bakersfield in 1877, and a verdict of guilty of murder resulted. Sheriff Madison P. Wells, desiring to perform his duty in the proper manner, sent a deputy to Stockton to examine its scaffold. Hayes was hanged; the rope was the same one used in five earlier executions, including that of the outlaw Tiburcio Vasquez.

As public executions were popular events, many people attended, some of whom were invited into the jail yard. Others peered through the fence, climbed trees, mounted roofs, or stood on wagons. While his execution aroused feelings of curiosity, Hayes' burial produced anger and outrage. The townspeople at Old Town would not allow his interment in the cemetery and so he was laid to rest outside the fence. Somewhere today, out near Old Town, lies James Hayes and, according to one oldtimer, his grave was at the top of the hill that was cut out when the Golden Hills Motel was constructed in the early 1970's!

Constable Godwin and his peers during the formative years were the law in the Tehachapi Valley. Appointed as peace officer for the Justice Court of the Tehachapi Township, the Constable had been "the law" since the formation of Kern County in 1866. After Tehachapi was established in 1876, for a time two Justice Courts and their lawful representatives upheld the laws. When extremely serious crimes occurred, sometimes there was time for the Sheriff to travel from Bakersfield. Until a resident deputy was appointed, local citizens carried a badge and a gun, although some oldtimers have said they were more for looks than enforcement, and political appointments at that!

A newspaper report in July 1891 mentioned, "A cowboy rode his horse into a saloon on Front Street last week. H. Spencer says nothing of that kind has happened here before in 15 years." Spencer, as a saloonkeeper in Tehachapi from the inception of the town, saw much of the early lawlessness. And there is no doubt that the expressions of violence seemed at times to overshadow the continuing efforts of the citizenry to develop a stable community.

Miners, cowboys, laborers in the lime camps, worked hard for six days, the seventh was to rest and play, which began on Saturday night. In from the ranches and farms, from the lime camps and isolated mining camps, came the single men, to revel and disport themselves in the manner of the day. It's no wonder that temperance workers visited the town and that local lodges were active in their work, with several busy saloons and cowboys riding horses into them. In February 1898 a comment appeared in the newspaper, "High life in town gives employment for the doctors!''

Sometimes outlaw gangs passed through the valley, using the Tehachapi Pass. Tiburcio Vasquez often rode through and one of his gang settled in the region. According to Earle Crowe, ''There was also Abalino Martinez, a diminutive Mexican herder, who had acquired notoriety in the Tehachapi country as the renegade who had acted as messenger for Tiburcio Vasquez, the bandit, in procuring ammunition and supplies'' (43).

J. J. Lopez of the Tejon Ranch, in 1879 conducted an historic sheep drive for General Beale from the ranch to Wyoming to escape the drought. Crowe continued: ''Martinez importuned Lopez for a place on the trail crew in order to escape hostility in the mountain country, and returned after the drive to live out his days in the town of Tehachapi.''

Abalino actually worked for many years as a vaquero on the Cummings Ranch, and continued to ride horseback until his death at about the age of 115.

A resident Sheriff, in addition to the omnipresent Constable, moved to Tehachapi in the late 1940's. Sheriff John Loustalot had considered appointing a deputy to be stationed in Tehachapi in 1940 and 1941, but lack of money prevented it, although the Town was assured the Sheriff's Department was ''prepared to be here in time of emergency.'' For a time in the 1940's, to afford additional county protection, the Chief of Police acted as a deputy sheriff and was paid by Kern County.

In the late Forties a resident deputy was assigned and for a few years the suburban areas were better served. For ten years, however, beginning in 1952, the area was again without its deputy, as calls were handled by the Mojave sub-station. In 1962 a resident deputy was permanently assigned to the Tehachapi sub-station, and today two deputy sheriffs are stationed in Tehachapi to cover a 590-square mile area, augmented on occasion by unpaid, but dedicated, reserve officers.

Two opinions about Tehachapi's early lawlessness are expressed by oldtimers. One day as we sat talking, two men explained that immediately after the turn of the century, even into the Twenties, Tehachapi was ''pretty wild.'' It was nothing for a ''guy on horseback to ride down the street, shooting out the lights. Anything went.'' But both of these men knew something of the more rugged side of life, as miner and law officer.

On the other hand, family men and active participants in the town's commerce, suggest it wasn't wild at all; just a simple Western-style town.

Despite the excesses of violence which occurred, the unspectacular efforts of a stable citizenry prevailed. There is no doubt that the earlyday unrest expressed in the documented events of the newspapers gave way to a more solid life in the 1890's. As Louis B. Wright commented, ''The conservation and perpetuation of traditional civilization in each newly settled region of the country have not received dramatic acclaim; they are not the subjects for stirring novels or sensational movies; but few characteristics have had a greater importance in the development of American society, as we know it today'' (44).

Abalino Martinez in 1940 at about 101 years old

The most difficult service for the community to organize was its fire department, which took years to develop. Fire was a constant threat. Wood frame buildings and wood sidewalks were allowed to deteriorate, contributing to the fearsome hazard. In fact, it was both the threat of fire and actual damage in the 1890's, which caused some downtown businesses to convert their buildings from wood to brick.

In 1891 as fire bugs threatened the community, a citizens' committee appointed additional night watchmen. A gasoline fire that year almost resulted in an old-fashioned shootout as several leading citizens, arguing about the origin of the fire, drew their guns. A hook and ladder company and bucket brigade were considered in 1892, but no action was taken.

Then in 1895 the town nearly burned down. A fire, discovered at eight o'clock on the evening of October 15 when flames were noticed at the rear of Harry Coleman's shoe shop, quickly spread to other cloth and paper-lined buildings which were "dry as tinder." In only half an hour an entire block was a mass of flames and the street was closed as the fire rapidly worked its way towards the Asher Building. By nine o'clock teams of wagons filled adjacent streets carrying loads of goods from the already burning and threatened buildings. Dull explosions punctuated the night air as the sharp rattle of rifle and pistol shots exploded when the flames reached boxes of cartridges and loaded firearms. A reported comment was, "There being no fire department or water works, the fire worked its own wild way and only stopped when it burned itself out."

An almost complete lack of fire insurance added to the tragedy, and the irony of the situation was the rates were too high because of a lack of fire extinguishers. Both the Summit and Piute Hotels were destroyed, as was the post office and postal telegraph building. Businesses owned by the Cuddeback Brothers, John Irribarne, H. M. Jacobs, Charles Lee, H. Wilkinson, Harvey Spencer, Charles Heath, David Clark, A. F. Buhn, Mrs. Mary Haigh, and a few others, were also burned down.

Reconstruction began within two days, some owners rebuilding frame structures, but others turning to brick. As the century ended the cry was heard, "Tehachapi should have fire protection, and at once." But it didn't have.

After incorporation, one of the Board's first communications was to the railroad "relative to making some arrangement with them whereby the town could put a connection to their waterplant at Tehachapi to attach a hose, to be used by the town in case of fire." As the connection was never made, the Trustees began to look at different types of protection apparatus.

In 1911 the street superintendent was instructed to "procure a reasonable amount of powder cans for buckets in case of fire and have them ready;" so the superintendent obtained fifty-seven buckets and four ladders and hooks, storing them at Jackley's Shoe Shop, Barrett's Restaurant, the Tehachapi Hotel, and in Tom Ellington's barn. Four barrels were also filled with water and placed in the downtown alley — for added protection. Meanwhile, the Clerk was instructed to investigate prices of chemical fire protection.

Two years elapsed before the Trustees made additional improvements. From the City of Whittier they purchased one hook and ladder cart, two hose carts, and from other sources a 500 pound fire bell, two nozzles, and 600 feet of fire hose. The bell was installed at the railroad depot because it was centrally located to alert the volunteers in case of an emergency. A new chemical fire engine was purchased from the Ajax Fire Engine Works in 1918, but it, too, caused a problem. When it was taken to a fire a few months later "the fire chief being absent, no one knew how to operate it." A facetious suggestion was immediately made that a public demonstration be held so people would know how to put out a fire.

As the third decade arrived, Tehachapi's fire fighting equipment included one hand ladder truck, two hand hose carts, and one two-wheel hand chemical fire extinguisher. Note the "hand." Even with automotive power a common factor in the community, still the fire brigade depended on man power rather than even horse. One young boy, however, learned to drive his dad's Model "T" and the firemen would hitch up the cart and race to the conflagration.

In the fall of 1913 a "temporary" 18 by 30 foot frame building was constructed and covered with galvanized iron. Tehachapi had a fire house, which was erected just south of the Town Hall on property owned by the Masonic Temple Association and remained there until 1939 when the Kern County Fire Department built a firehouse on Robinson between F and G Streets. The City soon shared the Temple Association's facility.

Fire Chief Sherm Chitwood had attempted to organize a volunteer fire department in 1934, but not until 1939 did a complete reorganization occur, necessary for the community to obtain a general reduction in fire insurance rates. Modernization had arrived.

A 500 gallon pumper was purchased. The volunteers were spruced up by the purchase of "hard-Boiled Tuff-Nut Hats," turn-out coats, badges, and boots, and Jack Vahanick, the new chief, was appointed under a new ordinance. The first volunteer firemen in the reorganization were also appointed, some of whom continued to serve for many years: Jimmie Cazacus, D. Van Ness, Al Hagenstead, Frank Cowan, Pete Errecart, Lloyd Pedigo, Pesky Valdez, Topper Navarez, and Ventura Guiterrez. The ordinance also established fire limits and regulated building construction.

Although the town now had an up-to-date protective force, it still had problems. A devastating fire at the high school in 1944 could not be controlled. According to Chief Vahanick, the mains which supplied water to that section of the city were too small to provide the water necessary to combat a fire of such magnitude.

An additional reorganization of the department occurred just after the end of World War II. In the years since, the department has evolved into an up-to-date volunteer fire department, including modern equipment and well-trained firemen.

—SEVEN—

As the town grew, so did its bank. Soon after the turn of the century,

Phil Marx came to Tehachapi to work as the Bank of Tehachapi's cashier. Albert Ancker was now the president, following the practice established by Isadore Asher of lending money based on a man's reputation for honesty and ability, rather than his tangible assets.

As its commerce increased, the bank outgrew the bounds of Asher's Store. About 1906 a modern building was constructed in the Keeley Block, next to the alley on the west side of Green Street, between F and G Streets, where it remained for many years. Money arrived in town via the railroad, handled by the local Wells Fargo agent. Such was the peaceful attitude of the town that, when Walter Marx was a little boy, he would take the money bag from the bank to the depot for shipment to San Francisco.

As early as 1927 Bancitaly Corporation, predecessor holding corporation to Transamerica Corporation, considered acquiring the Bank of Tehachapi and, from 1933 until 1937, Bank of America also was interested. It was not until 1944, however, that Transamerica Corporation acquired a majority of the capital stock for $70.00 a share, when loans were approximately $132,000 and deposits amounted to $1,020,000. At that time the president and major stockholder, Albert Ancker, was eighty-four years old and ready for retirement.

An interesting comment is found in a Transamerica report indicating the town of 1,200 inhabitants was a district "with little farming and cattle raising." Transamerica was impressed, however, with the cement plant, "a short distance away, and with a considerable payroll."

Six years later in 1950, Bank of America in a natural sequence of events attempted to purchase the business and assets of the bank, but the bank ran into difficulties with the Federal Reserve Bank and the Bank of Tehachapi was repurchased by Transamerica. In 1956 the Bank of Tehachapi became part of the Firstamerica Corporation. First Western Bank was its successor. In January 1974 the Lloyds Bank Group, twentieth largest banking corporation in the world, took over control of the local bank.

—EIGHT—

The isolation of the Tehachapis was partly a result of winding mountain roads on one side and a scarcity of desert development on the other. Even with the advent of the automotive age, not until almost half of the Twentieth Century had passed across the historical scene did the countryside population have easy access to the San JoaquinValley or the Southland.

And so in the context of their relative isolation the citizens developed a rural lifestyle not unlike many frontier towns of the West. In the 1960's when much of the land was opened to subdivision development on a grander scale than had ever before been known, it was the quiet country atmosphere of over 100 years of settlement that was a major appeal to modern immigrants on the road.

By the short span of years as well as a generation, the original settlers maintained a close affinity to the birth of the nation. What a joyful occasion was the earliest 4th of July picnic in the 1850's, attended by the Brites as well as those settlers who had joined them in pioneer living. Year-after-year the growing populace continued to celebrate their birthday in a fine manner: with picnicking, dancing, participating in games, and entertainments of the period.

"Tehachapi in autumn is undoubtedly one of the most seductive places for tourists in the Sierras," reported a newspaper in October 1892. "It's well known reputation as a hard town has died out and a most refined class of people are making their homes here . . . Clubs, both social and athletic, are numerous. Amateur theatricals, first class orchestras, and a brass band, contribute to furnish amusement after the busy day is done."

As the town's commerce and physical character matured in the 1890's, so did its sociability and culture.

Asher's Opera House, located above his store on G Street, was the scene of many events. The Piute Club, organized in February 1890, was a social group for gentlemen only; they met in Nicholson's Hall on H Street, where they kept a piano and gave elegant entertainments. Both halls were the scene of dramatic offerings. A popular one at the time presented by the Tehachapi Dramatic Club was the scenario "Ten Nights in a Barroom."

Baseball, the great national pastime, became an early favorite sport in Tehachapi. A remote descendant of the old English game of rounders, first played professionally when the Cincinatti Red Stockings pitched their first ball in 1869, the sport was a few decades old when an unknown Tehachapi hurler pitched the first ball on an unknown day. But the game quickly caught on and remained a favorite event well into the Twentieth Century.

At a Tehachapi baseball game on the 4th of July, 1914 (Ed Wiggins Collection)

An anonymous artist's rendition of an early day Tehachapi altercation. This painting hung in Jose Sola's barbershop for many years (Margaret Sola)

A delightful story is told by some oldtimers about a painting that hung on a wall of Jose Sola's Barber Shop. Although Sola never knew the true event depicted in the painting, the combatants shown appear intent on assaulting each other. Sola liked the explanation that the painting involved a man by the name of Boutcher, who was shot at Mrs. Ward's ranch west of Tehachapi in the 1890's.

Charlie Powell, however, told the story "straight from the horse's mouth." He said Harry Payne told him that he was the man in the painting who held the club. Only it wasn't a club, but a bat. The painting faithfully depicted the aftermath of one of Tehachapi's famous baseball games. Mr. Powell suggested it might have been one of the famous post-game brawls that usually occurred between the Tehachapi and Mojave teams. Residents from the two communities really did like each other; they got along well at dances and picnics. But a baseball game, that was a different matter. Not just the players usually ended up in a clash of bats, but spectators as well. However the event occurred, it was immortalized by an itinerant artist who was just passing through town.

At the end of the 1890's some businessmen organized baseball teams, and in 1899 the most popular dances were sponsored by the Tehachapi Baseball Club.

The postal telegraph, intended to relay messages of great importance and value, transmitted a message on a Friday in November 1899. "Quite a crowd gathered at the postal telegraph office in the Denison building," read a report, "to listen to the returns of the Shankey Jeffries (sic) fight last Friday. The general opinion of the public though was that the decision was given to the wrong man."

The male interest in physical culture was expressed by membership in the Tehachapi Athletic Club. Everyone had a grand time when they gave their opening exhibition at Asher's Opera House on August 27, 1892. The program with twenty-five members participating, included boxing — Greco-Roman and catch-as-catch-can — wrestling, horizontal bar, foils, high jumping, and kicking.

The sport of bicycling was also popular in this last decade; racing as well as just pedaling along the dusty roads. On May 1, 1897 "The bicycle races were well-filled, the track was in good condition and a fine crowd attended. One drawback was observable; a high wind was blowing and caused slow time to be made."

A bowling alley opened in August 1890.

And to enjoy the great outdoors, there was always the sport of bear hunting. Traps were laid and after the bear was caught, he was let loose, whereupon the dogs were set on him for the kill.

The women of the community had their own social and cultural activities. In the early 1890's the Golden Guild was organized as a social organization of young ladies to give entertainments and do benevolent work. They met almost every Saturday, and their membership of about fifteen included many of the community's leaders.

But they had their problems, mainly with others of their sex. On May 29, 1891 it was delightfully reported, "There seems to be trouble brewing between the married and unmarried ladies of this place or at least between some of them. Several married ladies here have formed a Ladies Aid Society while the unmarried ones have formed the Golden Guild. From some cause unknown a slight enmity has sprung up which promises to develop into a warm controversy unless it is nipped in the bud." The presidents were hoping to compromise their problems.

Whatever their difficulties, the women gathered into a literary society in those culturally formative years. In January 1894 some citizens expressed a need for a library, and in April of that year the Good Templars turned their reading room and effects over to a citizens' committee so that "place has a free library and reading room."

The organization of the Wednesday Club to "advance literary and educational interests of its members" may well have contributed to the development of a public library. It was first discussed at a meeting of the Tehachapi Board of Trustees in May 1911, at which time an offer of the County Board of Supervisors to provide books was accepted; the Trustees agreed the books could be kept in the Town Hall for the time being. Miss Anna Lorentzen was employed as the first librarian, replaced in 1914 by Mrs. Jean A. Durnal, who was followed in 1915 by Miss Verlie Jenkins.

The library was officially opened on November 1, 1912, with 235 volumes. It was open Tuesday, Wednesday, and Friday evenings from seven until nine o'clock, and Monday and Saturday afternoons for two hours. The library remained in the Town Hall until February 1917, when by a new agreement with Kern County, the library was moved to the "old

Freeman building.'' The Town paid the rent and other costs, while the County paid the librarian's salary. On October 3, 1931 the present library building on Green Street between E and D was dedicated and is a branch of the Kern County Library system.

—NINE—

One of the most popular organizations established in the 1890's, an interest in which continued for almost thirty years, was the melodious Tehachapi Brass Band. ''The Tehachapi Brass Band is no longer a thing of conjecture,'' reported the Tehachapi paper in August 1891. ''All the new instruments arrived yesterday, ten in number, and the band organized last night with Professor Roth as leader. There are three cornets, one clarinet, two altos, one tuba, one trombone, and drums.''

But the band didn't always play a harmonious tune. In the fall of 1892 it was ''making a great struggle to resurrect itself, but the fact is its members are at this time too busy to give their time to the divine heart.'' In 1897 Tehachapi ''organized a brass band'' which on St. Patrick's Day, gave a ball that was a huge success, using the evening's proceeds to buy new instruments. Two years later, however, Charles Heath reorganized the band.

After the turn of the century, residents in Old Town got into the act by organizing an orchestra in 1901, but it didn't last too long.

The Tehachapi Brass Band was reorganized in 1914. It had seventeen members in 1916, and band concerts were a regular Sunday afternoon occurrence. Again in 1918 the band was in a disorganized condition. The Country's entry into the First World War took instrumentalists from the

Tehachapi's Brass Band plays at the baseball game on July 4, 1914 (Ed Wiggins Collection)

area and the band disbanded. The Tehachapi Jazz Orchestra was formed in December 1919, and played for many dances.

One of the town's delightful historic events occurred during the peak of the brass band's popularity and exemplifies the type of politics possible and once prevalent, when men could laugh at themselves.

The year was 1916 — an era of vocal and demonstrable patriotism, a time of war, a time when small town enthusiasm overshadowed a major event. Democrat Woodrow Wilson was campaigning for his second term as President of the United States; his Republican opponent was Charles Evans Hughes.

The Democratic Central Committeeman from Kern County's second district was Henry Downs, a mercantile merchant, affectionately called "Unk," and a staunch party member and devoted worker. About a week before the November election "Uncle" Henry made a wager, declaring, "If our President carries California I will roll a peanut with a toothpick from the center of town to the city limits." He even promised to jump into the air and clap his heels together three times. From his own stock he selected a large double-jointed California peanut, hung it in a conspicuous place, and tied it with a pink ribbon.

"Gabe" Brite rests on a broom while to his right Henry Downs waits to roll a peanut down G Street in 1916. The Tehachapi Brass Band is in the background. (Herbert N. Force Collection)

The committee-in-charge, J. E. Durnal, F. A. Nejedly, and J. A. Cooper, wasted no time making preparations, apparently assured Wilson would carry the State. One can't help wondering if the growing excitement was because of the election or Downs' wager.

The history books have recorded the result of that election: Wilson not only swept the country, but also California. What was not recorded is the grand celebration which occurred soon thereafter.

The celebration was a Sunday as well as a holiday. Not only were most of the citizenry of Tehachapi present to watch Henry Downs pay his debt, but a large delegation of Democrats arrived from Bakersfield and Mojave and from other nearby towns.

At two o'clock in the afternoon Dr. N. J. Brown, Jr. declared "Uncle" Henry fit to proceed. Mrs. James Brite, a sympathizer, provided kneepads. Supervisor L. F. Brite, broom in hand, prepared to sweep the path clean as Downs made his journey "draped in an American flag, wearing knee pads, a broad Southern grin, and brandishing a huge toothpick." As the applause died down, one of the principals came forward, read a comedic biography of the fated politician and declared, "It is time." Down on his knees went Downs. Tehachapi's seventeen-piece brass band sounded the first notes of the day's official song. This song, sung joyously by a quartet to the music of "Tipperary," proclaimed the words especially written by another friend, Frank Reed:

Verse

Up in old Tehachapi
A Democrat one day,
Made a strong election bet,
And to his friends did say:
'If Wilson wins this state, by heck
Perform a stunt I will,
I'll roll a peanut on my knees
From here to Ferd's limekiln.'

Chorus

It's a long way to Snyder's limekiln,
When you can't go with ease;
It's a long way to roll a peanut
When you crawl upon your knees;
But keep the stick a moving
While Gabe Brite sweeps with care;
It's a long ways to Snyder's limekiln
But Downs will get there.

Verse

When he finished walking,
Then a friend stepped to his side,
Said, 'Old pal, I'm with you,
And I hope it's nation wide,
If your Woodrow wins this state
I'll sweep your pathway clear
That you may keep your promise true,
And never injury fear.'

O. D. Day brought up the rear with a cat-o'-nine-tails to urge the hero on. The band played. Hundreds followed behind him, cheering, laughing. What a day! True to his word, Henry Downs paid his wager, a quarter-mile's worth. Afterwards the peanut was tied up in its large pink ribbon and, together with the knee pads, sent to Downs' boyhood friend, Postmaster General Burleson.

Politically from the very beginning of its recorded history the Tehachapi region was strongly affiliated with the Democratic Party. The earliest settlers were primarily Southern Democrats, who brought a strong party allegiance with them in their migration Westward. Indicative of their attitude is a letter initiated by John Brite on June 4, 1859, to the Democratic Convention meeting in Los Angeles:

"We, the undersigned, claiming to be the Democrats from principal, would most respectfully represent to your honorable body, that we have learned that there has been a meeting held in this Valley, purporting to be a Democratic meeting, which said meeting has nominated and elected, as we believe, a Black Republican, as the only man to represent the Democracy of Tehachapi, and we take this method of remonstrating against such proceeding; and would respectfully ask that one Bascomb should not be admitted to take a seat in the County Convention, as there was not a general meeting of the citizens of the Valley, and as we hold that Mr. Bascomb is a Black Republican at heart; as in duty bound, we will pray, and et ceteras." The letter was signed by John M. Brite, Wm. C. Twitty, J. R. Lowery, W. H. Samuel, G. L. Farot, James C. Keer, John Gildon, David Wisdom, W. D. Holton, M. H. Hamilton, H. Hamon, Mitchel G. Kellar, T. J. Doss, M. Hart, W. P. Ayres, John Findley, Wm. Davidson, Aaron Hart, C. Garison, John M. Smith, D. Perkins, J. H. Campbell, Thos. W. Spiking, James Ayres, C. M. White, and J. Davies.

In his book "Pioneer Days in Kern County" Arthur Crites recorded one incident of Tehachapi's early political affairs:

"At one of the early elections held there and to the great consternation of all the members on the election board, there came out of the ballot box a Republican ballot. It upset the procedure of the election board for quite some time. What 'Black Republican' did they have in their midst? Who dared to vote a 'Black Republican' ticket in that precinct? How they would like to know who the 'Black Republican' was, and much more of this same sort of talk, with the addition of about all the other vile names they could think of.

"The vote was cast by a Mr. Buhn (a Dutchman who had recently come to this country). It so happened he was sitting by while the ballots were being counted and he listened to all the 'pet' names he was being called, but did not then, or for many years afterward, let it be known that he was the one who cast the 'Black Republican' vote.

"It was finally torn up and thrown into the spittoon and was not counted. It might be in order to say that the spittoon consisted of a box of sand well saturated with tobacco juice."

The brave Republican F. Lewis Buhn was born in Baden, Germany in 1843, and immigrated to California in 1863. He worked for two years in San Francisco as a gardener and then went to the mines of Butte County, finally settling in the Tehachapi Valley in 1870. For another eight years Buhn prospected and mined. He was also a farmer, the owner of 400 acres near Old Town, on which he planted sixty apple trees, 250 cherry trees, and twenty-seven pear trees.

Perhaps Buhn and Peter Greene, Tehachapi's other vocal Republican, were present at the Republican Rally held in October 1876. "Flaming Republican posters announce that Cutter and Smith of Bakersfield will orate," reported a Bakersfield paper, suggesting "The announcement creates no enthusiasm whatever, and I venture to say, that they will have a slim attendance if, from curiosity, our Democratic friends do not attend. Tehachapi is not a healthy location for Republican speakers."

But they were brave men, nevertheless, especially in the secrecy of the ballot box during the years of the Civil War. A Los Angeles newspaper commented in November 1864: "Tehachepy (sic) is the one precinct yet to hear from; . . . It will probably poll about thirty Copperhead votes and four or five Union votes" (45).

In August 1894 enough Republicans were located to form the Tehachapi Republican Club.

Indicative of the role politics played in Tehachapi is the 1934 election campaign for the county's Board of Supervisors. Perry Brite, who had represented the second district since 1927, was seeking another term. He followed in the footsteps of his father Lucas F. Brite, and grandfather John Brite, both of whom represented the district on the Board.

During the 1930's the management of Kern County General Hospital in Bakersfield was a hot and heavy issue; much controversy and turmoil filled the public's mind and spilled over into the supervisorial race. Brite was seeking re-election while he served as Chairman of the Board and was in a vulnerable position.

At the age of eighty-five years and a few months before his death, Mr. Brite recalled vivid memories of that campaign. He remembered that a doctor at Mercy Hospital "took out a lot of ads in the Tehachapi paper. It was a bonanza for the editor." These ads were in opposition to Brite's re-election and perhaps played a part in his eventual defeat at the polls by George W. Parrish on November 6, 1934.

It would take a political analyst's astute observations to determine the actual cause of the defeat. Nevertheless, early the morning after the election, a line formed at The Tehachapi News. If the News had been a bank, the line would have been called a "run." First in line were Mr. and Mrs. Charles Powell, owners of the Cameron Dairy, who also enjoyed discussing the incident, not because their friend and choice for supervisor lost, but because of the effect of the line. The Powells were followed by most of the community's businessmen, who advertised in the paper. They recalled the advertising was "mean and vicious;" the businessmen and loyal Brite supporters wouldn't stand for it. Out came their ads. In time publisher George Burris realized his mistake, but by then it was too late. He soon left town — ads support a paper.

Mr. Brite was later appointed by the Board of Supervisors to serve as County Tax Collector, and was eventually elected to the same office.

TEN

The ability of the citizenry to develop a growing sense of community in the waning years of the Nineteenth Century was proof at last that the forces of civilized living were permeating the actions of frontier townsmen. In Tehachapi much of the lawlessness stemmed from the saloons. It's actually with a sense of pride that some oldtimers talk about the thirteen saloons that were a source of merriment and entertainment in the years prior to prohibition. And the population in town then was only about 500!

But out in the countryside were those ubiquitous cowboys, miners, and quarrymen. Up the pass struggled several trains each day, and the trainmen sought a place to gather before the trip back down the mountain, so the social hall of the workingman became the saloon. Don't dare say "bar" to an oldster who insists saloon and bar weren't the same. True, drinks were served, but it was a place to meet and share thoughts and ideas with other men and, if the males of the family did spend too much time at the local pub, well, no wonder so many women joined the crusade for temperance!

Edwin R. Jones, another Tehachapi resident with vivid memories, many carried from childhoold, particularly recalls the saloons, as his father Clinton Jones owned the Palace Saloon from 1913 to 1918, when it was closed because of prohibition.

Mr. Jones' funniest recollection was of the day in 1914 when the saloon was moved. The Kessing Block was being constructed at the location of his father's establishment. The wood building was moved onto logs and rolled to the back of the lot, where it continued to dispense fun and games while the brick-block was being built. "French Paul and another fellow were cutting bricks in half to lay the building," he recalled during a visit a few years ago, "when I went over to inspect their work. They tried to run me off; but I took some of the bricks and started to pelt them." French Paul went to the elder Jones and reportedly suggested, "Take that brick-throwing kid away so we can finish this." The appelative stuck, and from that day forward he was known as Brick Jones.

According to Mr. Jones, there were so many saloons in the early days because running one was one of the easiest ways to earn a living. Jones said a carload of Old Crow Whiskey cost $4.00 a gallon, and his dad sold it in the saloon for fifteen cents a shot or two shots for a quarter. Mr. Jones added, "Men never drank at home in pre-prohibition days; they always went to the saloon which resembled a fraternal house."

An early consequence of Tehachapi's incorporation was restrictions on the operation of saloons. In no time some saloonkeepers were breaking laws and being warned; men were robbed while drinking, causing some citizens to express concern at Town Hall meetings. In 1911 there was a problem with "sidebars" through which women and children were passed drinks. In 1914 illegal dances were held in saloons, and it was decided to cover the "clear windows so the children couldn't see inside." That same year a new ordinance was passed to try and control the problem.

With the advent of prohibition in 1918, Tehachapi's thirteen saloons were closed. Then began the reign of the bootlegger who, at least in the folklore of this area, was something of a folkhero. Men didn't stop drinking just because of a law; as long as there was a demand, there was a supply, and the bootlegger was always around to supply the liquor. During this period men began to buy bottles of whiskey and bring them home to drink, so that when prohibition ended, drinking in the home was a natural way of life, and the new saloons that opened were fewer in number.

One of the most popular bootleggers of the day was Jim Davis, who operated a "still" in a secluded spot west of Willow Springs Road several miles from town. Up in Oak Creek, where that canyon is bisected by many another defile, the Payne Brothers also brewed their concoction for the benefit of the region's citizenry. And one popular lady of the day regularly transported bootlegged-whiskey into the area in her automobile, ably assisted by warnings of raids from a Bakersfield deputy sheriff.

But the law was enforced and raids were held often throughout those years in an effort to control the bootleg traffic.

It was in fact the charge of "possession of illicit liquor" that finally rid the town of its last bawdy house, which was located on East H Street. Especially after incorporation, some citizens were quite vocal in their complaints about the activities taking place in those sequestered houses. In April 1910 property owners on Robinson Street petitioned the Trustees "praying for an ordinance be passed prohibiting the erection of houses of prostitution on said street." H Street property owners submitted their petition in May. Consquently the Trustees notified any persons contemplating such businesses to keep them east of Robinson Street.

Over the years different ruses were attempted to find Madam Lottie Bustos with the "goods," meaning bootlegged liquor. The law had just about given up any hope of arresting her on a charge of prostitution. Lottie was a good businesswoman according to one who remembers her; always ready to earn a dollar, she chanced upon an easy scheme. One of the town's merchants had bought a slot machine to entertain the customers, but the customers didn't use it, so Lottie made a deal. She took the machine to her establishment, confident her waiting customers would use it more than the merchants. Each Saturday her partner came to collect half of the slot machine's earnings.

One Saturday as he headed for Lottie's place near H and Robinson Streets, Lottie's partner heard a shot. Out ran Lottie, exclaiming, "There's been a little trouble. You better not come over." "Little" was the understatement of the evening. When everything quieted down, two men had been killed and one was crippled. Before the night was over, a fourth hanged himself; no one knew why. The ladies of the establishment, meanwhile, went on about their business. Calm once more prevailed.

It wasn't until some years later that Lottie finally left town. On October 16, 1925 a search for liquor was made at her premises to no avail. On November 2 a number of citizens complained to the Trustees about the "disorderly place" kept by Lottie; a search warrant was issued, but again, no liquor was found. Less than a month later, however, on November 20 she was charged with the crime of "possession of illicit liquor." Figuring it was a good time to say good-bye to Madame Bustos, the Judge said, "You've got three days to leave town." And she did.

—ELEVEN—

No other institution more emphatically stated the virtues of the town or forcefully criticized it than Tehachapi's newspaper. From the first printed page of The Journal in 1888 until The Tehachapi News was purchased by Walter Johnson, father of the present owners, in 1943, the journey of the printed word was as circuitous and changing as the winding road in Tehachapi Canyon. A Bakersfield paper reported in 1888, "The Journal, published by McGrew and Houck, is the name of a new candidate for public favor. It is bright and newsy, brim full of enterprise, devoted to its section and deserves support. We wish it success." That first auspicious publication was so short-lived that there are no editions of it remaining and little memory.

The first sheets of The Summit Sun were lifted off the press on October 31, 1890, heralding the second weekly newspaper in the Tehachapi Valley. It, too, had problems. "With this issue of the Summit Sun," said the editor in his first issue, "we make our first effort in the field of journalism. As our name indicates, we are high up, geographically speaking; our desire is to be high up in the estimation of our readers. We have settled--not upon Mt. Ararat, as did Noah's Ark, but upon the summit of the Tehachapi Mountains, . . .

"We have come to publish the resources of this wonderful country of which so little seems to have been known until quite recently. We feel confident that whenever the resources of this part of Kern County shall be known, our population will so increase that it will be necessary to form a new county for the convenience of the great numbers who would naturally settle among us in order to be benefitted thereby.

"We have not come as the champion of any political party. We claim the right to criticize the acts of all persons holding any office of public trust, and this we shall do without fear or favor . . .

"Our columns may not always be filled with such reading matter as we might wish; but we beg you to remember that perfection is something that has to be attained, and we pledge you that our every effort will be made to give you value received for whatever assistance we may kindly receive at your hands."

Printed in a building located east of Nicholson's Drug Store on the corner of Curry and H Streets, E. J. H. Nicholson its editor and proprietor, The Sun began to inform the region. In March 1892 Nicholson hired another man as editor, and four men quickly moved through the title mainly because they enjoyed libations too much.

One of the editors in the early 1890's was former New Yorker F. M. Mooers who, in the 1860's, had worked for the Demas Barnes Drug Company in New York, and then joined the newspaper community as head bookkeeper of the Brooklyn Eagle. The West beckoned, and from city to hamlet to city Mooers worked his way to the Pacific Shore, arriving some time prior to 1891 in Tehachapi. In July he "returned . . . His friends are glad to welcome him back . . . and his services are badly needed now," in editing The Summit Sun.

The first issue of The Summit Sun, October 31, 1890 (Frank Tharp Collection)

Meanwhile down on the desert new gold discoveries were made and once again Mooers moved on. With his partner John Singleton, a Tehachapi resident and millwright, in 1894 Mooers prospected for gold in Goler Canyon. Singleton, a native of Tennessee, first made his way to

Texas as a youth and worked for an uncle in a cotton firm. In the late 1860's the lore of gold beckoned him, also, and he came West to seek his fortune. Singleton's millwright experience as well as his interest in carpentry was merely temporary employment; undoubtedly he was working in Tehachapi only in between his desert explorations for gold.

In April 1895 Mooer and Singleton, joined by C. A. Burcham of San Bernardino, while prospecting claims in the vicinity of what is now known as Rand Mountain, located gold. The Rand Mining District was born, the Yellow Aster Mine of Randsburg was born, three men made a fortune, and Tehachapi lost another newspaper editor.

The Summit Sun struggled along; the paper's problem was not lack of support, but "sheer neglect of its managers." Little news reached print until March 1892, when the Tehachapi Tribune made its first appearance, published under its new name by Nicholson and his associate, Mr. Perry. Nicholson and Perry sold the paper in September to Judge Wells and J. W. Jameson, who hired C. A. Seay, a foreman under Nicholson on the old Summit Sun, as the editor. Seay purchased the paper in 1893, resurrecting its original name, and published his first sheets.

Then in 1897 a new paper appeared on the scene eclipsing the Tribune, nee Sun, which had disappeared along the way. In November Grey Oliver, formerly of Bakersfield, located his press in Hop Lee's Blue Wing Restaurant, and printed a six-page paper he called The Times. He continued until August 1899, when he left Tehachapi to take a position on the Los Angeles Herald.

Much of these early papers consisted of reprints of political discussion rampant over the land, a good fictional serial, ads for out-of-town merchandise, and useful information, practical advice, anything of interest, in addition to a little local news and some ads, which filled only a couple of the pages.

Enter the Twentieth Century, and with it the birth of a new paper, when on October 13, 1900, The Tehachapi Tomahawk came off the press, edited by Seay, who was once again on the job. After only six months the paper was moved to Mojave and became known as The Mojave Tomahawk. Then Charles Heath purchased the type and press, returned The Tomahawk to its original home, and began to republish The Tehachapi Tomahawk in 1902.

Initially Heath printed the paper in a shed next to his E Street home; about 1910 he moved to a room in the Masonic Temple at Green and F Streets. Upon his retirement in 1914 his son Erle, later employed as a public relations representative for the Southern Pacific Company, published the paper until he sold it in 1916 to George Snell.

The new owner had some problems with local merchants because, as a minister, he refused to advertise the local saloons. During Snell's tenure the Kern County Press Association was organized in September 1916; the Association's first secretary was W. A. Wyatt, who represented The Tomahawk, apparently as one of its employees.

During publication of the paper by Franklin A. Meyer and Merle D. Hurlburt, who purchased it in 1919 from William J. Evans who had published the paper since 1917 along with the Mojave News, the paper's name was changed to The Tehachapi News. "After a long and lingering illness covering a period of almost seventeen years of intensive suffering," proclaimed the new owners, "Tom-A-Hawk, one of Tehachapi's pioneers, quietly passed away at midnight of June 12." When Meyer sold the paper in 1920, moving to Bishop, California, he took along all of the equipment.

A nephew of Senator John P. Jones' was the next publisher of the Tehachapi paper. After his discharge from the Army in 1919, Gregory Jones worked for a while in Los Angeles and, in the summer of 1920, arrived in Tehachapi to labor in the wheat harvest, and then in the various orchard jobs of the Ramina Ranch's operation.

"Meanwhile, my wife had joined me, and together we purchased and operated the little local weekly newspaper, the Tehachapi News," he recalled in 1975. "On a lovely spring day early in April, 1921 we were just completing the blossom spray, and we had about decided that 'This was the Life'. Alas! the following morning we looked out of our window at a howling blizzard, the thermometer registering 14 above zero. Not a pear to be picked that year! As soon as we could, we packed our belongings, and left for San Francisco."

Mr. Jones had already sold the paper before the spring freeze, announcing on February 5, 1921, he would discontinue publication even without a new publisher, in two weeks. A new paper was on the scene, however, and Archie Hicks published the paper of February 26, 1921.

In 1922, a year after he took over the paper, Hicks modernized printing when he bought a three-magazine linotype which enabled him to print all of the paper in the plant. Before that, news matter was cast on machines in Los Angeles, and the headings and ads were set by hand in the Tehachapi shop, together with local news.

The linotype, which was invented by a young German-American, Ottmar Mergenthaler, in 1884, and perfected two years later, enabled the printer to compose metal molds or matrices in lines, "justified" their spacing, cast lines of type in molten metal and redistributed the matrices to repeat the operation. One man could set up to seven lines of type a minute, or more than three times the speed of hand composition (46).

Hicks sold the paper in 1928 to W. L. Davis, and after two years George R. Burris assumed ownership. Ill-health terminated the interest of Grove Wilson's who, in 1943, sold the paper to Walter Johnson, after owning it since July 1935.

Mr. Johnson started in the newspaper business as a "printer's devil" when he was fourteen years old, purchasing his first paper four years later. He moved to California in 1927 to work for his brother, who owned a paper in Banning, where Walter stayed until he purchased The Tehachapi News in 1943. Upon Mr. Johnson's death in 1964, the paper passed into the hands of his sons Warren and Richard, who continue to co-publish the weekly sheets today.

—TWELVE—

An oldtimer who enjoyed describing the pleasure of the "good old days'' is Sherman Chitwood, a native son. "Young people gathered on Saturday night for the dances," he told me during a visit a couple of years ago. "Everyone mixed then." It was all congenial, although sometimes there were fights or somebody had too much to drink. The first big dances were held in Asher's Opera House, but dances were also held in the schoolhouse. Dancing was the big event of the week.

"Before prohibition, the cowboys would come to town," Mr. Chitwood recalled. "Tehachapi had thirteen saloons at one time and three or four bawdy houses across the tracks. Sometimes they got drunk and messed around, but it wasn't really bad."

"Across the tracks, northeast of H and Green Street, the land was undeveloped and a quarter-mile race track was laid out. Several ranchers had good horses, especially the Brite family. Sunday afternoons were also set aside for baseball. There were contests with Mojave, Lancaster, and Palmdale. Before the automobile," he added, "the few roads there were were very dusty — especially on the way to Palmdale. By horse and buggy it was a hard trip across the desert. Sometimes we'd go by train. All day we'd play in the hot sun and then return at night."

The opera house was also the scene of the traveling shows that periodically came to town. One of the most enjoyable was presented by the Chautauqua, which each summer arrived from its headquarters in New York. Large caravans came by train, later by truck and automobile, offering literary and moral entertainment as well as just plain fun wherever the caravans went.

From about 1900 on, a variety of social clubs provided respite for occasional leisure hours. They included the Tehachapi Drama Club, the Whist Club, the Knights of Pythias (established in 1893), and the Ladies Aid Society of the Methodist Church. The Eastern Star was organized in January 1901 with fourteen members. And the Tehachapi Lodge Number 313, F. & A.M. was established in 1907. The Lodge's property on Green Street was the location of the original Town Hall and in 1925 the post office was also moved there.

The Boy Scouts were first organized in November 1915, and reorganized in 1921. The Tehachapi Athletic Club was reorganized in 1915, and for many years offered boxing matches and provided tennis courts in addition to other sporting events. In 1931 the Tehachapi Golf Club was formed, its course located near the airport.

The Tehachapi Amusement Company was showing five-reeler Charlie Chaplin movies in 1916 at the opera house. Of those there, who would ever forget Grace Darling as Beatrice Fairfax in "The Story of the Missing Watchman!"

The movies were a popular pastime in Tehachapi, particularly because they were actually filmed in the region. The Al Jennings Feature Film Company was in town in June of 1918, making a movie. In 1919 the company was responsible for the only successful robbery of the Bank of Tehachapi, when Jennings filmed the "Bennington Bank Robbery" in July, complete with gunplay in the streets. In March 1920 W. S. Van Dyke, who had first been in the area with Jennings' Capitol Film Co. Incorporated of Los Angeles, was at the old Spencer place with thirty movie people from Los Angeles, filming part of a twelve-episode Jack Dempsey serial.

Jennings brought to his productions first hand experience in bank robbery, although his motion pictures depicted more successful crimes than those in which he participated. He was one of three sons of an old Southern gentleman who practiced law in Oklahoma. He and his brother Frank lived in El Reno, while Ed lived in Woodward.

On what proved to be a motivating occasion, a drunken brawl occurred in an Oklahoma saloon in which Ed Jennings was killed by a "swashbuckling attorney, Temple Houston, son of General Sam Houston," and Ed's brother Frank was wounded. The trail to crime was born in the courtroom when, as the result of a successful plea of self-defense, Houston was acquitted, and Al Jennings "left the courtroom very bitter, cursing the administration of justice and vowing vengeance."

Vengeance became thievery as the two remaining brothers began to rob express companies and traveling men. In a gang with three other men they attempted train robbery but were such amateurs that their loot was only a few hundred dollars. The gang's third train robbery was a failure because instead of stopping, the engine ran right through the ties which had been laid on the track to wreck the engine.

The law finally caught up with them in a spectacular long-distance gun battle in a ranch house after which, quite peaceably, Al, Frank and two others of the gang, surrendered. Al as their leader received the longest sentence: a life term in the Federal Prison at Columbus, Ohio, for "molesting the United States mails." Within five years, however, he was released, only to be reincarcerated for another five years at Leavenworth, Kansas, for robbing the trains. Through the intercession of friends he was again released.

A writer appeared to help him write his autobiography. In turn Jennings was a lecturer, evangelist, and motion picture actor. He journeyed to Tehachapi to put his earlier experiences to good use!

Skating was another popular activity in the late 1920's, when a rink was located at the American Legion Hall. The Oddfellows Lodge was built in 1930, but by the next year the "old Opera House," which was in addition to Asher's Opera House and located on the north side of F Street between Green and Robinson, was in such bad condition with paper hanging in shreds from the walls, that the doors and windows were nailed shut.

At the beginning of World War I some change occurred in Tehachapi, mainly affecting the personal lives of individuals. A Home Guard was organized in April 1917, composed of men who were beyond the age of enlistment. In July the first quota of draftees from Tehachapi numbered twenty-six men. A local branch of the Red Cross was organized in November and Liberty Bond sales were initiated. At the end of the war in 1919, nineteen Tehachapi men had served in the Armed Forces.

Immediately after the war, the American Legion Post was organized in 1920 and was for many years responsible for some of the big and popular dances in the region. As a sign of the times with the advent of the Charleston craze, in 1926 the dance was prohibited at Legion affairs because of complaints about the "contortions." The Charleston had already been banned in other cities. But complaints about the Charleston weren't the only ones; drunkenness and rowdyism were so frequent in 1924 that the Town's Trustees were encouraged to do something about it.

Mrs. Sarah Woods, wife of retired Justice Court Judge William Woods, summed up the social and cultural life one day, when she told me, "People worked harder then to make a living, longer hours, and were ready to rest when not working. Families visited with each other, there was church, school, and lodge activities, the atmosphere was relaxed. People would come to town and ask what we did in such a small place," she added. "But we were active and busy — we really didn't know any different."

—THIRTEEN—

Although the pioneer settlers were religiously inclined, the relative isolation of the community and lack of considerable numbers precluded an active church for some years.

Circuit riders were the main instrument for instruction for the people until the 1890's cultural explosion occurred. As early as 1863 a Methodist South preacher rode by horseback to preach to the few families then in the area. A visitor in the Valley that year recalled, "Strange as it seemed to us, there had been religious service in the valley that day. A Methodist South preacher was visiting a settler and held a 'Meeting' that day in a house, and all of the half-dozen families of the valley turned out." And in 1876 another observer commented: ". . . no professional cumbers Tehachipee (sic), save and except gentlemen of the church, but at the date of my visit a 'tracted meetin' was being held, and I am proud to say that I saw and appreciated a shade the roughest tussle with Satan which I ever witnessed. It was 'powerful' tough."

After the Kern River Circuit of the Methodist Episcopal Church was established in the early 1870's, the Reverend J. L. Bennett was the first minister assigned a vast territory which in 1871 included Tehachapi, Kernville, Havilah, Weldon, Isabella, Onyx, Bodfish, and Bakersfield. Called "walking parsons," they were provided lodging in private homes as the parsons provided sustenance for representatives of fifteen to twenty different Protestant denominations.

A Methodist church was organized as a part of the Kern River Circuit in the Mid-Seventies, with services held in the Old Town schoolhouse. A circuit rider from the Los Angeles Conference of Methodist Churches ministered there as did an "itinerant schoolteacher" who preached to the people during the late Seventies in unorganized services. The congregation did organize under the Methodist Episcopal Conference in 1888 with Reverend Lee serving as its first pastor. They met in a building constructed of wood donated by John Brite.

Meanwhile, in October 1876 a Baptist congregation held two weeks of religious revivals conducted by Brothers Riley and Freckeray.

Formalized Catholic services began in the Tehachapis in 1884, when Father Bannon was appointed the first pastor of Kern and Inyo Counties. No doubt the initial settlement of the area by Southern Methodists and the

Tehachapi Methodist Church about 1916, located on the southeast corner of D and Green Streets (Ed Wiggins Collection)

St. Malachy's Catholic Church in 1916, located on the corner of F and Pauley Streets (Ed Wiggins Collection)

lack of a large Spanish population precluded early development of the Roman Church before that time. In pre-parish days, however, when Bakersfield was a mission of Visalia, an assistant priest drove with horse and buggy to Bakersfield and through the mountains to Tehachapi and on into the Mojave Desert. The first recorded mass was on April 8, 1877, when Father Marion of Visalia visited the town. Semi-annual services were held at the home of Antone Pauly.

Both the Methodist and Catholic congregations initiated building programs towards the end of the 1880's. Although the Catholics had built a small church which was dedicated on June 13, 1887, in 1891 they contracted for a new thirty-by-fifty foot edifice and built it to plans furnished by Philadelphia architect Mr. Pierce. Tehachapi was formally made a parish in 1893 with Father Bannon as its pastor.

The Protestants first proposed a building fund for a permanent edifice in June of 1890. The new Union Church, constructed in the popular brick style coming into focus during that decade, was a welcome addition at the end of 1891, augmented by a parsonage a year later. After several years services were irregular, especially around 1908-1910. For two years there was no resident pastor and it was many months since any activities were held except for Sunday School and the Epworth League.

The members of what was then known as the Tehachapi Methodist Church requested release from the Conference in 1920. After reorganization and incorporation the Tehachapi Community Congregational Church was established, holding its first annual meeting in January 1921. The Congregationalists sold the brick edifice and for some time held services in the grammar school. In 1928 a new church was built, which still serves the congregation at the corner of E and Green Streets.

The Catholics rebuilt St. Malachy's Church in 1936, which served them until the 1960's, when they moved to a new location at F and Mill Streets.

Both the Catholic and Protestant churches conducted Sunday Schools; the Catholics organized one as early as 1901, and the Methodists in 1907.

In recent years the influx of residents to the region has created additional denominations, which today number about nineteen.

When Mrs. Alex Prewett died in 1858 just a short time after giving birth to what oral tradition says was the first white child born in the area, she was buried by her family on a small plot of ground on their land. As the years passed other families also buried their loved ones on the same plot which eventually became known as the "public cemetery." Later the property was owned by Jeremiah Shields who legally set the plot aside as a cemetery.

A meeting of Tehachapi's citizens was held in 1889 with a view of obtaining land for a new public cemetery. The Eugene Garlock family, which lived a few miles east of town, also used their land for family burials, and soon the area's residents were burying their loved ones at that location, which became known as the Eastside Cemetery.

In 1948 with the formation of the Tehachapi Public Cemetery District, the Garlock heirs legally conveyed the land to the District for a public cemetery. The District also operates and maintains two other cemeteries. The first is the Catholic Cemetery, located on land donated by the Clark family and blessed by Father Bannon in June of 1891. (The district has leased it from the Roman Catholic Church for ninety-nine years.) The second is a family burial plot now owned by the District in Sand Canyon, where a number of Indian people are buried.

—FOURTEEN—

The decided aspect of improvements which occupied the minds of the town's citizens in the early 1900's was exemplified in public education, which was important to the earliest settlers in the region. As early as 1861 William C. Wiggins conducted classes for the children living in the Brite Valley area. The Tehachapi School District was formed on November 9, 1866, when the Board of Supervisors established the boundaries of the first publically tax supported school district in Kern County.

At first classes were probably held in a private home, as it wasn't until June 27, 1868, when the school trustees were elected, that the citizens also voted to build a schoolhouse. A wood frame building was constructed and there Miss Louesa Maria Jewett instructed her first students, which included five Doziers, five Wigginses, four Brites, one Hosack, two Harts, four Cuddebacks, three Tylers, one from the Hale family, and Nellie Calhoun.

The Old Town School as it looked in 1934 (Camille Gavin)

Miss Jewett, who in later years was married to another Kern County figure, rancher Angus Crites, took her position on May 20, 1867, agreeing to teach for three months. But when the patrons of the school learned they could draw public money for her salary, she agreed to teach for five months. Miss Jewett used McGuffey readers, but a scarcity of books necessitated her reading most of the lessons to her pupils. The young teacher, who had arrived in Tehachapi on horseback, boarded with both the Doziers and the Wigginses, a custom followed by teachers for many years.

When the District's name was changed to Old Town in 1909 (neighboring Summit School District having assumed Tehachapi School District as its designation), the average daily attendance had dropped to five pupils.

Education for the youngsters in Tehachapi formally began on February 18, 1877, with the establishment of the Summit School District; fifteen students were in average daily attendance. In April 1878 the students met in their newly constructed two-story frame schoolhouse at the northeast corner of I and Curry Streets.

One of the big events of school days in the two-story white frame building across the tracks remembered by Mr. Chitwood, was the annual May Day picnic. There once was a beautiful grove of oak trees west of Tehachapi, not far from the tracks. The wildflowers in late spring were abundant. With picnic baskets in hand the children walked to the grove, played games, and danced around the Maypole.

The Tehachapi Summit School which was located on Curry and I Streets Circa 1890's (Ed Wiggins Collection)

One reason for changing the location of the grammar school was the danger of so many children crossing the busy railroad tracks. A new three-room brick school building was constructed in 1903 at a cost of $10,000 and located at E and Robinson Streets. That fall, tennis and basketball courts were built for physical education.

There are memories of those days, too. Mrs. Peggy Dickerson Pedigo attended all eight grades there, contained in four classrooms, two grades taught in each by one teacher. There was also an auditorium with a stage. Each morning grades one through four assembled outside at the east side of the auditorium while grades five through eight assembled on the west. When everyone was quiet and at attention, each student was allowed to march up the steps and go into their respective rooms with "no talking, no giggling, no gum chewing, eyes straight ahead, through the cloak room, deposit coats and country kid's lunches and into our own seats ready to begin our school days work . . . The school was heated using coal and more than once a piece of coal was used 'accidentally' to crack a window. The floors were pine and were coated with oil to keep the dust down."

An educator's 1918 report commented: "In the little old town of Tehachapi, three teachers are employed in the grades. Each year the school gives an entertainment that takes a prominent place in the community affairs. Last year it consisted of a musical operatta (sic) for the performance of which teachers and children deserved great credit. The training has had a marked influence on the children's ability to articulate distinctly in reading and speaking."

The original schoolhouse was sold in July 1903 to Frank Dufour who bid $625 for the building, moving it to the corner of F and Green Streets. It was sold again in 1905 to Mr. Barneche and, after a series of owners, it was last used as a drugstore. The Tehachapi Grange bought the building and moved it to their property on C near Mill Street, where in 1958 it was torn down. The original belfry was removed in 1907, and the school bell was housed for a time in the City's garage. The bell is now located near an entry to the Wells Elementary School.

By 1916 attendance at the Old Town district school was so low that portions of the District were added to the Tehachapi School District at "Summit." However, in 1914, classes began at a new school which was constructed near Brite Valley at a cost of $3,500 to the Old Town School District. Children from that area attended classes until 1922-23 when attendance dropped to an average of two a day. The school was damaged by a heavy wind during its first year when according to an annual report the "wind mill and tank during last winter were blown down in one of the unusually strong winds and have not been repaired. The boys' out-house was also blown over and over for fifty feet in the windstorm. We righted it temporarily where it stopped." That school burned down in 1923.

The Old Town School District was finally terminated in 1928 because of a lack of attendance and the area became part of the larger Tehachapi and Cummings Valley Districts.

One other school district functioned for a number of years as it educated a minimal number of children in its one room, one teacher schoolhouse. The Cameron School District was formed April 5, 1893 to serve the youngsters in the Cameron Canyon area. Its first Board of Trustees, D.

Monroe, J. W. Iles, and L. B. Killian, called an election for July 10, 1893, at which the District's electors passed a bond to buy lots for and build their schoolhouse.

The most central location was decided as a lot about two miles east of Willow Springs Road and on the north side of the Cameron Canyon Road. Beginning with an average daily attendance of ten pupils in its first year of operation, 1893-94, peak years of attendance were 1902-1905 when sixteen pupils were recorded for each of those years.

Then on August 27, 1915 the District's voters cast ballots at another election to move the schoolhouse to "near the bridge as possible on Oak Creek where Willow Springs and Mojave Road cross." Where freighters and stages had once kept Oak Creek Station a lively place, for about fifteen years, until the 1929-30 school year when attendance dropped to two children, lively youngsters learned and played in the relocated Cameron School, which at its new locale was popularly called the Oak Creek School.

Because of lack of attendance the Cameron School District was suspended on August 4, 1930, and was declared lapsed on November 28, 1932, when the District's territory was divided between the Aqueduct and Tehachapi School Districts.

A number of people who taught in local schools later achieved prominence in other areas. Leo G. Pauly, who attended school in Tehachapi, taught sixth through eighth grades in the original Tehachapi schoolhouse. Pauly was its principal after he graduated from San Jose State Normal School in 1896, serving until 1898. Mr. Pauly was also principal of the Kern City School in East Bakersfield, and a member of the County Board of Education from 1896 to 1917. He was active in Bakersfield business and banking commerce and postmaster there in the 1930's.

Alexander B. McPherson, who taught in Old Town in 1869-70, later served as Kern County Superintendent of Schools. Another Superintendent was J. H. Berry, a teacher in Keene from 1888-1890. Mrs. Jean A. Durnal served on the County Board of Education from 1914-1920 after teaching three years in the Aqueduct School. C. M. Vrooman, who taught in the Brite Valley School in 1886, also served on the County Board of Education, and was its president from 1884-1888. Alfred Harrell taught school in Tehachapi in 1885 and married Virginia McKamy, a Cummings Valley teacher. In 1897 he bought The Bakersfield Californian for $1,000 and became editor and publisher of a paper owned today by his heirs.

As early as 1909 an effort was made to provide a high school education for the area's schoolchildren. Until that time the children were sent to either Lancaster or Bakersfield to live with relatives, or boarded out. Otherwise their education necessarily ended; for many it did.

Mrs. Elizabeth Hill Jackson, who was in the eighth grade in 1909, recalled in 1974, "Our folks thought we were too young to leave home and enter high school — so arrangements were made for a freshman class at the elementary school. We were instructed in Algebra, English, General Science and History" (47).

Mrs. Jackson didn't know why, but the next year the class was discontinued and in 1911 "the majority of the class either moved from

Tehachapi or went to live with friends or relatives so they could continue their education.''

It may well be that the eighth grade in 1909 was a special effort of the Kern County Schools Office, as Mrs. Jackson also recalled that examinations were sent to Tehachapi from that office, and when she entered high school in Dinuba, after the family moved there, her transfer came from Bakersfield, not Tehachapi.

Another attempt was made in 1916 to provide a high school when a temporary building was erected. The building included two classrooms, an assembly room, and a principal's office. The school was located just east of the grammar school, renting the first year for $400. In January 1917 twelve students attended the smallest high school in Kern County, of which Professor R. Y. Glidden was the teaching principal. By that winter only five children were enrolled and concern was expressed that the school would have to close in the spring, which it did. The low attendance was attributed to parents' concern that the school was unsatisfactory. Many parents once again sent their children out of town.

In 1925 the Chamber of Commerce initiated a new move to conduct local high school classes, and in 1928 a high school district was legally established. That same year the Parent-Teachers Association was formed. The following year a three-year course was established for the high school which opened in a private home at 401 South Curry Street. Its first principal was Orris Imhof, with one teacher for the twenty-four students.

The district purchased property southeast of Snyder and G Streets in 1929 from C. A. Willis (who that year advertised a new subdivision, the Willis High School Subdivision). A new high school building was planned in 1930. At a cost of $50,000 the reinforced concrete building, which opened in September, consisted of four classrooms, a library, offices, and a combination gym and auditorium. Sixteen students attended the first year.

For fourteen years the building continued to serve the community until one night in 1944 a fire which started in the chemistry room, swept through the main building, destroying the auditorium, the music room and instruments, a fully equipped science room, and the home economics room. But repairs and improvements soon put the building back in order.

In 1955-56 an additional school was constructed on Curry Street south of town, to serve the expanding population. Known today as the Tompkins Elementary School, it was originally built to house the Tehachapi Junior High School, which consisted of seventh and eighth grades and relieved the pressure on the growing elementary school. Then in 1965 with the opening of the new Tehachapi High School on Anita Drive, the Snyder Street high school became Jacobsen Junior High School, and the junior high building became a second elementary school. Also in the mid-Sixties the Tehachapi Elementary School was renamed Wells Elementary School in honor of its long time principal Claude L. Wells.

As a result of a public election in 1957, the Tehachapi Unified School District, administered by a seven-man Board of Trustees, was established, combining the Aqueduct Elementary, Tehachapi Union Elementary, and Tehachapi Valley Union High School Districts. The District's first superintendent was Thomas J. Feeney, and the Board's first president was J. C. Jacobsen.

Jacobsen had initially opposed unification as he was concerned it would increase operating costs, but the State of California exerted pressure on the District, telling it that to continue to qualify for certain aid money, it would have to unify. Outlying country school districts had already become associated with the larger union districts in the 1950's, when consolidation was initiated.

In the 1974-75 school year the District was a major regional employer with a budgeted payroll of $1,833,589 for its 189 staff members.

—FIFTEEN—

A Santa Fe Railroad Business Directory in 1905 advertised the gamut of Tehachapi's services: Blacksmiths, "Ladies' and Gents' Furnishing Goods," several saloons, a meat market, general merchandise stores, stables, a painter and paperhanger, a tailor, a confectionary shop, hotels, and an undertaker, served the population. In all, twenty-two businesses subscribed to the ad. As the years passed slowly down the calendar of time, modernization changed blacksmith shops into garages, hotels to motels, and saloons to bars.

Inside Laura Wiggins Weferling's millinary store which was located in the Vernon Hotel on Green Street. The clerk is Rose Paulsen Walker — Circa 1912 (Ed Wiggins Collection)

When she first alighted from a train in 1914, moving to the Tehachapi Valley from a northern city, Mrs. Hazel Dickerson, not yet married to one of the area's dairy farmers, was left with this impression of

Tehachapi: "A small village, a small western town, with dirt streets and false fronts on buildings." In 1915 complaints were made about the "old Seeger Building and old Spencer Building which were both nuisances and had vagrants sleeping in them;" this only thirty years after the buildings were constructed. Complaints of this type continued, resulting in an ordinance controlling dilapidated buildings, some of which were torn down.

In the late 1920's when the young married couple of Sarah and William Woods moved to the region, their first impression of Tehachapi was also of an "old town, not particularly pretty." And until the 1952 earthquake, little new construction occurred in Tehachapi.

The business district remained static, centering between Curry Street, which was its westerly border where for many years Jim Brite's livery stable was the landmark to turn the corner and go south, and Robinson Street on the east. A few businesses were still established north of the tracks on H Street. To the south, Green was the major artery of commerce with little occurring beyond F Street.

Ever so slowly the commercial scene moved south on Green and then east on F, until the downtown section was more than just a block along the main highway. For years the railroad remained the core, and the commercial area as well as the residential neighborhoods evolved from this axis.

Fire and the fear of it, as well as a need to get away from the temporary appearance of wood frame buildings, created the new brick blocks of the early 1900's. At this time architectural change occurred. One project was initiated by Mary Kessing who, with her husband Bernard, arrived in Tehachapi with the railroad in 1876. The Kessings constructed the first frame building in town — The Summit House — which was a restaurant and hotel. After Mr. Kessing's death in 1890, his widow continued the hotel's operation. The Summit House was torn down in 1914, making way for a new "block" of brick, which housed several stores, the telephone office, an electric shop, and a shoe store.

The activities of the on-again, off-again Chamber of Commerce helped to bring new people into the community. Motion picture companies were in the region in 1922 filming the silents, which the Chamber declared was a good means of "advertising Tehachapi and the vicinity." After the demise of the Chamber in 1937, the Exchange Club was formed. (In 1952 the Chamber was re-established, first as the Tehachapi Businessmen's Association, and then in 1961 as the Tehachapi Chamber of Commerce.)

The Tehachapi Women's Club was active in the 1940's and lest anyone think women didn't have any power, besides their successful campaign to erect "sheep signs," they assisted in having directional signs placed at important places in the community, such as the park and the hospital. Back in 1915 the members of the club were so disgusted with the general unsightliness of the town that they organized a clean-up day, providing a team and wagon to pick up the debris.

By 1921 some new services were in the community and the businesses included a 24-hour telegraph service, four general merchandise stores, two markets, two dairies, a pharmacy, five hotels, two restaurants, two barber shops, a confectionary, a shoe shop, a tailor and cleaner, three real estate offices, three garages, an Opera House, blacksmiths, hay and grain yards, a lumber yard, three pool rooms, packing houses, a bakery, a cutlery dealer, and the bank.

The population just the year before, taken during the national census, showed the incorporated limits had 458 people living in Tehachapi, one of the smallest municipalities in California. The population of the general area was set at 1,323.

When Mr. Chitwood was a youngster, he remembers the only work available was in the hayfields, or on a ranch for $1.00 a day. The economy which fed the businesses was mostly farming, cattle, and lime kilns, and the railroad workers who kept the restaurants going as their helper engine crews laid over. "The horse and buggy days were much better," Mr. Chitwood insisted one day. "With autos, people moved around more, weren't settled down. Farmers used to come into town once a month or a little more often for goods. When they got cars, they came in several times a week and neglected their farms.

"Summer was the active season, when produce was teamed to the warehouses at the tracks; hundreds of cords of wood were stored from where the carwash is today on G Street to the depot. The only activity in the winter was the lime kilns; they, too, had storage sheds at the track. The railroad was really used then."

Mr. Chitwood felt the economy's limitation to agriculture and lime kept the population stagnant, as there was no other way to earn money. Then, with the years becoming drier, and the "rainfall not like it used to be," money tightened in the agricultural community. It wasn't until Monolith was in full swing in cement production that an increased payroll enabled town residents to begin to think about supporting more services. "If a man is only earning enough for his family," Mr. Chitwood explained, "he isn't spending it elsewhere." He added, "People were more congenial, more friendly. Everyone knew each other, everyone mixed. Not many wealthy people here; economically everyone was about the same level." And Mr. Chitwood's impressions were repeated over and over again as I talked with oldtimers and some not so old. There may not have been the modern conveniences of the 1970's, but generally speaking, people preferred the "old days in Tehachapi."

—SIXTEEN—

Before the advent of the automobile, the train was the main mode of travel out of town, but even so, people didn't go to Bakersfield too often. There was a local freight train on which a passenger could buy a ticket and ride the caboose. For children the year's big event was a trip to the "city" to see the Ringling Brothers' circus.

By car, in the beginning it was a good four-hour trip into the San Joaquin Valley. Returning to Tehachapi, automobiles usually had to stop, especially on the Bear Mountain Grade, to cool their engines.

The Halter Grade and steep stage road were circumvented in 1916 when a bond issue, which was approved July 18, 1913 for $2,500,000, culminated in construction of 28.2 miles from the Sand Cut to Tehachapi, and 20.8 miles from Tehachapi to Mojave.

Part of that road is still navigable as the Tehachapi-Woodford Road from Tehachapi to Keene, and further west from the Caliente cut-off into the old Edison Highway. It is a narrow, extremely winding road and, according to Mr. Hicks, who was working at the cinnabar mine in 1916 as the road was built past his retorts, one of the foremen told him the company was paid more for curves than straight-aways. Count the curves if you ever drive the scenic road . . . .

The Board of Trustees passed its first ordinance regulating automotive traffic in 1912, stating, "All vehicles on the streets or highways . . . shall be one mile in six minutes or the rate of 10 miles an hour . . . Slow signs to be placed on highway." Another ordinance regulated mufflers on motors or other engines "to prevent emission of loud and explosive sounds," with a penalty or fine of not more than $50 or imprisonment in the Town Jail or Kern County Jail for not more than twenty-five days.

But there was still horse traffic in 1917, when it was reported a tree in front of a house on G Street was being used as a hitching post and horses were getting on sidewalks. Rather than cut the tree down (it was a large shade tree), a "No hitching — Do Not Disturb The Tree" sign was posted on it.

In 1915 another ordinance regulated increasing automotive traffic, the same year that the Automobile Club of Southern California asked for permission to post signs for passing motorists. A sign was necessary in 1918 at the corner of G and Green Streets to control all of the traffic on the main boulevard. It simply said "Keep To Right." It wasn't until 1930 that a boulevard "Stop Sign" was placed at the same intersection.

In the early Twenties with more automotive horsepower, speeding on the streets became a problem. In 1926 Marshall Louis Boden, who had his hands full just trying to keep up with the lawbreakers and maintain the peace, was assisted by a Town Traffic Officer, but Robert G. Nelson, the traffic officer, quit in only a month and Boden resigned as Marshall in

186

Looking northwest at Tehachapi in the second decade of the 20th century. Denison's young pear orchard is at the left. The brick building in center

January 1927, to become Constable of the Fifteenth Judicial Township.

With traffic increasing in the Tehachapi region, in 1928 the State of California appointed the first area State Traffic Officer. F. R. Walker was stationed in Tehachapi to enforce the regulations. He remained on duty until 1931 when he was transferred to Bakersfield, from where the Tehachapis were covered. It wasn't until 1958 that a substation of the California Highway Patrol was opened at Cache Creek. The substation was elevated to an area office in 1969.

One of the earliest automobiles was owned by Jess Cuddeback, who also owned a saloon in nearby Mojave, as well as a livery business in Tehachapi in 1903, from which he hauled freight to the desert mines. According to Herb Force, a long time resident, Cuddeback claimed he bought the first car into the area, a 1900 Packard, to save horseflesh, except that every time he'd load the car, he'd have to hitch up the horses to pull it! Once, on a trip to Monolith with some cousins as passengers to show off his "contraption," they had great fun, especially every time the car got stuck in a chuckhole and everybody got out to push. This dependable Packard had only one cylinder. When Cuddeback wrote to the factory asking why there weren't more, he received the reply they "were having enough trouble with just one!"

While on one of his jaunts one day in 1903, Cuddeback stopped at the Monroe Ranch near Cameron Canyon. In recalling what happened when he asked the Monroes if they would like a ride, Mrs. Elizabeth Monroe Powell said her father adamantly refused to get into that "damned contraption," but her mother thought it would be a delightful experience. Besides, they were driving only a few hundred yards up the road where one of the neighbors was returning to his home.

Mrs. Monroe jumped into the back of the car which had only two seats, both up front, and off they went. When the short ride was over she walked the few hundred yards back home. There she was met by a greatly angered husband who, it turned out, was sure his wife was "trying to commit suicide" by riding in the car.

187

---

foreground is the Tehachapi Elementary School (Victor Phillips and Reverend Lewis Wakeland)

The Kessing Block on southeast corner of G and Green Streets. J. Iriart's Franco-American Hotel & Bar, and a ball court, are across the railroad tracks — Circa early 1900's (Herbert N. Force Collection)

Automobiles were such a curiosity that in December 1906, when a car with a driver and six passengers passed through town, the car was mentioned in the local paper as the "largest to pass over the mountain."

Motorcycles were quickly accepted, perhaps more as a means of enjoyment than locomotion. In 1910 W. N. DeSpain advertised Excelior, Yale, and Reading Standard Motorcycles. The same year White Wolf Grade, the horrendous obstacle to quick travel up the mountain from the San Joaquin Valley, was the scene of cycles being tested for endurance and hill climbing.

The Ramina Garage bridged the gap in their 1916 advertising, telling people the livery was operating, but they did garage repairs, too. And that same year a Ford dealer was in town at the Baker Garage.

Charles Kerr, owner of a distillate gas generator, according to Mr. Force claimed in 1914 that the generator was the best thing on earth and furnished the cheapest fuel known — he set out to prove it. First, with three passengers in his Ford automobile, he made a trip from the old Pauly home north of town, to the summit of one of the highest peaks, Tollgate Mountain. He burned coal, claiming it made an easier ascent than at previous times when he used plain old-fashioned gasoline. Using denatured alcohol in his next test, Kerr again was happy with the results. Then came the final test. Clint Jones, owner of the Palace Saloon, poured 40-rod whiskey into the car's drained tank. Holding his breath, Kerr turned the engine once and off he went, one and a quarter miles.

In 1918 the Standard Oil Company realized the business available at the area by increased use of the automobile, and opened a local plant consisting of three 20,000 gallon tanks, a pumping plant, a motor truck, and a tank wagon. Standard delivered its products in a wagon drawn by four horses.

Public transportation entered the automotive age in 1921, when the Packard Stage Line began operating between Bakersfield and Los Angeles, three trips daily in each direction.

Mrs. Kessing also recalled the town's early days. She once wrote, "The town has gone through several changes. First, the cattlemen were gradually driven out of the valley by the sheep men; then in their turn, they too, were driven out by the grain men, and now the grain fields are gone and in their place are the apple and pear orchards where the best apples and pears of the State are grown. Now Tehachapi is such a quiet little town with its electric lights and automobiles, so different from the old stage depot and cowboy town of the past."

—SEVENTEEN—

If the automobile was a source of amusement, the airplane as it flew across the Tehachapi landscape was viewed with awe. A landing field was first discussed at the Board of Trustees meeting in July 1921 because passing "aeroplanes needed a place to put down." Not until 1927, however, was a field actually established on land owned by the Ramina Corporation, when the Chamber of Commerce made arrangements with the County Road Department to grade the land, and also provide signals and other equipment necessary for the field.

The airport was initially merely a convenience for pilots flying over the valley, but the Chamber hoped it would bring additional prominence to the area. The first commercial flight landed in Tehachapi on a Sunday afternoon in February and passengers were taken for rides. The field was actually used the first time on the second of the month when a passing plane made an emergency landing for repairs.

An effort was made in February 1934 to get the county to lease or buy the airport site from the Ramina Cororation. Sometime afterwards the airport did in fact become part of the Kern County airport system.

Long before Tehachapi even thought about an airport, an event occurred in its skys that generated much excitement. In February 1914 Silas Christofferson intended to demonstrate the long-range ability of flight by flying from San Francisco to San Diego. He was hampered by several problems. His first attempt to leave San Francisco was delayed "because of heavy sands which clogged the running gear" of the biplane and "prevented him from rising." When he finally arrived at Lerdo he was forced down by darkness after flying forty minutes "by the light of the moon." While landing, a brace on the plane was broken.

The Tehachapi Mountains were the next barrier. Five attempts to fly over them were failures, as Christofferson had insufficient engine power for the "heavy air." After a train trip to San Francisco, he returned to Bakersfield with an eight-cylinder, 100-horsepower engine to replace the sixty horsepower machine he started out with.

On February 16 he was airborne again. A newspaper commented: "Christofferson today set a new record in the field of aviation when he successfully negotiated the air spaces over the Tehachapi range, flying above the mountain summit and on down to the desert and to Los Angeles, where he arrived at 12:30. He lost nearly an hour and one-half adjusting his carburetter (sic) at Bena, this side of the mountains, so that he was really in the air but two hours and fifteen minutes. From Bena he rose rapidly . . . at the summit with its 4,000 feet elevation, he was in the clear by 800 feet.

". . . at 10:32 he was sailing over the summit of the mountains against a 15-mile gale which was blowing full in his face. He was at an altitude of 800 feet at this point and was in plain view of the mt. folk who turned out in large numbers to see him pass."

A local report said: "Those on the lookout at Tehachapi first sighted the airship as it emerged from the canyon northwest from Tehachapi . . . the aeroplane was in a direct line with G Street when it was turned to the east and sailed directly over the Tehachapi Valley. The daring aviator was hailed with shouts by the spectators at Tehachapi and he returned the greeting with a wave of his hand."

There was another sighting in the Tehachapi skies in 1918 when three military planes flew over the valley, mapping an aerial route for the United States Mail. Six years later in 1924, David Pitts posted the first airmail letter from Tehachapi. It went first to San Francisco and was then flown cross-country to his niece in New York. It took forty-one hours to arrive, compared to the railroad time of 120 hours.

In the late 1950's a young pilot was in Southern California looking for a suitable location for a unique form of flight, soaring. Fred Harris had been working at Minter Field in Bakersfield for about six months, when he selected the Tehachapi Valley as a perfect location to open the Holiday Soaring School in 1959. It was one of only two commercial soaring operations in the United States.

Under a contract with the National Aeronautics and Space Administration in the early 1960's, Harris helped develop a prototype for the modern hang-glider. For about two-and-a-half years he also worked with the astronaut program, training men whose names are now household words: Neil Armstrong and Edward Aldrin, among them. At the school these men learned the art of free soaring through space, a part of the training program before their historic moon flights.

Walt Disney Studios was in the Tehachapis in the late 1960's. With Harris' assistance they filmed a television-movie, "The Boy Who Flew With The Condors," starring Tehachapi High School teen-ager Chris Jury. Most of the long distance shots in the film were flown by Darwin Wilkins, who is a seasonal resident in Tehachapi each spring as a frost forecaster for the United States Weather Bureau.

Golden West Airlines inaugurated the first daily commercial passenger flights in 1973, connecting with Los Angeles in conjunction with the land promotion at Bear Valley Springs. After the franchise expired, however, customer service declined so drastically that in the mid-Seventies daily service was discontinued.

—EIGHTEEN—

During the depression years some employment was affected, although residents at that time have said, "If a man was willing to work, he could always find some kind of a job." A large number of itinerants were in town in the early Thirties asking for free meals. The Board of Trustees decided to pay them twenty-five cents an hour in exchange for street cleaning. And the Tehachapi Relief Committee assisted the transients in getting fed at a local restaurant.

An excellent picture of the community during this period was presented in a letter to Bank of America in June 1933. W. R. Powers, Cashier of the Bank of Tehachapi, obviously presented the facts in the best light possible inasmuch as the bank was seeking a sale to Bank of America. However, he showed the impact nearby areas had on the Tehachapi region, writing in part:

"The community served by this bank consists of the following several towns: Randsburg, Cantil, Mojave, Monolith, Tehachapi, Inyokern, Keene and Caliente. They total about 3000 population.

"The Town of Tehachapi has a population of about 750 and is an incorporated town . . . Our town is in excellent financial circumstances, no bonded indebtedness and a substantial balance in their treasury.

"The Monolith Portland Cement Company has a large plant four miles from Tehachapi with an annual payroll of between $300,000 and $500,000. The Cudahay Company operates a mine at Cantil where they mine the Old Dutch Cleanser product. There are large salt deposits being developed at Saltdale, near Cantil. There are several valuable gold properties being developed at Randsburg. The principal mine is the Yellow Aster Mine.

"The County of Kern has a fine tuberculosis hospital at Keene which has a payroll of $50,000 or more. The State has recently completed a new state prison for women near Tehachapi. This institution will soon be occupied and its payrolls will benefit this community.

"The State Highway Department has recently purchased a site for a [road] camp in Tehachapi where a number of men will be employed.

"I know that it is hard to accuratly (sic) state the amounts of the various payrolls in our surrounding community, but would state that they would total well in excess of a million dollars annually.

"There are a number of large ranchs (sic) located nearby with valuable acreages and many cattle and sheep. The water conditions in our community are very good, and the land is fertile and well suited for orchards, grain hay and produce. A number of San Joaquin Valley potato growers are interested in securing acreages for raising seed potatoes for planting in the valley. The soil is adapted for potatoes and the weather also suitable. Our summer climate is moderate and never extremly (sic) warm.

"The mountains have many desirable sites for summer homes.

"The Pacific Portland Cement Company owns quarry sites and holdings a few miles from here.

191

"Our citizens are sturdy and substantial. These qualities of our people have made the Bank of Tehachapi a profitable institution throughout the many years of the existence of the bank."

In the midst of the depression a building boom was actually experienced in the Tehachapi region. One hundred thousand dollars in civic and business building improvements was spent in the first two years of the 1930's. Included were a new Odd Fellows building, the County Library, the high school, a new grammar school unit, the Iriart business block, new residences, the Keeley business block, and the new City Hall.

But the largest venture, by far, was the construction of a state prison.

Tehachapi Women's Prison — Circa 1932 (Herbert N. Force Collection)

—NINETEEN—

Originally in the State's history of incarceration, women felons were imprisoned along with their male counterparts, at San Quentin Prison on San Francisco Bay. During the 1920's an effort began to find a new and separate location for the women; over 100 sites were inspected throughout the state.

The Cummings Valley ranch of Lucas F. Brite was chosen. The reputed purchase price in June 1930 for the 1,700 acres was $114,056.65. By June

1932 four permanent buildings were erected and dedication ceremonies held. According to G. Perry Lloyd, the first superintendent of the later men's prison on the same grounds, ". . . although these beautiful new buildings had been completed and made ready, they could not be used because of legal difficulties that developed. The Attorney General ruled that the women prisoners had been sentenced by the courts to San Quentin prison and could not be legally transferred elsewhere.

"Through a change in Legislation, the unit was declared a branch of San Quentin and was finally opened . . . in September of 1933 with the receipt of the women prisoners."

The first contingent of twenty-eight inmates arrived in the early part of September to a prison; guards and wire fences protected the grounds. But the Norman-style architecture situated in this verdant valley was not like the facility they had come from. One reporter likened the buildings to a castle and quipped, "There will be no knights mounted on white chargers to rescue them, however, unless the state parole board starts using horses."

The prison had a capacity for 170 inmates; they were housed in two cottages. There was also a detention building, as well as the administration building.

The philosophy of the new prison was exemplified by a statement of Mrs. Ernest Wallace, then Chairman of the Board of Trustees, California Institution for Women, in 1930:

"Prisoners are people. Women prisoners are much like women everywhere. Some of them take a great deal of pride in their work. Some of them will give to the uttermost for the joy of doing a good piece of work. Others, the greater number, will require careful watching, and an

G Street between Curry and Robinson Streets before the 1952 earthquake as shown in series on next five pages (Edwin and Laura Jones)

incentive to do good work.

"They [the Board of Trustees] believe that if they can turn their women out, when the time comes for the doors to swing wide for them, equipped with the knowledge of how to keep house and with one other vocation, one in which employment can be readily secured, and with healthy bodies accustomed to work eight hours a day, with the blessed knowledge that they can earn their own living, they will have an excellent chance of making good in the outside world from which they were banished."

Eventually all of the 145 women who were at San Quentin moved to Cummings Valley. Additionally a commissary building, three open-type dormitories, temporary shops, and school buildings were built. Soon the inmate population reached 240.

The original trustees had hoped to run the facility entirely with women without fence or guards. It was to be an honor system, but that didn't materialize. While the superintendent was a woman, the deputy warden was a man. The one guard at the gate, as well as a mounted guard, were also men. And as time went on, certain maintenance jobs also brought men to the scene. But mainly, the Women's Department of San Quentin at Tehachapi, as it was called until 1936 when an amendment to California's Constitution created the California Institution For Women, was for women and by women.

There's a delightful lady living in Tehachapi today who remembers vividly when the fairer sex hoped for a better day at the old Brite Ranch. Mrs. Ruby Attryde was employed at the prison from 1944 until 1952, and retired from the system in 1960. By the time she joined the staff, the population was stable. Three large cottages housed the residents, who originally had their own rooms, but as the population increased, bunk beds were introduced and they had to "double-up."

The daily program was geared towards rehabilitating prisoners. There was an education plan to upgrade individual deficiencies. The work experience plan included an industrial factory, a dressmaking establishment, a bakery, and a beauty shop. The women wore dresses in

194

their own choice of prints. Social activities were provided within the scheme of institutional life. The food was good. Outside entertainment was brought in. In fact, Mrs. Attryde remembers telling one girl, "You have a better life here than on the outside."

In all the years she spent in prison work, Mrs. Attryde can't remember any serious problems. "We weren't allowed to know why the women were in, so no questions were asked," she explained. But the women came from every walk of life, and their crimes ranged from minor to murder.

In the early days the women inmates were older, in their thirties and up. But as the years passed, not only were the inmates younger, into the early twenties, but their numbers increased.

The remoteness of the institution from any considerable population center made it difficult to recruit and maintain a sufficient and competent staff for the increased population, which had reached 300 in 1948. (In fact, as an economic contributor to the region, the prison offered little. Most of the custodial staff were women who commuted to other areas on week-ends or their days off, and spent little of their salaries in Tehachapi. And most of the goods used in maintaining the unit were imported from elsewhere in the State.) The California Legislature was stirred into action. As early as January 1945 there was discussion about moving the prison. In 1946, according to Mr. Lloyd, the board of trustees advocated the abandonment of the old plant and the construction of an adequate institution elsewhere. A new site was purchased in 1949, and construction of a new prison near Corona, California, began. While some of the town's leading citizens opposed the prison's original construction, in June 1951 the City Council passed an ordinance opposing the proposed relocation.

But before the new facility was finished, the 1952 earthquake struck the area. With their cottages damaged, the residents moved into tents on the grounds, where they lived for about six weeks until they could be moved. To Mrs. Attryde's knowledge, no escapes were attempted. Everyone pitched in and made the situation workable, she recalled. Within a few weeks the women completed their move to Corona, however, and the

195

grounds were placed on a caretaker status.

—TWENTY—

Growth during the two decades prior to the Second World War had been slow, but steady. While little new business was introduced, in the first eight months of 1940 forty-nine building permits were issued, mainly for residences valued at $2,500. A former editor of The Tehachapi News, Harry Hollins, commented in 1974, "That the leaders, while not being against growth, didn't want the flashy type, but a solid kind that meant more permanent homes and families" (48).

During and after the War, the City Council acted to maintain the downtown business district as it was to insure continued prosperity for its established merchants. "Fly-by-night" peddlers who paid no taxes were a problem. There was little the merchants or the council could do, however, about "good highways, fast automobiles, and stores that operated from trailers." This was the situation facing the Council in 1940, one of vital concern to the smalltown businessman. At a meeting to discuss the problem, Councilman Phil Marx explained, ". . . if the local merchants wanted to compete with each other by broadening their line of merchandise it would be a good business practice and attract the local consumer, but everything possible should be done to prevent outside merchants from infringing on their rights, which are protected by the ordinances of the Town."

The Councilmen could protect their established businessmen, but they couldn't keep consumers at home. At the beginning of automotive travel, people tended to stay home, the necessity of transporting themselves over the crooked, winding road into Bakersfield especially keeping them there.

In 1937 with prison labor as the work force, the construction of a modern highway began at the Bear Mountain Ranch and continued until 1943 when governmental restrictions on materials stopped the project. The final link of the new two-lane road, which was moved north of

196

Tehachapi Creek after it left Keene for the east, was completed on October 31, 1948, when the section between Keene and Tehachapi was finished, marking twenty-four years of effort to provide a safe road between those two communities, and linking Tehachapi also with points east.

The biggest construction problem of the new highway was the creek which had caused devastating damage during periodic floods. The highway actually passed through the creek's gorge which, while normally a small stream, became a raging torrent when storms of cloudburst proportions created peak floods (49). The new highway circumvented the flooding problem with a bituminous surface treatment three inches in depth and shoulder dikes or berms composed of the same material.

The Second World War brought some changes to Tehachapi; events took place directly involving the population, but there was no great impact. In October 1940 the community recognized a need for "guarding precautionary measures for the protection of vital points in this section as a defense measure, and also to cope with the present influx of migrants."

The American Legion worked directly under the County Sheriff in a National Defense Program in 1941, providing an observation post for airplanes first at the Community Hall, later at the elementary school. Air raid exercises were a periodic occurrence. In 1942 sand was deposited at various locations to be used in the control of incendiary bombs in the event an actual attack occurred. Another war effort was the collection of tin cans. Even the bars contributed by closing at midnight.

Highway 58, a major east-west route, was regularly used for military activities and troop movements, creating a great deal of traffic through the Tehachapi Valley.

Tehachapi had a local unit of the State Guard in 1944. Walter Hicks recalls one episode concerning the "home boys." As a platoon leader one bright day, he was drilling his men on the high school's grass field near the highway. "Hup, two, three, four," they marched along the field, until, suddenly facing the squad appeared "the enemy;" the field's water

sprinklers were operating. As Mr. Hicks laughingly commented, ''For the life of me I couldn't think of the command to reverse march; we were up to our knees in water and I finally just threw up my hands and said, 'Oh, hell, turn around and go back.' ''

During the 1940's, particularly toward the end of the War, Chief of Police Jackson reported a problem to the Council: the general conduct of Marines stationed at the Mojave base while the men were on leave in Tehachapi had reached a point where it was necessary for something to be done. Jackson was able to get little, if any, help from the base officials. But the base did provide a source of employment for some Tehachapi residents during the war years, and despite Chief Jackson's occasional problems, relations betwen the City and the Marine Base were good. After the War several men who had been stationed on the desert returned to Kern County, to make their homes in Tehachapi.

The Earthquake

In an emergency City Council meeting Tuesday afternoon it was decided upon by the Council to ask Governor Warren to declare Tehachapi a disaster area.

In The Tehachapi News,
July 24, 1952

—ONE—

It was the time of morning when stillness reigned. The darkness of the sky was kindled by the rising sun as birds in their nests and animals in their lairs stretched and scratched. In their homes, only a few people had begun the day's ritualistic ambulations.

It was still.

And then, at 4:52 in the morning of Monday, July 21, 1952, the earth began to move as the second most disastrous earthquake in California's history struck the Tehachapis. In its wake, the forty-five second tremor left eleven people killed and several injured. Almost all of the downtown business section was in ruins; approximately seventy percent of it so damaged it had to be torn down and rebuilt.

Mrs. Blance Cantana and four of her nine children, asleep in the second floor of a G Street building, were buried under an avalanche of debris, but her husband and their other five children escaped with only minor injuries. In an adjoining building, three children of Louis Martin's, owner of the Martin Furniture Store, were killed, as was an overnight guest, Marilyn Taylor. While the Martins were residents, the Cantanas had arrived in Tehachapi only the evening before from Silver City, New Mexico.

A tenth victim was Walter Nolen, about fifty, a guest at the Summit Hotel, where he was trapped under falling debris. Out in Brite Valley sixteen-year-old Florence Ann Fillmore of Los Angeles was visiting her sister and asleep for the night in the stone milk house. She was trapped and killed under the falling rock.

A number of people were treated at the Tehachapi Hospital, which was also severely damaged and had to be abandoned. At the Tehachapi Fire House and on the hospital lawn, where the patients were assembled, a morgue and first aid center were established.

From throughout the surrounding area, aid came quickly. The United States Air Force at Muroc (now known as Edwards Air Force Base), the Naval Ordinance Test Station at China Lake, various Red Cross units, Boy and Explorer Scouts, as well as innumerable individuals, expedited relief to the quake victims. The State National Guard was on duty to prevent looting. Doctors from Bakersfield flew to Tehachapi to aid the injured. The county airport was extremely valuable during the emergency when roads were closed and giant DC 3's had to fly in cargo and medical supplies.

By nine o'clock in the morning crews from the county and state highway departments were on the job, assisted by volunteers with heavy equipment, cleaning away the rubble from fallen buildings that littered the streets. That evening most of the rubble was removed and by Tuesday evening all of the work that could be done at the time — knocking down dangerous walls and clearing the streets — was completed and the salvage operation was transferred to property owners.

Southwest corner of G and Green Streets after the July 1952 earthquake
(Ed Wiggins Collection)

G Street in Tehachapi, July 22, 1952 (Ed Wiggins Collection)

A few buildings were left practically unscathed; those constructed of reinforced concrete: the Bank of Tehachapi, the Tehachapi Lumber Company, the two schools, the Catholic Church, the Beekay Theatre, the I.O.O.F. Hall, required little or no repairs.

The gigantic quake which wreaked the damage had a force magnitude of 7.7 on the Richter scale. It originated at a depth of about ten miles, at latitude 35 degrees 00 minutes North longitude 119 degrees 02 minutes West, near Wheeler Ridge. The White Wolf Fault, sometimes called the Bear Mountain Fault, had been known to geologists for many years; its general trace was plotted on a geological map as early as 1906. It was known to have moved in recent geological time, although it was not considered active in the sense of constituting a threat.

The scope of its force was magnified by the fact that 6,900 foot Bear Mountain moved three feet, railroad tracks in the vicinity were twisted into an S-shape, and earth deplacements were up to ten feet. (It was about one month before the railroad was able to resume moving traffic over the tracks.) The Caliente Creek region burst forth with new springs, and for about two years the State Department of Fish and Game planted fish that provided sport and recreation, until the earthquake-spawned water dried up.

The Tehachapi earthquake was the strongest shock in California since the San Francisco earthquake of 1906, and in Southern California since the Fort Tejon quake of 1857.

"The days following the earthquake were hectic ones indeed for everyone," wrote Walter Johnson, editor of The Tehachapi News, soon afterwards. "Housewives faced the mountainous task of cleaning up their houses and cooking meals while they dreaded the thought of returning to the homes where the memory of fury was still all too fresh in their minds. In town businessmen were anxious to see what losses were and to try and get back into business again. In the fields," he added, "farmers anxiously surveyed the damage to their crops and water pipes."

He described the havoc along G Street:

"Starting at the east end of town on Highway 466, the Tehachapi Supply Co. had all its pane glass shaken out and some structural damage. Vern's Auto Parts and Service was a great loss with its walls crumbled, its front knocked out and water from the fallen Southern Pacific water tank had caused great damage to its stock and fixtures. The Economy Mercantile had some structural damage and great stock damage as a result of the water from the S.P. tank. The building housing Pruitt's, Helen's Cafe, the Post Office, Byrom's Barber Shop and the Round-Up Cafe and poolhall was a total loss." Across the street another building housing a hotel, drug store, and cafe "were never to house another business again."

Mr. Johnson eloquently attested, "Yes, Tehachapi looked like a town God had forgotten. Common words were: 'Well, that finishes Tehachapi; Who would want to build here again anyway?' . . . spoken mostly by the sightseers and those without faith."

An estimated seventy-five homes received major damage, although in the country, not just houses had to be rebuilt, but a number of wells and springs went dry, and almost all of the reservoirs cracked.

"Tehachapi is far from dead," Johnson wrote a year later. All along the main street new buildings housed old businesses and new businesses were in new buildings. In the aftermath of the quake, which was said to be the equivalent of an explosion of one million tons of TNT, a new, modern facade evolved as once and for all the Western aspect of a frontier town disappeared from the business district. As fires in the 1890's influenced rebuilding in brick to avoid destruction, so the earthquake sixty years later restructured the town as the brick that withstood fire fell to the earth's movement and cement was the salvation and future, of others.

Immediately following the earthquake the City Council was determined to "adhere strictly to the building code;" it was seen as an opportunity to once and for all do away with the "old brick structures which seemed to have suffered the greatest damage."

The Mojave Corporation undertook some of the reconstruction, including the Masonic Temple, erected at a cost of $60,000, and the Squires Block of five buildings on Green Street, between E and F Streets.

Vaughn Squires, who had operated the destroyed drug store on G Street, is viewed by some residents a score of years later as a folk hero because of his initiative in rebuilding part of the downtown area. His faith in Tehachapi's future was exemplified in construction of a five-store all concrete building, and his later construction across the street of a two-story combination store and office building — all of which added the final touch to the architectural change downtown. This also extended the business district south on Green Street.

Besides Squires, Lou Kanstein and Frank Baumgart, partners in the 1930's purchase of the business block on the east side of Green Street between F and G, rebuilt that area into a store and a modern service station for the Union Oil Company. On F Street east of Green, Al Lange was encouraged to construct three new buildings, and was the first to have them ready for occupany after the quake. Across the street from the City Hall the Tehachapi Cleaners built a three-business structure.

On the southwest corner of Green and G Streets, where the Juanita Hotel had stood, a concrete block building was constructed to accomodate several businesses. West on G Street the "old red brick" buildings which were not destroyed were remodeled with a "brilliant new front of redwood" and new businesses opened. On the west side of Green Street between F and G, still another concrete block building was constructed next to the alley, housing two new businesses.

The two destroyed hotels were permanently displaced. In the intervening years the motel entered the economy. Right after the earthquake Don Carroll constructed the Ranch House Motel on East G Street.

As a native daughter eloquently expressed it recently, "Not only the familiar structures but the old slow pace of life was disrupted." Mrs. Pedigo recalled, "Old hotels are gone; in their place motels and inns, boarding houses replaced by restaurants; separate dry goods stores, meat markets and a drug store by supermarkets and a variety-drug store."

TWO

The Tehachapi earthquake shook the area at a time when change had already begun. In 1948 Don Carroll initiated the first annexation to the original incorporated town limits when he constructed the Ranchotel on Curry Street as a home for his in-laws, as well as an economic operation. About the same time he purchased an adjacent eighty acres of potato farmland. He had determined the only direction the town could grow was south and west. Initially Mr. Carroll planned to do some farming and subdivide ten-acre parcels at a time and "let someone else do the building." Today, better than 350 Carroll-constructed homes later, one can look over the Tehachapi Valley and see the impact of his early vision of general growth through the region.

In order to control the quality of homes, Carroll decided to build them himself. He was then the only housing contractor in town. But not for long, because Al Small of the Tehachapi Lumber Company, and Jim Iriart and Jim Cazacus, as partners, entered the home construction business at about the same time in the mid-1950's, building a substantial number of homes in the city.

The attitude of many area residents as the houses went up was, "Who's going to live in them?" At that time Monolith was doing away with some of its housing, the men's prison was opening and Cal Portland had begun production — buyers were always available.

Mr. Carroll annexed property of the Tehachapi Fruit and Land Company tract immediately south of the town's limits and west of Curry Street in 1950 and 1951. The next year, southwest of the corner of Valley and Curry, another annexation occurred. Throughout the 1950's and 1960's, additional annexations took place as subdividing continued, adding land to the city in the southeast and southwest so that at the end of 1974 the incorporated boundaries included 2,747 acres of land.

At the end of the 1950's the City Council inaugurated a Tehachapi Area General Plan in an effort to both guide and control the future growth and expansion of the city and to implement effectively, through its Planning Commission, the goals of the citizens as expressed through their governing body.

In the years after the earthquake, even without the perspective of time it is possible to detail some changes which have materially affected the growth and economy of the Tehachapis.

Madge and Harold Schlotthauer, both doctors of general medicine, moved to the Tehachapi Valley in the mid-1930's under an agreement with the union at Monolith-Portland Cement Company to care for its employees. In no time at all as obstetrical patients knocked at their door, among their first patients were new-born babies. While there was another doctor in Tehachapi when they arrived, out on the desert and in the Antelope Valley, the population was barely served by the medical profession, and patients began to drive up the hill to see Doctors Madge and Harold, as they were affectionately known.

The need for hospital care was apparent from the beginning. On March 1, 1934, the original Tehachapi Valley Hospital, a two-bed facility in an old residence-apartment house on the corner of Curry and E Streets, opened. Within just a couple of months, on the 1st of July it was moved to a large two-story building that had once operated as the Capdeville Hotel at 115 West E Street. Licensed for fifteen beds, it served the area with some adequacy, for a new wing was in the planning stage at the time of the 1952 earthquake.

The Tehachapi Valley Hospital was a total loss; its patients were first moved onto the lawn and then into a hastily devised house-hospital. Eventually, on March 1, 1953, the Schlotthauers moved their hospital to Mojave. That summer, meanwhile, construction began on their new Tehachapi Medical Center at the same site as the original hospital. Initially only outpatient care was provided, but the continued need for a bed-facility brought about groundbreaking ceremonies on May 16, 1956 for the Tehachapi Valley Hospital, which admitted its first patients on April 8, 1957.

The Doctors Schlotthauer continued to operate their private medical clinic and hospital until the late 1960's. On January 1, 1969, upon their retirement, the Tehachapi Valley Hospital District purchased the twenty-eight bed facility.

Out in Cummings Valley, with the women's prison in need of earthquake-caused structural repairs, the anticipated move of the prisoners to Corona was stepped up. A temporary camp was established for an inmate clean-up crew and inspection crews from Chino, after which a caretaker moved in to protect the "mothballed" facility.

By 1953 the increasing population brought about increased crime, as well as a need for additional custodial space within the State. That year the State prison authorities decided to reopen the Tehachapi prison as a branch of Chino. Necessary repairs and new construction materially changed the decor of the facility, as the high-pitched tile roofs were removed and replaced with a lighter roof.

The first male inmates arrived on January 3, 1955, and at the same time a complete renovation and alteration program began. Originally developed as a minimum security prison, in 1957 medium security felons were added. In 1961, with the creation of the California Rehabilitation Center as a control and treatment program for narcotic addicts, Tehachapi received its first commitments as a branch of the Center. But in May 1963 the facility was returned to the California Institution For Men.

Finally in 1964 a State prison for the confinement of males under the custody of the Director of Corrections, known as the California Correctional Institution at Tehachapi, was established by an Act of the State Senate. During the next few years major construction changes occurred, and a medium security unit was added adjacent to the original buildings.

At the end of 1974 CCI had an inmate population of 1,226 and was at almost full capacity. Of its 382 employees, 210 were residents of the greater Tehachapi region, earning a payroll of $2,800,000.

The only industry within the boundaries of the incorporated city limits opened its doors in 1958. Lillian and Spencer Lees had operated a small five-sewing machine garment company in Minnesota, manufacturing children's lingerie and sleepwear. When they sold the business in 1956, the company had grown to forty machines.

"Spencer-California" opened in Tehachapi with only two employees, the Lees. Since then children's sportswear and sleepwear manufacturing has increased so that in 1974 fifty residents of the Tehachapi region were employed with an annual payroll of $225,000. They originally marketed their designs only in Southern California, but interest in their stylish clothing spread into other states and to other countries as well, where the Tehachapi-manufactured clothing is now shipped.

Subdivision of the once secluded ranches and farms in the early 1960's began with the promotion of Oak Knolls. The purchase of four ranches in Old Town by the Murchison Brothers of Dallas, Texas, was heralded as a major development of 5,500 acres, first known as Oak Knolls. It was later acquired by Boise Cascade in October 1968, who substantially improved the property. They were also responsible for the subdivision of a large acreage in the foothills south of Tehachapi, known as Mountain Meadows. While there were only two residences in the Meadows in early 1975, and the land was then criss-crossed with weed-chocked, rutted roads, a flood-control system was constructed to control some of the water which has historically swept out of the canyons and caused considerable damage on the valley floor.

The sale of the Rex Ellsworth Ranch in the southwest corner of Cummings Valley to Benquet Corporation created Stallion Springs; while the acquisition of the Fickert Ranch by Dart Industries at the end of the 1960's maintained the closed atmosphere of that secluded valley as a guarded retreat.

The improvements of the Pacific Telephone Company at a large facility in Mojave; the increased personnel of the Mojave district office of the California Highway Patrol; the opening of California-Portland; the development of the space agency program at Edwards Air Force Base on the Mojave Desert — all have brought additional families on the long road to the Tehachapi region, increasing population and services alike.

In the 1910 incorporated census Tehachapi's population was 385. In 1970 the City's expanded limits included 4,211 people. From 1910 to 1920 only seventy-three new residents were counted. In the next thirty years the increase was greater each decade by a few hundred, until in 1960 the combination of annexation and new employment opportunities, in one decade increased the population to 3,161, almost doubling its 1950 census of 1,685. There was a noted decrease in new population at the 1970 census which was 4,211; and in 1973 a special population estimate actually showed a decrease in the official census which reached its high of 4,370 in 1972. Interest in suburban living has been partially blamed for the drop.

The extent of growth in the future is for another historian to record. Dwindling employment at Monolith Portland Cement Co., partly because of modernization; the uncertainty of space exploration and its concomitant effect on NASA's program at Edwards; the state prison project at the mercy of state officials — all bode uncertain projections for the last quarter of the Twentieth Century.

In Old Town, Bear Valley, and at the Chanac Ranch, the uncertainties of exploited suburban living and second-home attractiveness in a time of an irrational economy, preclude any prediction of the future.

And so, the long road to Tehachapi is at an end. This journey is over. Not just has the pioneer morale which impelled the first settlers and sustained them on their long voyage over sea and land disappeared, but some of the pioneer descendants who contributed unstintingly to this record by reaching with their memories into the distant past, have journeyed to a new experience.

There is little but ruins in isolated canyons and near modern by-ways to speak of Tehachapi's early history; and fenced lands as well as locked gates preclude exploration by the curious and adventurous.

In such a short span of years, less than 125, the Four Valleys of the Tehachapis have experienced in about twenty-year spurts material change in agricultural pursuits, mining industries, and physical character.

Do the personages herein appear as heroes? They're not. Innumerable closets were opened in the search for the past out of which many skeletons emerged to tell their stories, and then were returned, to rest in peace. It is the peoples' efforts, contributions, and rewards, that are the concern of this historical narrative.

All of the oldtimers with whom I visited, time and time again expressed a wish to return to the "good old days." They enjoyed the personal camaraderie of an earlier time, the closeness of community, the lack of rush. They may have forgotten in their desire for lost youth the harshness of pioneer living, the long days in the fields or mines, the drudgery of home life without conveniences, even the long walk to the outdoor privy.

The Tehachapis are different in the modern scheme of late Twentieth Century life. The land has been cut up and divided; trees and running streams have disappeared; few indeed are the descendants of pre-1900 settlers who remain in the region.

A new road of interest brings new settlers onto the land. It's a shorter journey, not fraught with danger and the fear of the unknown. But history continues to unfold as the road invites travelers and settlers, while the future awaits new dreams and new vistas.

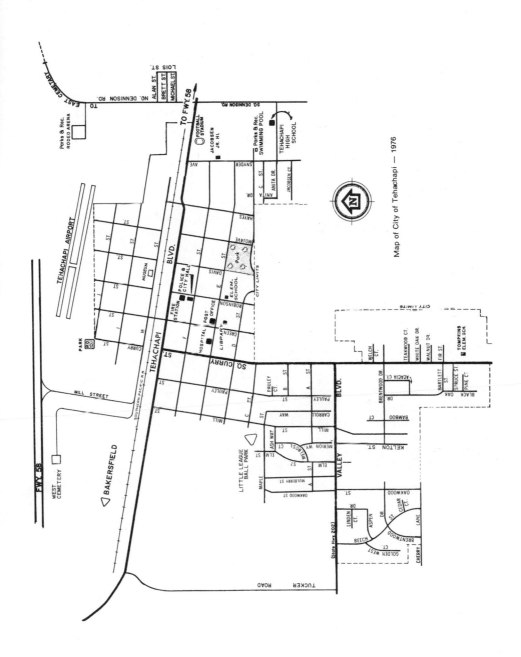

Map of City of Tehachapi — 1976

209

Notes

(1) Spanish explorers had crossed the desert seventy-five years earlier when the Anza expedition traveled a similar road, in a small measure affecting the future of the Tehachapis. That story is told in The Farms.

(2) Although several other routes were available, the most often traveled was Cooke's road.

(3) The same last names of the Wiggins' wives suggests they could have been sisters.

(4) George Foley was a brother of Francis, and also ranched in the Tehachapis during the 1870's.

(5) In **Daniel Boone** by John Bakeless (Pennsylvania, 1939), Thomas Hart, Sheriff of Orange County in North Carolina, and his brother Nathaniel, are mentioned as lifelong friends and business associates of the Boones. Nathaniel Hart was involved in Boone's Kentucky ventures when Josiah Hart was born there. Although I have not been able to prove a kin relationship between the Tehachapi and Kentucky Harts, it is an enticing possibility which may yet come to light.

(6) Adelia O'Brien Ward, a native of Boston, was a widow when she opened a hotel in 1875 at Greenwich, in the Tehachapi Valley, and also an early hotel in Tehachapi Summit in 1878. That same year she married Jack Eveleth who assumed charge of the hotel and also ran his cattle ranch.

(7) While the memories of several Tehachapi oldtimers have been invaluable in preparing this book, wherever possible primary sources and original research have been used to corroborate and elaborate on the oral history. In some instances the early recorded information differs from the oral tradition, and is used here.

(8) His brother Peter J. McFarlane was Tehachapi's postmaster from 1904 to 1913.

(9) Lest anyone wonder where all the trees have gone, in 1888 for instance a Summit Lime Company kiln, which produced 780 barrels of lime, required seventy cords of wood for burning, averaging one cord of wood for each ten to twelve barrels of lime.

(10) In addition to everyday necessities, Cooke brought with him "one great Bible and four olde books." See **Mayflower** by Kate Caffrey (New York, New York, 1974). Two United States presidents were also Cooke's descendants: William Howard Taft and Franklin Delano Roosevelt.

(11) Mrs. Haigh was one of the earliest residents of Tehachapi Summit and operated a restaurant on G Street.

(12) Until her death in 1963 at the age of 102, Mrs. Ida May Jameson managed the various family interests after her husband died in 1934. They included the J. W. Jameson Corporation, the Burbank Canning Co., and the J. W. and Ida M. Jameson Foundation, which today oversees the estate's trust. In 1974 the Foundation donated $2,500 to the West Kern Oil Museum Association for its purchase of a 2.97 acre site from Jameson Trust Co., on which it intends to erect a museum.

(13) Besides the Department of Water and Power Library of the City of Los Angeles, a valuable source of information on the whole Owens Valley — Los Angeles Aqueduct story is Nadeau's **The Water Seekers** and Chalfant's **Story of Inyo.**

(14) Cowles Book Company, Inc. **Cowles Encyclopedia of Science, Industry and Technology.** (Toronto, Canada, 1969).

(15) The St. Francis Dam was the cause of a major scandal for the City of Los Angeles. Just after midnight on March 12, 1928, because of what later was determined to be improper design, the dam collapsed, causing a massive wall of water to rush 53.8 miles to the Pacific Ocean. It resulted in between 400 and 500 deaths, and $13,500,000 in damage claims. This story is well told in **Man-Made Disaster; The Story of St. Francis Dam** (Glendale, California, 1963).

(16) Harvey Hicks of Tehachapi, eighty-nine-year-old grandson of Mahala Hicks, told me this story. After this book was ready for print, however, Mrs. Phyllis Chappell McCarthy of Bealville, a great-granddaughter of Mrs. Hick's, provided me with a completely different background as substantiated by another granddaughter, Mrs. Frances Elizabet Chappell Engerman. They said: "Mahalia Mackay was born February 10, 1819, in Otwah, England. It is northeast of London and the name has now been changed to Witham. The Mackay and Burns families came to America in 1826. The Burns had been neighbors and friends of the Mackay's in England and had one son, Daniel, born April 15, 1817. The Mackays and Burns settled in Whiskey Town, Texas. The name has since been changed to Dallas.

"In 1836 Mahalia and Daniel were married, she was seventeen and he was nineteen. They had two children, Daniel, born in 1837, and a daughter, Sarah, born in 1839. Daniel, Sr. was fighting in the Mexican War and

210

was killed in 1847. Mahalia stayed on and was helped by the Burns family as her parents had died and left their property to her.

"Later about forty families decided to come to California. They sold their property and there were about fifty wagons in the train. Some carried supplies. All who were old enough and could handle a gun had one, in case of Indian attacks, and they had several but finally made it to California."

Mrs. McCarthy indicated the family Bible with all of its records was destroyed in a fire at her parents' home, and that it contained confirmation of this version of Mahala's saga.

The difference of opinion about Mahala Hicks' origins is not unusual. Time-and-time again discrepancies were found in biographical material, a problem that is a particular enigma to the historian.

(17) Their daughter Sarah Burns was first married to Sie Glenn, a brother of Jerry and Bob Glenn of Old Town. Her second husband was Ed Chappell, a well-known cowboy in the Tehachapi pioneer period.

(18) An account in the Los Angeles Star of September 21, 1854 graphically describes Ellington's murder on the previous Sunday and the eventual arrest and execution by hanging of his killer Felipe Alvitre, on January 12, 1855. Ellington's murder is considered the first in El Monte's history. Mahala Ellington then married Vol Gentry by whom she had two children, and after his death was married to Bob Hicks, who Mrs. McCarthy and her aunt describe as "half Cherokee Indian," a matter disputed by the Hicks' descendants, who insist Mahala was the part-Indian member of the family.

(19) Letter from Mrs. Ruth Cuddeback Hall of Menlo Park, California, granddaughter of Grant Price Cuddeback, dated May 4, 1975.

(20) Letter from Harrison Doyle of Vista, California, dated April 21, 1975, a descendant of the Cuddebacks, in which he indicated Grant Price Cuddeback was accompanied on his journey to California by a brother, John Cuddeback, who later located where Red Bluff, California, is today.

(21) In later years Clinton, as he was known in the Tehachapis, married Sarah Davenport, another pioneer daughter of the region.

(22) The Los Angeles Star, February 23, 1861, reported that Joseph Fountain and John Bright, also from the Tehachapis, were given similar appointments at the same time.

(23) Another daughter, Catalina, married Geronimo Lopez, who built a large adobe which later became Lopez Station, a major stage stop. The building was buried under the waters of Van Norman Dam in the San Fernando Valley.

(24) Permission to quote from "HM 4376 Francisco Lopez de Belderrain manuscript" was graciously granted by The Huntington Library, San Marino, California.

(25) J. J. Lopez claimed the family was descended from Estevan Lopez who, in 1602, was with Vizcaino as a boatswain on the frigate Tres Reyes.

(26) The word California is generally accepted as originating from a Spanish novel, **Las Serges de Esplandian**, by Ordonez de Montalvo. This romance, which was popular from 1510 to 1526, described an "island of California on the right hand of the Indias very near the Terrestrial Paradise," peopled with black women, griffins and other creatures of the author's imagination. While there is no historical proof of the application of this name, the coincidence is so striking that most authorities generally agree that the name of California was derived from this source.

(27) An obituary notice in a June 1930 issue of The Tehachapi News commented on the passing of a daughter of General Andres Pico, Mrs. Carolina Pico de Sais, who died June 12, 1930, at Pasadena. All official biographies of Andres Pico indicate he died a bachelor. In a letter from William M. Mason, Curator of Archives and Southern California History, Los Angeles County Museum of Natural History, dated April 28, 1975, however, he said: "I have several indications that Andres Pico was married to Catalina Moreno of Los Angeles, at least by the early 1850's. They are listed together in the census of 1860 at San Fernando, and had adopted at least three children — Carolina (Moraga) Pico, Romulo (Moraga) Pico, and Catalina (Brent) Pico."

(28) Fremont was in the Tehachapis in 1844 as an official topographer for the United States Government. His diary is an outstanding, fascinating tour of California. It is only a coincidence, but Andres Pico, as a descendant of the Anza expedition, met with two different Americans who played preparatory roles in Tehachapi's history: Fremont and Cooke.

(29) A notice in the August 26, 1865, issue of The Los Angeles News, refers to Bailey Tungate as a judge in a county election, the polls located at Brite's house. This may be the same man.

(30) See **Pleasures and Palaces, The Memoirs of Princess Lazarovich-Hrebelianovich** (1915), and the November

6, 1974 issue of The Tehachapi News, "A True Fairy Tale of Old Tehachapi." Another daughter, Virginia Calhoun, also appeared on the stage, and wrote as well as acted in the play "Ramona" which was based on the Helen Hunt Jackson classic novel.

(31) Used with permission of the publisher of the current edition, New American Library, Inc.

(32) In a letter from Gregory Jones of Sonoma, California, dated March 25, 1975, he said: "The name Steam Farming came from the fact that the combine harvesters and the plows were drawn by giant high wheeled tractors that resembled the old steam locomotive."

(33) The personal papers of Senator Jones, as well as the files of the Ramina Corporation, were read by the author in the Special Collections Library, University of California at Los Angeles.

(34) In a letter from Gregory Jones dated March 25, 1975, he said: "The name Ramina is suggestive of the Spanish word, meaning branch, or the Latin word rami, meaning branches. In this case, it was derived from the first names of the Senator's four children: Roy, Alice, Marion and Georgina."

(35) As a result of Williamson's report the region was named. After exploring the Walker Pass area the Williamson party marched over the mountains and found a camping site next to a stream of water where there was good grass. He wrote: "There was another rancheria close to the place selected for our camp, and from the Indians we learned that their name for the creek was Tah-ee-chay-pah. It is the one called Pass creek by Colonel Fremont, and is the same one he ascended when he crossed the mountains in 1844." Unfortunately the Lieutenant failed to translate the word, and to this day speculation as to its meaning continues.

(36) Stanford was one of the "Big Four" of Southern Pacific railroad fame. The other three were Charles Crocker, Colis P. Huntington, and Mark Hopkins.

(37) See **The Pacific Tourist**, edited by Frederick E. Shearer, and reprinted in 1970 by Bounty Books, a division of Crown Publishers, Inc., New York.

(38) In 1975 Curry Street is still graced with a few "stately mansions" which have escaped the scar of progress. On intersecting avenues other pre-1900 homes are additional architectural reminders of the dignity of the Victorian age.

(39) Although the bank advertised in the Tehachapi newspaper as the "oldest commercial bank in Kern County" it was apparently overzealous as the Kern Valley Bank of Bakersfield incorporated in 1874 and the Bank of Bakersfield incorporated in 1890. Letter from Gerry Findley, Economic and Research Consultant, Temple City, California, dated January 30, 1974.

(40) This area became populated in the late 1920's when C. A. Willis, who had purchased considerable land in 1924, began to sell it. On July 14, 1931, a map of the Union High School Addition was recorded, which added Snyder Avenue, at the corner of which with G Street Ferd Snyder operated a lime kiln some years earlier. Involved in the subdivision was the Western Trust and Savings Bank which filed the map, and Albert Ancker and Phil Marx, on behalf of the Mountain Orchard Co. Also, in December 1929, Willis deeded to the Tehachapi Valley Union High School District, property which became the site of the new high school.

(41) In the spring of 1975 inflation hit the City's pocketbooks. With garbage disposal operating at a deficit, after much discussion the service was franchised once again to a private concern.

(42) Midway Gas Company was founded by William G. Kerchoff, who was connected with the Kern River plant that supplied Tehachapi's electricity. It was acquired by Southern California Gas Company in 1928.

(43) See "General Beale's Sheep Odyssey" by Earle Crowe (**Kern County Historical Society 24th Annual Publication,** Bakersfield, 1960).

(44) See **Culture On The Moving Frontier,** by Louis B. Wright (New York, 1961).

(45) Webster's **New World Dictionary of the American Language** defines a copperhead as a "northerner who sympathised with the South at the time of the Civil War. Contemptuous and hostile term used in the north."

(46) The linotype was retired in 1967 and replaced with an offset printing machine. In 1974 another modernization occurred with the introduction of a computerized typesetter, a Compugraphic.

(47) Letter from Mrs. Jackson to The Tehachapi News, printed December 18, 1974.

(48) Letter from Harry H. Hollins of Bakersfield, California, dated March 1974.

(49) Peak floods occurred in 1932 and 1945 during summer rains, carrying water at an estimated 33,000 second-feet. There was loss of life and heavy property damage, most severely in Keene, and to a lesser degree in the Tehachapi Valley.

Bibliography

(The listed material represents only a portion of the research for this book. Only material that directly pertained to the subject has been catalogued.)

BOOKS* PERIODICALS* PAMPHLETS

Allen, Gary G. "Narrow Gauge in the Tehachapis." (**Pacific News**, No. 157, November 1974, Vol. 14, No. 11, pages 10-15.)

Aubury, Lewis E. **The Structural and Industrial Materials of California.** (San Francisco, California, January 1906, California State Mining Bureau Bulletin No. 38)

Austin, Mary. **The Flock.** (Boston, Massachusetts, 1906)

Bancroft, Hubert H. **History of California — 7 volumes.** (San Francisco, California, 1884-1890)

Bancroft, Hubert Howe. **Register of Pioneer Inhabitants of California, 1542 to 1848.** (Los Angeles, California, 1964)

Barras, Judy. **Tehachapi: The Formative Years.** (Tehachapi, California, 1973)

Banning, William and Banning, George H. **Six Horses.** (New York, New York, 1930)

Bell, Horace. **Reminiscences of a Ranger, or Early Times in Southern California.** (Los Angeles, California, 1881)

Bell, James B. "A Log of the Texas-California Cattle Trail, 1854," edited by J. Evetts Haley. (**The Southwestern Historical Quarterly**, **Volume XXXV**, July 1931 to April 1932, Austin, Texas, pages 208-237)

Bieber, Ralph Paul. Ed. **Southern Trails To California in 1849.** (Glendale, California, 1937)

Bixby-Smith, Sarah. **Adobe Days.** (Los Angeles, California, 1931)

Blanchard, L. Judson. "A Noted Gem Field in Kern Co." and "History And Geology of Horse Canyon, in The Heart of Kern County." (**Mineral Notes and News,** April 1950)

Blanchard, L. Judson. "The Horse Canyon Agate Area." (**The Lapidary Journal,** April 1950)

Bolton, Herbert Eugene. Ed. **Anza's California Expeditions. Six Volumes.** (Berkeley, California, 1930)

Boyd, W. Harland. **Land of Havilah, 1854-1874: The Story of Keyesville, Kernville, and Havilah, in the Kern River Country, California.** (Bakersfield, California, 1952)

Boyd, W. Harland. "The Stagecoach in the Southern San Joaquin Valley, 1854-1876." **(Pacific Historical Review. Vol. XXVI, #4, November 1957** Berkeley, California, pages 365-372)

Boyd, William Harland. **A California Middle Border. The Kern River Country, 1772-1880.** (Richardson, Texas, 1972)

Brewer, William H. **Up and Down California in 1860-1864. 2nd Edition.** (Berkeley, California, 1949)

Brown, G. Chester. **Kern County.** (California Division of Mines Bureau Report No. 14, 1916, pages 471-523)

Burmeister, Eugene. **The Golden Years: A History of Caliente, Walker's Basin, Twin Oaks, and Loraine, California.** (Arvin, California, 1959)

Buwalda, J. P. "Geology of the Tehachapi Region in California." **(California Division of Mines Bulletin 170,** Chapter 2, pages 131-142)

Buwalda, J. P. and Lewis, G. P. "A New Species of Mercychippus." (U. S. **Geologic Survey Professional Paper,** 264-G, 1955)

Buwalda, John P. "New Mammalian Faunas From Miocene Sediments Near Tehachapi Pass In The Southern Sierra Nevada." (Geology Bulletin Vol. 10, No. 6, pages 75-85, **University of California Publications,** November 18, 1916)

California Division of Mines. **Earthquakes in Kern County California During 1952.** (Bulletin No. 171, California, November 1955)

Chalfant, Willie A. **The Story of Inyo.** (Bishop, California, 1933)

Comfort, Herbert G. **Where Rolls The Kern.** (Moorpark, California, 1934)

Cooke, Philip St. George. **Journal of the March of the Mormon Battalion of Infantry Volunteers Under the Command of Lieut. Col. P. St. George Cooke, from Santa Fe, N.M. to San Diego, California.** (Washington, D.C., Senate Documents, 30 Congress, Special Session No. 2, 1849)

Coues, Elliott. Ed. **On The Trail of a Spanish Pioneer. The Diary and Itinerary of Francisco Garces, 1775-76.** (New York, New York, 1900)

215

Crites, Arthur S. **Pioneer Days In Kern County.** (Los Angeles, California, 1951)

Crowe, Earle. **Men of El Tejon, Empire in the Tehachapis.** (Los Angeles, California, 1957)

Drago, Harry Sinclair. **Roads To Empire, The Dramatic Conquest of the American West.** (New York, New York, 1968)

Duke, Donald and Kistler, Stan. **Santa Fe-Steel Rails Through California.** (San Marino, California, 1963)

Elliott, Wallace W. & Co. **History of Kern County, California, with Illustrations, Descriptive of Its Scenery, Farms, Resources, Public Buildings.** . . (San Francisco, California, 1883)

Fishburne, Karen J. **The Building of the Railroad Down the San Joaquin Valley.** (Master of Arts Thesis in History, 1967, California State University, Sacramento, California)

Fremont, John C. **Memoirs of My Life, Including in the Narrative Five Journeys of Western Exploration During the Years 1842, 43-44, 45-6-7, 48-9, 53-4.** (Chicago, Illinois, 1887)

Galvin, John. Ed. **A Record of Travels in Arizona and California, 1775-76, Fr. Francisco Garces, a New Translation.** (San Francisco, California, 1965)

Goodyear, W. A. "Kern County." (**Eighth Annual Report of the State Mineralogist,** California State Mining Bureau, Sacramento, California, 1888)

Harrington, Edmond Ross. **A History of the Office of the Kern County Superintendent of Schools.** (Bakersfield, California, 1969)

Hittell, John S. **The Commerce and Industries of the Pacific Coast.** (San Francisco, California, 1882)

Jackson, Joseph Henry. **Anybody's Gold.** (San Francisco, California, 1970)

Jackson, William Turrentine. **Wagon Roads West; A Study of Federal Road Surveys and Construction in the Trans-Mississippi West, 1846-1869.** (New Haven, Connecticut, 1964)

James, George Wharton. **The Wonders of the Colorado Desert. Vol. I.** (Boston, Massachusetts, 190—)

Johnson, Henry W. "Where Did Fremont Cross The Tehachapi Mountains in 1844?" (**Annual Publications of Historical Society of Southern California, Vol. 13,** part 4, 1927)

La Fuze, Paulina B. **Saga of the San Bernardinos.** (San Bernardino, California, 1971)

Lawson, Andrew C. "The Geomorphogeny of the Tehachapi Valley System." **(University of California Publications Geology Bulletin, Vol. 4, No. 19, pages 431-462)**

Lewis, Oscar. **Sea Routes to the Gold Fields; the Migration By Water to California in 1849-1852.** (New York, New York, 1949)

Lewis Publishing Co. **A Memorial and Biographical History of the Counties of Fresno, Tulare, and Kern, California.** (Chicago, Illinois, 1891)

Lewis Publishing Co. **An Illustrated History of Los Angeles County.** (Chicago, Illinois, 1889)

Lloyd, G. "Tehachapi -- Ups and Downs at 4000 Feet." **(Correctional Review,** Sacramento, California, 1966, pages 1-6)

Los Angeles, Board of Public Service. **Complete Report On Construction of the Los Angeles Aqueduct.** (Los Angeles, California, 1916, pages 98-110)

Morgan, Wallace M. **A History of Kern County, California.** (Los Angeles, California, 1914)

Nadeau, Remi A. **City Makers. The Men Who Transformed Los Angeles from Village to Metropolis during the First Great Boom, 1868-76.** (Los Angeles, California, 1965)

Nadeau, Remi A. **The Water Seekers.** (Garden City, New York, 1950)

Newmark, Harris. **Sixty Years in Southern California, 1853-1913.** (Boston, Massachusetts, 1930)

Norris, Frank. **The Octopus. A Story of California.** (New York, New York, 1964)

Outland, Charles. **Stagecoaching on El Camino Real.** (Glendale, California, 1973)

Palmer, William J. **Report of Surveys Across the Continent, in 1867-68, on the Thirty-Fifth and Thirty-Second Parallels, for a Route Extending the Kansas Pacific Railway to the Pacific Ocean at San Francisco and San Diego.** (Philadelphia, Pennsylvania, 1869)

Peirson, Erma. **The Mojave River and Its Valley; An Ancient River, and the Story of Its Discovery, Its Paradoxical Nature, Its Service As A Pathway For Migration, and the Progress of its Valley.** (Glendale,

217

California, 1970)

Perkins, Arthur B. "Rancho San Francisco: A Study of a California Land Grant." (**Historical Society of Southern California Quarterly,** June 1957)

Pourade, Richard F. **Anza Conquers the Desert; the Anza Expeditions From Mexico To California and The Founding of San Francisco, 1774 to 1776.** (San Diego, California, 1971)

Pourade, Richard F. **The Silver Dons.** (San Diego, California, 1963)

Powell, Lawrence Clark. **California Classics: The Creative Literature of the Golden State.** (Los Angeles, California, 1971)

Robinson, William W. **The Story of San Fernando Valley.** (Los Angeles, California, 1961)

Simpson, Alice Fisher. "San Fernando Pass." (**California Highways and Public Works,** September-October 1954, pages 34-37)

Smith, George I. **The Geology of the Cache Creek Region, Kern County, California.** (Thesis for Master of Science, 1951, California Institute of Technology, Pasadena, California)

Smith, Wallace. **Garden of the Sun.** (Los Angeles, California, 1939)

Southern Pacific Company. "From Trail To Rail." (**Southern Pacific Bulletin,** Chapters 30 and 31 of the series, June and July 1928)

Starr, Kevin. **Americans and the California Dream, 1850-1915.** (New York, New York, 1973)

Treadway, F. Q. Ed. "Southern Pacific Bulletin, 1927-8." (**Southern Pacific Company,** 1927-8, San Francisco, California)

Troxel, Bennie W. and Morton, Paul K. **Mines and Mineral Resources of Kern County, California.** (San Francisco, California, 1962)

U. S. War Department. **Reports of Explorations and Surveys, to Ascertain the Most Practical and Economical Route for a Railroad from the Mississippi River to the Pacific Ocean, Made Under the Direction of the Secretary of War, in 1853-54. Vol. 5.** (Washington, D.C., 1855-60) (This is the report of Lt. R. S. Williamson.)

W.P.A. **Early History of El Monte, Vol. 1.** (El Monte, California, 1936)

Wentworth, Edward Norris. **America's Sheep Trails.** (Ames, Iowa, 1948)

Wood, R. Coke. **California-Colonial History. Time-Line 1769-1783.**

(Sacramento, California, 1974)

OFFICIAL RECORDS

City of Tehachapi, California. City Council Minutes, 1909-1960.

County of Kern, California, Hall of Records. Birth and Death Certificates, Grant Deeds, Patents, Homesteads.

County of Kern, California, Surveyor's Office. Maps and Minute Notes of Surveys.

United States Government. Census Reports for El Monte, California, July 1860; and for the Tehachapi area for the years 1860, 1870 and 1880.

United States Government. General Services Administration, National Archives and Records Service.

NEWSPAPERS

Havilah Miner, Havilah, California, June 1872-May 1874

Havilah Weekly Courier, Havilah, California, October 1866-December 1869

Kern County Californian, Bakersfield, California, December 1879-March 1891

Kern County Weekly Gazette, Bakersfield, California, 1876-1885

Kern County Weekly Courier, Bakersfield, California, December 1869-May 1876

Los Angeles News, Los Angeles, California, 1864-1867

Los Angeles Star, Los Angeles, California, 1851-1864, 1868-1875

The Bakersfield Californian, Bakersfield, California, February 1897-December 1899

The Bakersfield Californian, Bakersfield, California, Centennial Editions of April 2, 1966, May 21, 1966, August 20, 1966 and October 8, 1966

The Daily Californian, Bakersfield, California, April 1891-February 1897

The Southern Californian, Bakersfield, California, May 1875-December 1879

The Tehachapi News, Tehachapi, California, 1919-1954

The Tehachapi News — Earthquake Anniversary Review, Tehachapi, California, July 23, 1953

The Tehachapi Tomahawk, Tehachapi, California, 1900-1919

Tulare County Record (Visalia Delta), Visalia, California, 1859-1860

Visalia Delta, Visalia, California, August 1866-December 1867

Index

Heath, Erle, 171
Hendrickson, John J., 38-39,
    51-52, 114, 123
Henning Ranch, 112
Hickey, John, 81, 94, 95, 142
Hicks, Archie, 172
Hicks, Bob, 67
Hicks, Charles, 152
Hicks, Harvey, 55, 69, 70, 186
Hicks, Jess, 67, 69, 70
Hicks, Mahala, 67
Hicks, Walter, 78, 197-198
Hill, Roland, 78
Hill, Ross, 78
Hill, Russell, 78
Hirschfield, H., 136
Hollins, Harry, 196
Holton, Dade, 90, 165
Hood, William, 119
Horse Canyon, 46-48
Hosac, ———, 92
Hosack family, 178
hospitals, 81, 201, 205-206
Houston, Jim, 13
Huntington, Henry E., 146, 147
Hurlburt, Merle D., 171

Iles, J. W., 181
Imhof, Orris, 182
Indian attacks and uprisings,
    13, 26-28, 31, 35, 68, 91
Indians, 7, 10, 13, 24, 26-28,
    40-41, 67, 82, 87, 178
Inyo Mountains, 51
Iriart, Jim, 205
Iriart, Sam, 113
Irribarne, John, 136, 156
Isthmus of Panama, 90-91, 125

Jackley, J. M., 141, 142
Jackson, Chief of Police,
    198
Jackson, Elizabeth Hill, 181-
    182
Jacobs, H. N., 136, 156
Jacobsen, J. C., 111, 112, 113,
    182, 183
Jameson, Corporation, 42, 60;
    Foundation, 60; Mountain, 52,
    60; Ranch, 61, 180
Jameson, Ida, 60
Jameson, J. W., 55-56, 58,

80, 171
Jasper, Robert, 114
Jenkins, Verlie, 161
Jenkins, W. W., 77
Jennings, Al, 173-174
Jennings, J. W., 106, 107
Jewett, Louesa Maria, 178
Johnson, Jerky, 89
Johnson, Richard, 172
Johnson, Walter, 169, 172, 203,
    204
Johnson, Warren, 172
Jones, Clinton, 167, 188
Jones, Edwin R., 145, 167
Jones, Gregory, 172
Jones, John Percival, 105-109,
    172
Jones, Roy, 106, 108, 109, 110
Jordan, Luis, 77
Jury, Chris, 190

Kaiser, William, 81
Kanstein, L. J., 108, 204
Kearny, Stephen, 7, 84
Keene, 55, 69, 70, 78, 132-133,
    181, 186, 191, 197
Keene, James R., 132
Keer, James C., 165
Kellar, Mitchel G., 25, 165
Kelley, Allen, 89-90
Kelso Valley, 25, 27
Kentucky, 10, 14, 22, 127
Kerchoff, William G., 146, 147
Kern County, 24, 31, 65, 67,
    78, 86, 87, 89, 91, 95, 107,
    110, 111, 119, 124, 129, 136,
    146, 153, 154, 157, 163, 178,
    182, 189, 198
Kern County Board of Super-
    visors, 86, 92, 93, 133, 161,
    166, 178
Kern County Fair, 104
Kern River Valley, 26, 27, 28,
    92, 146, 147
Kernville, 91, 105, 131, 146,
    175
Kerr and Jones, 99, 105
Kerr, Charles, 105, 106, 188
Kessing, L. E., 142
Kessing, Mary and Bernard,
    184, 189
Killian, L. B., 181
Kingsbury, Douglas, 152